THE CECILS

THE DYNASTY AND LEGACY OF LORD BURGHLEY

For my grandfather, Frederick Arthur Lee, whose perseverance, wit and legacy lives on in me.

THE CECILS

THE DYNASTY AND LEGACY OF LORD BURGHLEY

DAVID LEE

PEN & SWORD
HISTORY

AN IMPRINT OF PEN & SWORD BOOKS LTD.
YORKSHIRE – PHILADELPHIA

First published in Great Britain in 2023 by
PEN AND SWORD HISTORY
An imprint of
Pen & Sword Books Ltd
Yorkshire – Philadelphia

ISBN 978 1 39908 377 5

A CIP catalogue record for this book is available from the British Library.

Typeset in Times New Roman 11/13.5 by
SJmagic DESIGN SERVICES, India.
Printed and bound in the UK by CPI Group (UK) Ltd.

Pen & Sword Books Limited incorporates the imprints of Atlas, Archaeology,
Aviation, Discovery, Family History, Fiction, History, Maritime, Military, Military
Classics, Politics, Select, Transport, True Crime, Air World, Frontline Publishing,
Leo Cooper, Remember When, Seaforth Publishing, The Praetorian Press,
Wharncliffe Local History, Wharncliffe Transport, Wharncliffe True Crime and
White Owl.

For a complete list of Pen & Sword titles please contact
PEN & SWORD BOOKS LIMITED
47 Church Street, Barnsley, South Yorkshire, S70 2AS, England
E-mail: enquiries@pen-and-sword.co.uk
Website: www.pen-and-sword.co.uk

Or

PEN AND SWORD BOOKS
1950 Lawrence Rd, Havertown, PA 19083, USA
E-mail: Uspen-and-sword@casematepublishers.com
Website: www.penandswordbooks.com

Contents

Acknowledgements

I owe a great deal of gratitude to many supportive, influential and encouraging people, whose belief in me has been instrumental during the production of this book.

My husband, Victor. Your support means so much to me. Thank you for your patience and always taking the time to listen to my fears, hopes, dreams and woes. My love for you knows no bounds.

My parents, Mary and David, for their continued support and belief in me. My brother, Conor, for his encouragement from the very beginning of my writing career.

My mother-in-law, Vera. Your belief in me is overwhelming, and I am eternally grateful for your support. You have given me my life's greatest gift. I owe you more thanks than can ever be expressed in the English language.

My friend Sandra Vasoli, who believes in me far more than I will ever believe in myself. You have shown me true kindness, guidance and friendship. You are a fountain of knowledge!

My supportive work colleagues, Mariana, Filipe and Sanja, who have had put up with perhaps hours of history lessons which they probably didn't want!

My dearest friend Carina. Thank you for all your love, support and laughs!

My editor Sarah-Beth Watkins, and all from Pen and Sword publishing, who have contributed to the production of this book. Particular thanks to Claire Hopkins for her patience and encouragement throughout this journey.

Introduction

The reign of Elizabeth I continues to be one of the most celebrated eras of English history. Without Elizabeth's long reign, Britain may have become an entirely different country. We refer to this period as 'The Golden Age', a time of prosperity and intrigue. Elizabeth herself continues to be revered as a virginal icon – 'Gloriana'. Yet, for all of Gloriana's iconography, virginity and victory, she would never have survived her tumultuous reign without the men who advised her. Two men in particular steered Elizabeth though her reign. Without them, she would have found it impossible to navigate England though some of its most raucous periods. Their names were William and Robert Cecil.

William Cecil, or Lord Burghley as he is often referred to, was Elizabeth I's longest serving statesman. He was her chief advisor and Secretary of State for most of her reign. He also became Lord High Treasurer. He had a profound influence on the establishment of Protestantism as the state religion. His political influence over the queen made him perhaps the most powerful man in the kingdom. The second half of the sixteenth century in England was dominated by religious and political turmoil and cultural changes. Despite the difference in the status of their birth, William and Elizabeth formed a close bond, and the queen depended on him for numerous tasks that she could not have undertaken alone. William's grandfather, David Cecil, was a favorite Yeoman of Henry VII, Elizabeth's grandfather and the first Tudor monarch. He was also the cousin of one of the queen's favorite ladies, Blanche Parry, and had even served as an administrator in Elizabeth's household when she was a princess.

William devoted his life in the service of Elizabeth's government and to the cause of making England a Protestant nation. His dedication to the protection of the Protestant state, the safety of the sovereign and the preservation and legacy of the Tudor dynasty are all key elements that mark the modern British sense of national identity. His dedication to the service of the English state was inherited by his son, Robert Cecil, Lord Salisbury. Robert was like his father in many ways: politically astute, highly intelligent, loyal and dedicated to the preservation of the Protestant religion. Yet he was likely far more ruthless than his father. William may have survived the bloody reign of Mary I and veered England towards its most glorious period, but his son Robert's position remained intact during the transition of power from the House of Tudor to the House of Stuart upon Elizabeth's death in 1603. Robert may have been loyal to the state, but his loyalty to his family and ensuring its legacy was even more important. William Cecil began a dynasty of powerful men and women, but his son Robert ensured its longevity and legacy.

The relationship between Elizabeth, William and Robert has long been a topic of discussion and debate. William was certainly influential in many of Elizabeth's decisions regarding domestic and foreign policy, but also her personal issues. He continued to encourage his queen to marry. This would not only serve to ensure the succession of the Tudor dynasty, but also served to preserve the position of the Cecil dynasty at the centre of Tudor society and government. It was also his job as her chief advisor to put pressure on her regarding such matters. Yet, despite the enormous pressure he put on his queen, and her many tantrums, Elizabeth found loyalty and friendship in Lord Burghley that she would never have found in a husband. His loyalty not only lay with her personally, but with his vision for England as a Protestant kingdom. Elizabeth knew that William would never betray her. It could even be argued that he acted, whether consciously or not is uncertain, as a father-figure to a woman who never truly had a close bond with her own father, Henry VIII. Like many of the queen's favourites, William was given a nickname – her 'Spirit'.

Robert Cecil also became a favourite of Elizabeth's. He was shrewd, calculated and a mastermind regarding foreign policy. Overtly pompous and staunchly Protestant, Robert represented the very essence of a loyal and incorruptible English statesman. He was considered short for the period, and he likely suffered from scoliosis, which gave him a hunched back. Despite his 'deformity', and the ridicule he endured at court for it, he remained steadfast in his endeavour to serve the crown just as his father had. Because of his appearance, Elizabeth referred to him as her 'pygmy'. Though derogatory in today's terms, this nickname may not have been intended as offensive. As his father and queen grew old, his advantageous nature further blossomed as he took on more and more responsibilities in the governance of the nation. Long after his father's death, and with the queen on her own deathbed, Robert communicated with the most appealing of her successors, King James VI of Scotland. James was the son of Mary, Queen of Scots who was executed for her involvement in the Babington Plot to assassinate the virgin queen. Lord Burghley's hand in her demise cannot be overlooked.

However, Robert was not his father, and King James was not his mother. As he was a staunch Protestant, Robert worked tirelessly to ensure the crown would rest on James' head after Elizabeth's death.

Despite his schemes, he greatly mourned the death of his queen. Over the years, he had an ongoing rivalry with Robert Devereux, 2nd Earl of Essex and favourite of the queen, which will be explored in this work. His later navigation during James' reign as James I of England, particularly his role during the Gunpowder Plot of 1605, is a prime example of the lengths he would go to, to ensure the preservation of Protestantism in England. He became a favourite of the new king, though remained generally disliked at court. The king nicknamed him his 'beagle'. While William and Robert's relationships with the queen differed, this has been a point of discussion among historians for decades. Their relationship as father and son however, has been often overlooked. We think we know almost everything there is to know about Elizabeth I. She was glorious, pious, virtuous, vane, pragmatic and highly intelligent. Her reign is not often remembered for those who stood next to the throne. Every victory and tragedy experienced by Elizabeth was witnessed by the men closest to her, or rather, the real power behind the throne. The Cecils.

Despite the Cecils' strong grip on the administration of English politics, they were human. This book will not only explore the political careers of William and Robert Cecil, but will also delve into their personal lives, relationships, particularly that with the queen, their religiosity and accumulated wealth. The purpose of this book is not simply to regurgitate the already-known facts of the Cecils. It will attempt to present a much more nuanced yet relatable portrayal of their lives and experiences. In order to fully understand the importance of Elizabeth's long reign, we have to first understand the men who made her and shaped her long reign. Ultimately, this book presents an unbiased yet chronological interpretation of the Cecil dynasty and legacy.

The author of this book has carefully consulted contemporary Elizabethan documents, in both re-printed and digitised archival format. Much of the primary evidence consulted throughout this book is catalogued online and is accessible to the public. The secondary sources, in both journal and book format, have been carefully selected due to their readability, relevance, accuracy and discipline.

Chapter 1

The Origins of a Great Family

William Cecil was born at Bourne in Lincolnshire on 13 September 1520. His father was Sir Richard Cecil and his mother was Jane Hekington. Though a Lincolnshire man to the bone, William was well aware that his family, and indeed the Cecil name, had originated from the Welsh Marches. The original spelling of the Anglicised family name would likely have been Seisyllt.[1] The family came from Wales probably sometime during the last quarter of the fifteenth century. William's later career during the reign of Elizabeth I, and the queen's favoritism of him, was in no way constructed by chance. Notably, both the Cecils and the Tudors had Welsh heritage. Though his grandfather began the family's service to the crown during the reign of the first Tudor monarch, his father Richard really paved the way for the success of the Cecil dynasty. Richard Cecil was a page in the chamber of Elizabeth's father, Henry VIII. His mother's family were members of the elite class in Bourne, where William's life began. The Hekingtons had long enjoyed success as town councillors, traders and landowners.[2] This is likely where William inherited his fine abilities for counsel and governance.

When William was born, England was in the midst of great change. Henry VIII, the second Tudor king, occupied the throne. Just before William had taken his first breath, Henry VIII had met with King Francis I of France at the Field of Cloth of Gold between 7 and 24 June 1520. This lavish and public ceremony was England's way of keeping hold on the balance of the friendship between the two nations. The frivolous ceremony may have been a bid for both England and France to display their wealth and power, but its results would also become an omen for Henry VIII's later reign, and the reigns of his three children.[3] William's father Richard served Henry VIII during this event. As Richard's father David was a client of Margaret Beaufort, Henry VIII's paternal grandmother, it was due to her influence that Richard found his post. It is likely that the king took notice of Richard, as his father was then granted the office of bailiff of the king's water, Wittlesey-mere.[4] While the political and religious situation in Europe in general was going through a period of great change, William's parents would have been none-the-wiser of their newborn son's future at the head of

1

governance of England. By the time he took his last breath, he had helped change and reform England and the future of Great Britain forever.

But who were the Cecils really? It is clear that William changed the spelling of the family name. David Seisyllt or Syssill as he likely spelt it, was the youngest son of the family and by the reign of Richard III, they were minor gentry and living on the Welsh border. Beckingsale states that David's father's name was Philip.[5] However, on close inspection of the Cecil family pedigree, his father's Christian name is shown as 'Richard'.[6] This Richard mentioned would have been known as 'Richard Cecill ap Philip Seisyll'. The prefix 'ap' in the name comes from the Welsh patronymic system used in family trees, and is a contraction of the welsh word 'mab' meaning son. Therefore translating as 'Richard Cecill son of Philip Seisyll'. Above his name on the pedigree is 'Philip', confirming this. Notably, most of the Cecils on this document share similar names, often going between Richard, David, Philip and William in differing orders. It is also likely that he went by both Richard and Philip.

David Cecil was in his thirties by the time Henry VII came to the throne after defeating Richard at the Battle of Bosworth in 1485, thus ending the Wars of the Roses. David's eldest brother Richard was heir to the family inheritance and would remain in the Cecil family home at Alltyrynys. His son then inherited it upon his death. It is ironic that though David Cecil did not inherit the family seat as the youngest son, it would be his descendants and his dynasty that would bring the Cecil name a glorious legacy due to his grandson William. The Cecils that remained on the Welsh border would eventually fade into obscurity, overshadowed by the grandson of David Cecil, who himself likely fought at Bosworth on Henry Tudor's side. It was through his mother's relative, Sir David Philips, that he came to support the Tudors, and therefore, in the aftermath of Bosworth, came into favour with Margaret Beaufort. Philips was a servant in Margaret's household. David later became a personal bodyguard of the first Tudor king and therefore it is unsurprising that his son Richard later ended up in the king's household.[7]

When David married Alice Dycons in 1494, he would have stepped up even further amongst the urban elite. Alice's father was a relative of David Philips' wife and this is likely how they were introduced. The Dycons family were prosperous merchants. However, the origin of David's wealth prior to about 1500 is difficult to obtain. Though he may have been rewarded for his loyalty and given a modest position at court, it appears that he was wealthy enough to enter into a marriage to a woman of a prominent family. Richard Cecil was born sometime in the following year. David became a Yeoman of the Chamber in 1506 and was thrice elected alderman between 1504 and 1526. Another son was born sometime after, also named David. The factor of which monarch he served under mattered little in terms of the security of his position. Indeed, when Henry VII died in 1509, David enjoyed further, if not more, bounty under the reign of Henry VIII, being granted further titles, properties and even a pension in 1513. David's marriage to Alice was likely harmonious and happy. However, when she died sometime around 1520, David decided to remarry to Jane Roos, the widow of Edward Villiers of Flore in Northamptonshire. Apparently an heiress of some substance, she was decades younger than her new husband who was considered an old man approaching his sixties. They had one daughter named Joan. Jane seems to have outlived him.[8]

David Cecil lived a rather long life, into his late seventies. He would prove to be an influential figure for William, who grew up witnessing his grandfather's continuous rise in power. Notably, David remained active until his dying days. In 1532, after having previously acquired the attention of Henry VIII's illegitimate son, the Duke of Richmond in the 1520s, David rose again as Sheriff of Northamptonshire. If that were not enough, he was also noted to hound Thomas Cromwell for the sum of £100. David's connections with Henry VIII during the period of his 'Great Matter', in which he sought a divorce from Katherine of Aragon in pursuit of Anne Boleyn, Thomas Cromwell during his rise to power, and the Dissolution of the Monasteries, of which he was certainly involved in, set the path for his grandson William. William's father Richard was also responsible for the growth of the family's prosperity. He used the family fortune as a means of expanding their power and generating more wealth. The Cecils continued to acquire property during the 1530s, likely a direct result of the dissolutions. But his attentions were not limited to just monastic properties. His proximity to the king grew as he became the Groom of the Wardrobe. However, the reason for his family's prosperity must be noted as being due to his diligence and his caution towards expressing too much ambition, a trait known to have influenced the downfall and deaths of many male and female courtiers during Henry VIII's reign.[9]

For their service during Henry's reign, the Cecils were remembered in his last will and testament. The apparent lack of Richard Cecil's ambition may have been the reason for this, despite his obvious loyal service to the crown – a trait he passed on to his son. However, though Richard and William often avoided putting their lot at risk, that is not to say that they lacked ambition entirely. Rather than outwardly seeking their numerous positions and accumulated wealth, which they likely welcomed, it was their ability to harmoniously work alongside their sovereign that appealed the most. To have the monarch's ear not only brought position, wealth and prosperity, but also significant influence on state policy. The influence William would later gain during Elizabeth's reign was much more important to him than the reaping of its rewards, yet reap he did.

William would emulate his grandfather in his ability to navigate the choppy waters and changing winds during the reigns of the Tudors. Though it could be thought that William's life prior to his rise during the reign of Elizabeth was of little consequence, it is important to understand why he became the man who the queen solely relied upon for proper counsel. William's birthplace, particularly the house in which he was born, has long been a topic of debate amongst his previous biographers. Some have argued that he was born in his paternal grandfather, David Cecil's home. However, Nares was of the opinion that due to his mother's position as sole heiress to the Hekington fortune, he was likely born at his maternal grandfather' William Hekington of Bourne's family seat. He was also likely named for his mother's father and he was baptised at Bourne.[10]

William was the only son and therefore heir to his father's lands and fortune which he had accumulated throughout his service to Henry VIII and Edward VI. He did have three sisters; Margaret, Elizabeth and Anne, all of whom married rather well.[11] There is little to go by in terms of William's early childhood and his relationships with his parents and sisters. However, there is evidence regarding his education, the foundation from which he would carve out his own lasting legacy. He certainly attended the grammar school at Grantham, where he likely boarded due to his long distance from Bourne. When his family moved to Stamford, he was moved to the local grammar school there.[12] William was described as a delicate child, with Smith noting that he 'played no games' but was careful to observe the adults around him.[13] His time at grammar school however, seemed to have made little impression on him and his learning. Whether he was a precocious child or not, the circumstances of his upbringing, education and heritage would later have an impact on his shrewd political nature and ability to keep in Elizabeth's favor.

The gaps in William's childhood are by no means an impediment to understanding his psychology and development into adulthood. He was a mere boy of nine years when Henry VIII's Great Matter began to have an effect on the governance of the kingdom and English body of religiosity. The religious tensions brewing in England were yet to erupt to the same capacity as other European states and so at this point probably had little effect on the boy's life. Indeed, his change to Stamford would also have little effect on his later ideology towards policy and religion. He was simply far too young for the political and religious turmoil to have any lasting influence on his life. It would be his teenage years at university that would make an immediate difference to his ideology, love for study and overall development.[14]

When he was just fourteen in 1535, William then went up to St John's College in Cambridge. This establishment was founded in the memory of Margaret Beaufort, who had died in 1509, the same year as Henry VIII's ascension.[15] It was here that William made the most important connections of his life, which would sow the seeds for his family life, political career and rise to power. William showed great scholarly ability at Cambridge. He could speak Greek in a comfortable and natural manner by the time he was nineteen according to his earliest, though anonymous, biographer. However, it has often been suggested that his early intellectual abilities are somewhat mythical.[16] It must be noted that both Mary I and Elizabeth I were also well-adept in foreign languages. Elizabeth displayed a great talent for speaking in several languages as a child. William's academic ability may have been great, but it is also likely that a number of intellectuals were able to promote their superior ability as a means of propaganda, later secured by Elizabeth's accession and religious reform in England. Though this would prove absolutely crucial in forming the man behind the power of the throne, he often had such a zeal for learning and study that it had a permanent effect on his health.

According to the aforementioned biographer, who is believed to have been a member of his later household, his want for knowledge and appetite for learning had a terrible effect on his legs, which was thought to be the original source of his gout. He awoke every morning before four, which may have been a habit he carried throughout his life.[17] This author is a well-known source for authors, biographers and historians. The narrative in which this work was preserved, whether wholly accurate or not, has led to the current historiography surrounding William's early career. Though Nares attested in his version of *Memoirs of Lord Burghley* that the said servant attended William for the last twenty-five years of his life, there is no name mentioned to indicate the identity or rank of this individual. However, the author may have been Michael Hicks, one of William's principal secretaries. Nares pointed out that though the narrative of these memoirs was noted to be originally written by a *domestic*, the notion that the author was of little or no rank is to misunderstand particular positions of servitude. Referred to as retainers, many men of well-to-do families with good reputations served men like Lord Burghley as menials on particular occasions. Whether or

5

not Hicks was the author of the anonymous memoirs, he continued in his service to the Cecils under Robert, Earl of Salisbury, and had a successful career.[18]

Despite William's young age upon entering St John's, education on a third level began much earlier during the sixteenth century. Though childhood was not understood in the way it is today, any sense of it would have left the young William upon his entry to Cambridge. William exercised an ability that soon caught the attention of his peers and lecturers. He was noted to have been a reader of the *Sophistic Lecture* at just sixteen years old and by the time he was nineteen, he read the *Greek Lecture* '...Upon pleasure, without pension'. He was noted to be 'beyond expectation of a student of his time, or one of his yeres of birth', and by the time he was twenty, his Greek was perfected.[19] William's grandfather David would become his greatest influence. Though his father outwardly lacked great ambition, William was more like his grandfather, but carried his father's caution. David died when William was around twenty. Though his reaction to this bereavement is unknown, it clearly had a profound effect on the young William, who went on to emulate his grandfather in so many ways. Despite the pressures put on the family by this patriarch, they were close-knit. This closeness, though not unheard of for the period, would have an effect on William's later family life, particularly on his marriages and relationships with his children. The characteristics embedded in him from an early age were the essence of his later success. By the time he came of age, any connections to their Welsh roots were severed and this was replaced by a cautiousness and ability to avoid offending others as they rose in stature and prosperity.[20]

Despite his hunger for knowledge, William also had time to make friends during his first year at Cambridge. Some of these friendships would last his lifetime. William Bill in particular, known as the 'Protestant Divine', later worked in service to William when he became Lord Burghley. However, the most poignant friendship that he established was with John Cheke, a student of the classics. He also struck up a close friendship with Thomas Smith, who would a play an important political role later on.[21] These men not only allowed William to form close bonds prior to his rise in power, but they also helped to shape his intellect and ideology. By 1540, John Cheke became the first professor of Greek at Cambridge and William was already well-adept and reading the very latest related to its study. Though he enjoyed it, he was more pressed with the kind of learning relative to an active life in politics. Something he craved. Though he was an eager student, William had other interests that he found himself absorbed in for the rest of his life.[22]

The sweeping Protestant sympathies across England would most definitely have reached Cambridge. These young men, in their most influential and formative years, became interested in the movement of reform. The zeal of the Catholic church had lost its charm, and men like William were looking for inspiration, rationality and perhaps some form of youthful rebellion. The words of Luther would have been intoxicating.

However, though corruption in the English Church was much lower than that of the German Church – the very reasoning for Luther's reforms, William had a lot to gain from the confiscation of church wealth and the Dissolution of the Monasteries. Many families, particularly courtiers, would have benefitted from the new vast wealth of the royal coffers. His father's estates in particular expanded, his wealth augmented. Notably, when the time came for him to be addressed as Lord Burghley, most of his estates, holdings and many houses had once belonged to the church prior to Henry VIII's break with Rome.[23]

This is not to say that William's ideology for reform and belief as a staunch Protestant was merely, or rather only, influenced by a means of financial gain. On the contrary, his beliefs were quite real and his faith unmovable. However, despite his father's prosperity, William would have been brought up to know that he was destined for royal service. Though his tumultuous career in politics was anything but smooth, as will become clearer, he would have expected to find a high position in the service of the crown. Therefore, it made sense that his religiosity reflected that of the monarch's. Richard Cecil was particularly convinced of the Protestant ideology sweeping across the kingdom by the 1530s. Henry VIII's position as the church's Supreme Head was welcomed by the Cecil family, ever loyal to the will of their Tudor masters who made them. If men did not move with the changing tides and failed to rise in favor in spite of their pride or religiosity, they often found it difficult to secure their family's prominence.

By the time Anne Boleyn was well on her way to securing the crown for herself and supplanting Katherine of Aragon – a staunch Catholic, Richard Cecil was cleverly securing his family's station. Despite his lacking want for rapid advancement, his convictions lay in another place. He openly preached during a sermon at Stamford on Justification by Faith alone. He had two opponents in Dominican friars. Richard's defence of this new radical doctrine likely gave him a greater purpose outside of his other obligations at court, and likely created ties to likeminded men who his son could later look to for aid in his own ambitions.[24]

William's stay at Cambridge may well have come at a time of great change, particularly with the weaving together of the humanist cultural revolution and the religious reformation, but this is not to say that he was wholly influenced in terms of his religious ideology there. Many differing reformers of his age drifted between Catholicism and Protestantism, seeking meaning and relevance to their studies. Yet, William's steadfast drift towards the new faith was already instilled in him, partly by his father's influence, partly due to his own thoughts. Cambridge simply allowed him to absorb the differing versions of theology, resulting in a man of true conviction and staunch Protestantism.

Though he had great zeal for languages and study in general, William became quite popular simply for his character. He was said to be merry, witty and of a generally humorous temperament. Yet, this led him to distraction. He apparently gambled away his money, books, clothes and even his bedding. However, it would be William's romantic interests that worried his father the most. William came into contact with his friend John's sister, Mary Cheke, and became besotted with her. It is not known when their paths first collided, but it is generally believed that it may have been during one of John's Greek lectures. When Richard Cecil was informed of his son's interests in Mary, he promptly removed him from Cambridge and enrolled him into Gray's Inn. William never completed his degree at Cambridge, likely to his own regret; for despite his father's attempts to chastise his son, William's infatuation for Mary did not wane. The reason for Richard's apprehension towards this relationship was likely somewhat snobbish. Mary's father was a beadle at Cambridge, which also explains her presence at her brother's lectures. Her mother ran a wine shop. Though it was not a bad match, and indeed, the Cheke's were not a lowly family by any means, Richard had great hopes that his son would marry well, perhaps to a daughter of some influential courtier.[25]

However, some scant evidence could suggest that a young William was familiar with the exploration of his emotions prior to meeting Mary. Though it must be taken with a grain of salt, for no other reference has been made to such a rumour, its existence at all poses some interesting questions, and possible reasons for Richard Cecil's concerns for William's attachments. By 1565, William was secure in position of service to the crown. Elizabeth I was queen, and he himself was married and attempting to persuade his queen to take a husband. A former pupil at Cambridge and one-time friend of William's, Sir Thomas Smith, wrote to him informing him of the French Queen Mother Catherine de Medici's admiration for him. If William thought this admiration was relevant to his service to his sovereign, he was poorly mistaken.[26]

The letter revealed that the queen mother thought William a good example to the young king, who had sired an illegitimate child with a mistress. This hint insinuated that Cecil had a fondness for fornication during his years at Cambridge, and that he had even produced an illegitimate son. This letter was probably intended to embarrass William and slander his good name. Perhaps it was merely a means of friction between Cecil and Catherine de Medici. However, though an interesting thought, there is unlikely any merit in Smith's letter, who by 1565 was definitely no true friend of Lord Burghley. This is the first and only hint of a glitch in William's morality and as it was revealed thirty years after the supposed event, it is doubly unlikely to have substance. It is also notable that by this time, William had accumulated many enemies both at home and abroad. Any such event would have been hard to keep a secret, and there is no evidence of his enemies ever using such slander against him. Furthermore, there is no mention of a mother's or child's name, or any reference to their circumstances. It must be considered that Smith's letter was simply an attempt at slander or simply a report of the French queen's words.[27]

If there was the slightest hint of truth to Smith's letters, then it was certainly one of William's best-kept secrets; and he did have many. Some may consider William's sense of morality and duty came from such a mistake in his adolescence. Yet, as mentioned before, his respectable behaviour was imbedded in him prior to his move to Cambridge. Therefore, it is much more plausible that his relationship and evident love for Mary Cheke was his first. The fact that this was a love-match is evident in Mary's lack of any real social stature or riches. Her only standing, despite her likely virtue to William's taste, was due to her brother's position at Cambridge. Such a match was probably a poor tactic, seeing as William's family had long made good matches in matrimony as a means of gaining further prosperity. Yet, his steadfast determination came through in his feelings for Mary. This factor reveals so much more about the famous Lord Burghley than we have previously considered. Despite his sense of duty to his family and his ambitious nature, there was a much more human side to William than his later contemporaries and enemies could have imagined.

By 1540, David Cecil had died. He would not live to see his grandson's early career, nor his first marriage. His will, which was drawn up in 1535, he requested that his body be buried in the parish church of Saint George in Stamford. He provided for his wife and younger children. He left his daughter Joan twenty pounds and he left his son two complete featherbeds. Richard was also the executor of his will, which was proved on 16 March 1541.[28]

William was twenty years old when he began to court Mary. At the very same time, his studies at Cambridge would end. His father may have thought that his high hopes for his son's future were now tainted, but William's relationship would have the opposite effect. While he stayed at Gray's Inn in 1541, William got a real taste for London and this allowed him to move in circles that could prove to be an advantage for his future career. The inns were basically a form of finishing schools for young men, usually the sons of gentlemen. This would have proved an education for William in terms of knowing his enemies, friends, and being capable of defending himself in the future. Learning the law was absolutely necessary for any young man who wished to work in government.[29] Whether William was a reluctant student at Gray's Inn is debatable. He certainly learned some useful tactics during his stay, for it was there that he lost money when gambling.

It must be noted that though William came from a relatively rich and successful family, his father would have greatly disapproved of such frivolity. Yes, the Cecils had money, lands and high positions, but William had not yet found a position in government. Squandering money on gambling sessions may have been the norm for his peers at Cambridge and the inn, but William would prove to be different and learned from his folly. However, his choice of bride would create a rift between him and his parents, which he evidently never regretted. On 8 August 1541, William married Mary Cheke. He recorded his marriage in his diary: 'Anno 1541, Aug. viii nupsi Maria Cheke...'.[30]

Almost exactly nine months later, on 5 May 1542, Mary gave birth to a son, named Thomas. Thomas would one day become the 1st Earl of Exeter. As he was born in Cambridge, it is likely that Mary was staying with her own family during the time of the birth. Whether or not this had something to do with the Cecils' disapproval of the marriage is unclear. It is much more likely that she retired there for her confinement period. Yet despite her victory in producing a healthy son and heir for the great family she married into, Mary died on 22 February 1543.[31]

Though William was already making connections that would prove useful in the future, it was his close bond to the Cheke family, even after his first wife's death that made all the difference to his cause. Despite his parents' objections to his marriage, his brother-in-law John Cheke was called to court to become the tutor of Prince Edward. At the same time, his friend, the famous Roger Ascham was appointed as the Lady Elizabeth's tutor. Prince Edward himself recorded in his own journal that Cheke was a 'learned' man.[32] At twenty-three years old, William found himself a widower, with a young son to provide for. However, despite his friends' grand appointments, he was younger and so had to accept his position on a borough seat as

Custos Brevium in the Court of Common Pleas.[33] He may have been over-ambitious, but this was a promising start. His father's position may have helped him along his way. The power that Parliament obtained in the latter years of Henry VIII's reign would have significant influence on the direction of William's career. His introduction to Tudor politics at such a young age served him better than his time at Cambridge or Gray's Inn.

As William began to piece his political career together, he also began to think towards his personal future. He had a young son who needed a mother figure. And he needed a wife. To secure his own dynasty and legacy, he had to move on from Mary. He never lost contact with her family. On the contrary, it seems that he kept a close bond with the Chekes for much of his life, and they too held him in high regard. By 1545, his career was on the rise; he decided to marry Mildred Cooke, the daughter of Sir Anthony Cooke. Though it was his first marriage that allowed him to obtain some precedence at court, it was his second marriage that would elevate him to a higher status. Perhaps this was the marriage his parents had hoped for from the beginning. Certainly this time round, his marriage was more advantageous in nature and would have had little to do with love. Indeed, Mildred was not known to be a great beauty by contemporary standards, but she was dutiful, diligent and well-learned. She proved to be strong enough as a wife to William, for a different woman may have found it difficult to play second fiddle to Elizabeth I later on.[34]

Mildred was one of five daughters and had grown up in Essex. She was twenty-two years old to William's twenty-five.[35] The couple married in December, and by the next year, his relationship with his father seemed to be on much better terms. It may have been Mildred that aided this reconciliation. It has been said that Richard initially disinherited William due to his marriage to Mary Cheke. However, it is likely that his remarriage to Mildred led Richard to destroy his original will. Either way, this has confused historians for decades.

William's new marriage drew him ever closer to the throne. He befriended like-minded men with strong Protestant convictions. These men were connected to Prince Edward and his uncle Lord Edward Seymour, Earl of Hertford, later Duke of Somerset. Seymour was a prominent councillor to the king and would later become Lord Protector upon Henry VIII's death in 1547, as the new king Edward VI had not reached his majority. Once old King Henry was out of the picture, the men that Seymour surrounded himself with, Protestant men like William, could now work towards building their careers under a new regime. William was still young at twenty-seven. His long years in education, experience in law, radical ideology and sympathy towards the new religion gave him the chance to better his lot. He was able to secure a position among the Lord Protector's companions. However, what William had in academic training he lacked in military experience. He had not yet been abroad, nor had he the stamina to be a soldier. He was a courtier through and through. He found employment in the Marshal's Court as a judge during Seymour's 1547 expedition to Scotland that summer, which likely suited his fine scholarly attributes.[36] However, during battle on 10 September, known as the Battle of Pinkie, William barely escaped the shot from a cannon fire.[37]

Regardless of the dangers during this expedition, William observed the campaign's performance in terms of policy. He took a keen interest in any military administrative issues. This would prove a useful platform for his future involvement in the art of warfare, of which Elizabeth I could not have done without. His sympathies towards Seymour's zeal for the continuation of the religious reformation, which had more-or-less been paused for the latter years of Henry VIII's reign, began to shift. He no longer wanted to be a bystander of this reform. If he wanted to remain at the peak of Edward VI's court circles, he had to do something. Luckily, he had an ally at the very epicentre of Tudor reformist society, the dowager queen, Catherine Parr.[38]

Catherine Parr wrote a three-part pamphlet *The Lamentations of a Sinner* in 1546, while Henry was still alive. By November of 1547, he was long dead and Seymour had continued the religious reform that Henry began, only this time in the young Edward VI's reign. Catherine was a staunch reformer, but she was not as hard-headed as the new Lord Protector, who would in due course become her brother-in-law. Her publication was a more passive approach towards the reformation. Indeed, it likely was written to encourage ladies of a particular class to gracefully embrace the new faith.

William was still only a minor member of the protector's household, but as Catherine was pressing for publication towards the end of 1547, it is striking that William was permitted to write the introduction. This not only indicates that his sympathies had evolved into something much more radical, but it also indicates the strong connection between reformers, despite the obstacle of rank and also the issues between Catherine and William's employer, Seymour, in terms of their personal elucidations of their faith. William was clear in how he perceived the new faith. He wanted to stress the virtue of the dowager queen, while also emphasizing the consequences of repenting one's sins, as Catherine had. This would have been exactly what Catherine wanted as an introduction, and William had proved that he could have a serious impact on the direction of religious reform during Seymour's time as protector.[39] He was also clearly capable of encouraging religious change without bringing about chaos and social upheaval at a very delicate time for the monarchy.

William cleverly encouraged his own take on reform by encouraging women, as Catherine had. His language was mild, pious and deliberately so:

> '...And, to all the ladies of estate, I wish as earnest mind, to follow our queen in virtue as in honour, that they might once appear to prefer God before the world, and be honourable in religion...so shall they, as in some virtuous ladies of right high estate it is with great comfort seen, taste of this freedom of remission of everlasting bliss...'.[40]

Edward VI was still a child, and Catholic rebels across England were giving the protectorate no respite; men of William's faith remained unsure of their positions, as many others of high rank such as Stephen Gardiner were unwilling to accept the reformist approach to religious doctrine. Indeed, perhaps William's greatest failure prior to his further elevations was the fact that he could not convince Gardiner to accept the articles that he was assigned to prepare. He attempted on many occasions to entice Gardiner into using his notes during sermons, which Gardiner always flat-out ignored. William wholly denied any idea of transubstantiation, to which Gardiner accused him of ignorance. Yet, despite William's seeming attempts at friendship, he was likely not fond of Gardiner at all, for he had attacked his teacher, brother-in-law and friend, John Cheke, in the past over his abilities in the Greek tongue.

Gardiner was at this time the Bishop of Winchester and continued to defend the traditional doctrines of the Roman Catholic Church, for which he was deemed 'arrogant' by many such as John Dudley, Earl of Warwick, a close confidant of William's.[41] But there were others such as the Bishop of London, who had to be dealt with, for the crime of secret, private masses would also become a bane to William. Though, he was likely not as extreme in his beliefs as others, which Beckingsale has noted.[42] The introduction in Parr's pamphlet is the earliest known sample of William's early writings. In comparison to the many other works he wrote during his long life, his introduction in *Lamentations* is rather bland. Far from suggesting that he was not radical in his ideology at this time, but rather, cautious and tactful. Once he was well-established as the Master of Requests, appointed to him by the protector, he became used to dealing with many requests and could decide what the protector would read and respond to. His position allowed him to help those close to him when necessary, and John Cheke even took the opportunity to write to William in pursuit of an appointment.[43] This may seem mundane and menial in contrast to his later position under Elizabeth I, but it was absolutely influential on his meticulous attitude towards domestic policy. Indeed, it also reveals that William was a man of great integrity and could be trusted. His integrity and cautious nature would serve him well, for the years ahead would not go as smoothly as he perhaps anticipated.[44]

Chapter 2

The Path to Power

In September 1548, William replaced Thomas Fisher as the protector's private secretary. He wrote this in his diary. This appointment would have been his reward for his services as the Master of Requests. Clearly he had significant influence over his employer. His new job was to serve in Seymour's office. Though he did not serve the Privy Council in this appointment, he was now of the same standing as the king's secretaries; notably, Sir Thomas Smith. However, as Loades notes, Seymour was paying less attention to the advice of the Privy Council and therefore, it is likely that William had more influence on final decisions than Smith.[1] In July 1547, new church decrees were issued in the name of the boy king. Holy images were banned, and the lighting of candles was forbidden. On November 4, the Act of Six Articles and Treason statute were repealed. The king's sister, Lady Mary, was absolutely opposed to the changes, and her situation became dangerous as she continued to hear up to four masses a day, despite the possibility of punishment. Further confrontation came by 1549, when the *Book of Common Prayer* became the only legal way of worship in England. To Mary, this went against her father's directions, as it was stated that no changes to the acts could be imposed until the young king Edward came of age. Mary's defiance astonished the protector, and created a rift between her and her brother the king, as it had done with her father.[2]

William also sat at Edward VI's first Parliament as a member of the Stamford Borough. It was this Parliament which repealed the Acts of Six Articles. Though William attended, it is difficult to know how much influence he had on the proceedings and decisions. A number of rebellions and uprisings arose due to the banning of masses. However, such reactions from the people would have been expected. By 1549, the new prayer book was forced upon the English. William's dealings with Bishop Gardiner had resulted in the Bishop's arrest and imprisonment in the Tower. However, during the winter of 1548/49, Parliament had a much more difficult task to endure. Thomas Seymour of Sudeley, the Lord Admiral and the protector's brother and king's uncle, was condemned for treason. His greed and ambition had gotten the better of him. Firstly, he attempted to marry the king's half-sister, the Lady Elizabeth, who was still a teenager. When this was denied him, he married her step-mother, dowager queen Catherine Parr. Lady Elizabeth's governess, Kat Ashley, revealed to Thomas Smith that Thomas Seymour had often entered Elizabeth's chamber early in the morning before she had risen and dressed. He reputedly struck her, slapped her on the buttocks and was rumoured to have kissed her on one occasion.[3] The event could be described as molestation in today's terms. Though it is important not to apply modern terms to sixteenth-century contexts, Thomas's behaviour was most definitely a violation of great proportion. The evidence was most likely gathered and kept by William, and the documents used for this trail remain in the Hatfield Collection known as the Cecil Papers.[4]

The Privy Council had been aware of Thomas' bid for more power. On 16 January 1549, he attempted to break into the young king's apartments at Hampton Court Palace. He killed the king's spaniel, who barked upon his entry. It was believed that he was attempting to take the king into his own custody as a means of gaining some influence. He was arrested the next day. The council, of which William was a now a member, gathered their evidence and his house was searched. By 24 February, Thomas Seymour's death was imminent. The council laid thirty-three charges against him, and the next day, a bill of attainder was introduced to Parliament, whereby every member had to find him guilty. Nobody dared opposed it. He was officially declared guilty on 5 March and was executed by beheading on Tower Hill on 20 March.[5] Elizabeth was also investigated for any involvement in Thomas' schemes. She had declared her innocence in Thomas's plots and condemned him.[6] At this point, William was not close to Elizabeth as he would one day be. Nor was he aware during this period of scandal, of which he was a witness, that he would one day serve Elizabeth as her most trusted advisor. As he was a witness to the damage to her reputation as a young woman, this may be the reason for his sympathy towards her cautious attitude for marriage and courtship as queen.

However, though William was lucky enough to have little or no involvement with Thomas Seymour, it was his connection to the protector, that would eventually find him ill-at-ease. Like Seymour and William, the Earl of Warwick was a man of staunch Protestant conviction. He was a product of the religious revolution of Henry VIII's reign. He was also the son of a traitor, who was executed during the same reign. The family, much like the Cecils and Seymours, had benefitted greatly by the Dissolution of the Monasteries, despite their earlier disgrace. Warwick was known as a good soldier, but his ambitions to have Seymour removed from his position, likely in favour of himself, were hidden behind his seemingly devoted service. During his time in Scotland, the protector had allowed Mary, the baby Queen of Scots, to be spirited away to the French court overseas. A rising against the leading government in Norfolk lent an opportunity to Warwick. Warwick needed payment for troops to quash the rebels, but the protector could not pay it. This was when William, as the protector's secretary, began to feel on-edge.[7]

William likely thought that Warwick and the protector were on friendly terms, considering his correspondence with Warwick earlier, where the latter asked William to thank Seymour for particular 'advertisements' which are not specified. Indeed, rather than implying that he had been long against Seymour, it seems that Warwick simply took the opportunity that the rebellions in the north presented. Therefore, William would not have been aware of any upcoming friction between the pair. Despite his friendliness towards Warwick, he knew where his duty lay as the protector's secretary. For without the protector, who was he? Loades states that Seymour, with all his pride and sense of purpose, too often forgot that he was in fact, not the king.[8]

Not only was Seymour feeding a faction of greedy courtiers, seeking favour in pursuit of land and riches, but his extremity towards Lady Mary due to her refusal to stop attending mass was making him even more unpopular amongst the public and nobles. By This time, Gardiner was in the Tower, and England was at a political breaking point. Catholics were persecuted mercilessly and thus, the French and Scots in allegiance with one another, dominated the English Channel. Warwick openly blamed the threat on the protector and summoned the officers of his army to Ely Palace. The Earl of Southampton, Thomas Wriothesley, who was totally opposed to the protector's rise to power in the first place, proved useful for Warwick and helped him convince notable Catholics that he was the right man for the protectorate.[9]

By October, William, as the corrupt protector's secretary, was in a dangerous position. And yet, this is where we begin to see how deep his loyalties lay. Whether it was out of duty to his employer or rather a decision based on the security of his position, of which he had worked tirelessly to obtain, William warned Seymour of the upcoming rebellion against him, by the group referred to as 'the London Lords'. On 6 October, the protector moved the king and those who had not defected, to Windsor Castle from Hampton Court. The fact that he had the king in his custody was likely the only tactic he had left. Correspondence from Warwick, who was in London by then, indicated that he was willing to negotiate. However, the next day, some deal was agreed upon, whereby Seymour's assets and particular

17

servants, probably including William as his secretary, were removed. William's own account of this period is rather scant, but it does appear that he himself was already held in the custody of the Lord Chancellor by 27 September. He had his liberty for most of October, but was sent to the Tower in November. Many servants of Seymour's household joined him there, along with the protector himself.[10]

On 25 November, many men including Robert and William Kett, captains of the Norfolk Rebellion, confessed to high-treason and were sentenced to be hung, drawn and quartered. A knight named William Shirington, who had previously been condemned for the rebellion was pardoned.[11] By January 1550, Warwick had risen to power as 'Lord President of the Council'. Both Seymour and William were released from prison by April, the former protector having been given a seat on the council. On 8 April, Seymour arrived at court at Greenwich. King Edward received him and swore his position on the Privy Council. An honour considering how low he had fallen. He then retired to one of his houses at Savoy.[12] William's initial direction after being released is unclear and it is not known how active he was after his release in 1550. He did not have a seat that year but it is likely that he remained in service to Seymour in some form for some time. In November, Katherine, the Duchess of Suffolk and a good friend to William, wrote to him conveying sympathy for his situation and for the loss of his position with Seymour's family.[13]

Warwick, much like Seymour, was in need of a man like William. He was loyal, discreet and tactful. For his services to Seymour, William was rewarded a manor and rectory at Wimbledon. Though he probably continued some form of service, not entirely severing himself from court, he retired there for some time with his family. From there he could watch, be informed and plan his way back to the very pinnacle of power. His friend Cheke had remained in the king's service as a tutor, and had the boy king's ear. Surely the Chekes wouldn't allow him to fall from grace? Warwick was careful during his ascent to power, but William Cecil was the least of his worries. According to Henry VIII's will, the Lady Mary was Edward's heir, a worrying thought for members of the council. Yet, despite popular belief, the king was generally healthy at this point, and it was thought that he would live to marry and sire an heir. Warwick just about put Mary out of his mind. The council were also relieved to hear that his religious policy was sympathetic to the reformist cause.[14]

The Earl of Warwick, though the son of a traitor, was much admired. He had experience as a soldier, was a family man, much adored by his wife and children. His position as Lord President made him king in all but name. Many thought that his rise to power would be a positive change. The Imperial Ambassador, for one, thought that the changing wheel of fortune might have some beneficial impact on Lady Mary's life. During Christmas 1550, when William would still have been licking his wounds, the Lady Mary was at court to join the young king for celebrations. The king was dressed eloquently, probably as an attempt to make up for his short stature and boy-like appearance. However, Edward may have appeared as a mere child, but his mind was razor sharp, a result of his lessons with Cheke and other scholars. His staunch approach to Protestantism made him a thorn in Mary's side, and he chastised her for her continuation of masses. Though she tried to defend herself, it did little to help her cause. The king was slowly but surely coming into his own, and Mary blamed it on the men surrounding her brother.[15]

Though Mary was able to get away with her defiance during Seymour's time as the Protector, under Warwick, she was much more severely punished. Her household was put under strict surveillance. Services in Latin were outlawed and uniformity was established. It was essential that Warwick had the support of the council to be successful in his ambitions for the religious reforms to take hold. He also needed to haggle with the French; that meant reversing the previous foreign policy under Seymour's rule. He did this by negotiating the marriage of Edward to Elizabeth, daughter of the French king. While this was all settling, and both Seymour and William were recovering from their brush with ruin, Warwick found that he was in need of a man of Protestant conviction, vision and learning. He soon found that the piece he was missing was William Cecil. No better man could undertake such a task as William. Warwick may have considered Smith for the position, but he was untrustworthy as he had sided with the protector. By the time Mary and Edward were openly hostile to one another in terms of religion, William was busy settling into his new role. He was now Secretary of State. The recordings of the Privy Council confirm that he was given this position on 5 September 1550, but the king's journal states the date as 6 September.[16]

William had shown that he could not only prevail through the storms brought on by the warring factions of the boy king's court, but he could also prosper in hindsight of his close call with imprisonment and disgrace. From September onwards, William was referred to as Mr Secretary, and was a respected and sought-after member of the Privy Council. He had the Earl of Warwick's ear, he had the Duke of Somerset's (formally the protector) ear, who was still the king's uncle, and he most notably, through his connection with John Cheke, *de facto* had the ear of the king. In this way, as a man of only thirty years, William was already beginning to emulate his father and particularly, his grandfather. Warwick was quick to learn that he could depend on William for everything. Though the workload may have been more than heavy, this was all part of William's education for much later on in his career. At his house in Canon Row, he would sit at his desk for hours; reading, writing, planning and recording all that was necessary. In essence, William Cecil, the grandson of a once lowly, youngest son of a Welshman, was now running the kingdom of England. And it suited him well.[17]

Some have insinuated that William went even further than his grandfather in his ambitions, implying that he planned an understanding with Warwick; that when he assumed power and supplanted the protector, that William would rise in rank and position for his support. This would portray him as a cunning, manipulative man with ingratitude for his former master who had helped him establish his early career. However, as Charlton stated, there is no evidence to suggest that William plotted with Warwick. It does however, make for an interesting interpretation. William may have been cunning and articulate, but he was by no means willing to sacrifice his honour, when he would likely have continued to rise under the patronage of the protector anyway. Contemporaries of William's who recorded such versions of events were likely attempting to blacken his name, and thus, their interpretation of events have inevitably filtered down through history and into some historical interpretations of his character and ambition.[18]

Indeed, William's loyalties lay with neither duke, nor earl, nor common man, but with the sovereign and God. For his services, he was only too happy to accept numerous new properties and riches. He soon proved that he was more than capable of his office. In fact, he was rather the perfectionist. He took note of everything, and did so methodically, without error or doubt. Given his young age for such a position, even for the period, it is unsurprising that many found William's manner and ability to prosper, despite the changing winds, a dangerous trait.[19] Behind William's outwardly servile disposition towards the crown, lay an inward desire to learn, prosper, and probably most importantly, survive. However, the question, or rather, the problem of the former protector was far from settled. William may have had a new role, but his survival now depended on further distancing himself from Seymour, for the pride of the Duke of Somerset led to his demise.

Edward Seymour could not accept that he now had to bow before those who had once served him as protector. After being released from his imprisonment and surprisingly retaining some position on the council, accepting his lot would seem the most intelligent thing to have done. But he did not. He plotted, and schemed, and eventually it was discovered that he was planning the destruction of Warwick. He was arrested in October, brought to trial, charged, and was eventually executed for attempting to re-take power over government on 22 January 1552. The king was unable to save his uncle, and it is possible that by this stage, as he was coming into his own, he did not wish to. It was clear to all that if Seymour were to be allowed to live, the stability of the current form of government in the name of the king was more than precarious. William was the right person for gathering evidence, and although Charlton states that he was unwilling to partake in his former employer's downfall, he began to gather the incriminating evidence against the duke.[20] Interestingly, the Dowager Duchess of Somerset stated that she believed in William's loyalty to the duke, and knew that he was not guilty in aiding her husband's downfall. She would later leave him a token of her friendship in her will as a sign of her gratitude and friendship. However, William's hand in Edward Seymour's downfall cannot be denied.[21]

The conflicting arguments regarding William's involvement in Seymour's demise matter little in terms of the benefits of it. He received a knighthood and was happy to celebrate the rise of Warwick to his dukedom. The Marquis of Dorset, father of Jane Grey, was also given the dukedom of Suffolk. If William were to not only survive but rise amongst the ranks, he was clever to keep in with these men. Yet, he would not have known of the dangers in doing so. For all his talents, he could not predict the future.[22]

It seems that though prior to the former protector's second and final downfall, William's drift from his service to Warwick's had not created any coolness between the pair. Indeed, though William was agreeable to the changes of fortune, and was prepared to go with it, come what may, there is no evidence suggesting a public disagreement or spat. In fact, though William was always friendly towards his former employer, prior to his role in the trial, it was his unusual friendship with the Duchess of Suffolk, that is far more illuminating and unusual. Upon his appointment as Warwick's secretary, the Duchess of Suffolk wrote to him, congratulating him on his promotion. Oddly, she mentioned that she was fitting out a ship at Boston, indicating that the pair were conducting some business together. But her language may have simply been symbolic of something else. The Duchess was also indifferent to the former protector and complained to William of his 'unkindness'.[23] By November, when her husband was imprisoned, she again wrote to William to ask for an amended warrant for the purchase of Spilsby Chantry. She had also previously asked him for help regarding a dispute between her cousins, which he gave.[24]

The Duchess of Suffolk and Warwick were not William's only friends or confidantes at this time. He may have been moving amongst those in government and with influential women such as the duchess, but he had also struck up a friendship with the Lady Elizabeth by this time. It is unclear how William's friendship with the princess began, or why it came about at all. It may be that the time of the scandal between Elizabeth and Thomas Seymour in 1548, which resulted in Kat Ashley writing to William, set the foundations of some form of acquaintance between them. Perhaps there existed an eventual educational bond between the pair. William as a form of tutor and Elizabeth as his pupil. By 1550, Elizabeth had finally been given the estates and annual income left to her from her father, as stated in his will. William would have played a role in allocating her inheritance as was his job at the time. He then became somewhat of a secretary for the princess, though unofficially and it is unlikely that he had any role in the daily management of her estates or households. He was simply there as an aid if needed. Why he chose to give advice and aid the princess in any form at this point is unclear.[25] What is clear, is that Elizabeth began to trust William from a very early age, and he too may have been sentimental by the time of her accession. He would witness, after all, the deepest depths of her despair and her greatest triumphs.

By the time of Edward Seymour's execution in 1552, the king was now fourteen. Many were undoubtedly readying themselves for the time when he'd take power into his own hands, or at least, more power. William was also developing his genius. Many men of the court and Privy Council were busy engaging themselves in petty disputes, which most of the court had descended into, but he was busying himself with his daily duties as secretary. His capability as a statesman is evident and we get a sense of the greatness that was to come. One issue that he immersed himself in was the task of the state's expenditure. Edward's debts, or the 'king's debts' as they were referred to, were not just based on his own expenditure and that of the court, but of the whole kingdom. The grand sum was a huge liability to the nation, and it often resulted in the borrowing of money from merchants at a high rate of interest as Charlton stated. Such debt could be ruinous for the country in general, but particularly for the new religious reform being directed in the king's name. The improvements that he made to the system which allowed England to take a break from the money-lending of other rich nations, meant that William's reputation as a man of commerce soared.[26]

Warwick, who himself was younger than William's thirty-two years, was also preparing himself for the maturity of the king. Within the space of a year, it was clear to him that he would soon be managing a young man as king, not a boy. The late Duke of Somerset's plans to divide the council had failed and it seemed for a time, that the Reformation would succeed.

Certainly, by this time, the execution of the once Lord Protector was an example to the Lady Mary that the men in power had no qualms about removing the highest man in the kingdom in the name of power, prestige and religion. If the king's own uncle could lose his head, then so could she. Warwick was evidently more ruthless than the Seymours had ever been, and with William Cecil at his side, he no doubt felt that the kingdom was in safe hands. However, the king was fond of his eldest sister, who by this time was in her late thirties. Warwick had to tread carefully not to alienate the princess, but not to welcome her with open arms either. Indeed, when Mary entered court in April 1552, no mention of a conversation of religion was recorded. By this point the new Act of Uniformity was enshrined in law. This meant that religious worship became overtly more Protestant than it had in 1549. The religious prayer book was circulating, allowing for contemplation, religious interpretation and reflection. Mary however, continued to be wholly opposed to what she saw as heresy. She did have the sympathy of some remaining members of the Catholic clergy, but it did little to help her cause.[27]

Towards the end of that year, Mary was continuing to argue that the Church of her father's time adhered to the Roman Catholic faith and that it should remain so. But her fight was not a public one by this stage. By Christmas, the king had caught a cold, but he was believed to be strong and had survived worse. Though it was often stated that Edward was a sickly boy, he was on the contrary, a virile child, much like his father. However, it eventually became clear that he was short of any recovery, and those around the king began to frantically prepare themselves for the inevitable.[28] William may have been the man of the hour regarding the direction of the king's new religion, but he knew, according to Henry VIII's will, that Lady Mary was next in line to the throne; and she would undoubtedly reverse any Protestant policy in England, and clear the Privy Council of men like Warwick and Burghley. If Mary were to be barred from the succession in some manner due to her apparent illegitimacy, then that also meant that the Protestant and favorable Lady Elizabeth should also be barred.[29] Thus, the only other true Protestant heir of legitimate standing was the wife of the Duke of Suffolk, Frances Grey, Henry VIII's niece by his youngest sister Princess Mary Tudor, later Queen of France and Duchess of Suffolk. Most notably, her eldest daughter Jane was similar in age to the king, staunchly Protestant, and likely controllable.[30] Conveniently, she had married Warwick's son Guilford on 25 May 1553.

It is unclear when exactly Edward's health began to deteriorate beyond repair, yet he himself was true to his Protestant convictions and was committed to the Reformation in his name, or so it appears. Whether it be due to his own will or of another we will never know, but in early 1553, probably prior to or just after Lady Jane Grey's nuptials, he drew up a document called his 'Device of the Succession', declaring that Lady Jane Grey and her heirs were next in line to the throne, thus excluding his half-sisters on the grounds of illegitimacy. William would have wholly approved of a Protestant succession. It is unclear how he felt about Elizabeth's exclusion, but it is probable that he was simply happy to avoid Mary's succession in any case. In February, prior to the king's definitive decline, Mary visited him at court. She continued to ask for the removal of restrictions for mass in her house. By March, the king was so unwell, that he could not open Parliament. By the time the new succession was drawn up, few knew of the king's plan including Warwick, and William.[31] Both had signed the king's instructions for the succession on 21 June, as did John Cheke, the Archbishop of Canterbury, amongst other members of the council.

In December 1552, during the celebrations and festivities, Warwick was beginning to feel dismay, and in a letter to William, described himself as 'constrained to seek some health and quietness' and questioned 'what should I wish longer this life, that seeth such frailty in it?' He also expressed his need for friends like William. There was also the problem of the new prayer book, which was finding much criticism amongst the public. The king had previously endorsed and encouraged the people to diligently attend to sermons from the common prayer book, and blamed a sudden outbreak of plague on their disobedience to God.[32] John Knox, a Scottish Minister and theologian who found refuge and exile in England, was tasked with using the new book, yet adapted his use of it on the basis of reform from the continent. He was successful and soon had a large following. However, Knox wanted to go further than the new book allowed, and complained that it sanctioned idolatry, which resulted in him coming into conflict with Thomas Cranmer, Archbishop of Canterbury.[33] Northumberland also wrote to William expressing that he wished the king to appoint Knox as the Bishop of Rochester as a means of dealing with resistance in Kent.[34]

By March 1553, the king was well enough to close Parliament. He was even able to get out for walks in April. This led to talks in early May of his complete recovery, and William, amongst others, may have been able to take a sigh of relief and plan towards the future. However, after the wedding of Jane Grey to Guilford Dudley, the king's health began to fail again. Notably, Jane was not Warwick's first choice of a wife for his son, and indeed, it is clear that he had no ambitions for her to be queen just yet. Equally, Jane felt that Guilford was her inferior and was not pleased to marry him. It went ahead, and just in time for Warwick as the king again began to decline. It must be noted however, that though Jane was named as Edward's heir, her marriage to Warwick's son may simply have been a typical aristocratic marriage in every sense, and to judge Warwick's character based on his choice of wife for his son, is to assume that he knew the king would die, at which point nobody could have predicted, as sickly as he was. The king also gave his approval for the ceremony, but did not attend.[35]

The device initially specified that the heir's male of the many female heirs including Frances and Jane Grey were to inherit the throne. However, Frances was not pregnant by the time of the king's decline, nor was the newly wedded Jane. Thus, he had to change the wording to allow for Jane to inherit 'and' her heirs male. The will was not sanctioned by Parliament, and Edward likely struggled with this fact. But his commitment to the Protestant cause is evident here. Was Mary aware that her brother had actually excluded her from inheriting the throne? She likely thought upon it, but she would not have known who he would pick in her stead. Loades states that the device was technically an illegal document, unsanctioned by Parliament and written in the hand of a king who was a minor.[36] Many council members were torn in their loyalties to the king and his true successor, Mary. But the king became insistent, even furious. So, they had little choice but to sign when ordered. As Tallis put it, 'they were full of foreboding for the future'.[37]

The most notable members of the council may have known of the king's changes to the succession, and Mary too may have had her suspicions. However, by mid-June, rumours began to circulate. Indeed, perhaps one of the members called to witness and sign the device failed to keep the secret. Whatever the case, the Imperial Ambassador, Jehan Scheyfve, wrote to Charles V, Holy Roman Emperor and Mary's cousin that the '…great lords and powerful men have been ordered to repair at once to Court, it is believed in order to deliberate and come to a conclusion of the same question of the succession.' The ambassador continued, reporting that the council planned to 'exclude the Princess [Mary] and the Lady Elizabeth, and declare the true heir to be the Duke of Suffolk's eldest daughter…'[38] It made clear that Mary was excluded due to her religion. Though the device itself was never made public, rumours also proposed that both Warwick and Suffolk would rule the kingdom in Jane's name, as joint regents.[39]

In March 1553, prior to the king's rapid decline and death, William also had to deal with the issue of his inheritance. On 19 March, Sir Richard Cecil died. Richard's will, disinheriting his son due to his marriage to Mary Cheke was likely destroyed once William married Mildred Cooke, seeing as there was no dispute thereafter. However, dates concerning the will (if any existed thereafter) appear to be rather contradictory and it is likely that at the time of Richard's death, there was no will. William was informed of his father's death on 25 March in a letter from Roger Alford.[40] William's grievance that March over the death of his father was noticed by none other than the Princess Elizabeth who granted him, some time after the 20th, lands such as LadyBrigg Close in Northamptonshire. These lands were formally owned by his father and it is interesting that at this point, long before any notion of Elizabeth's ascension, that the pair had formed such a bond and mutual respect.[41]

It is also notable that by April, William took vacation. By this point he had a house at Wimbledon as well as his property at Canon Row. But he withdrew to Canon Row that month. Was he there on personal business as some believe? State Papers for the next month indicate that he received prescriptions of several remedies by John Lord Audley on 9 May. Oddly, the very next day he received another letter from Audley who rejoiced in his recovery, and also sent him on a bill.[42] It was only when Cecil was informed of the king's declining health that he returned to his usual duties. It was also due to his new appointment as a knight of the shire for Lincolnshire. The king himself had requested William's presence for the ceremony at court in Greenwich.[43] When he returned, he was immediately confronted with the problem of the succession, or rather, the problem of the king's new succession plans. This is not to say that he wished for Mary to inherit the throne, but the storm over the succession that had been brewing for some time was about to come to a head. But what were William's thoughts on Mary, in contrast to that of her sister Elizabeth?

William may not have wanted Mary to succeed Edward in the event of his death, but did that mean that he was wholly indifferent towards her in general? Probably not. He knew that he would have to tread carefully; Mary was the lawful heir to the throne by English law and by the late Henry VIII's last will and testament. Perhaps his retreat to Wimbledon was also a time to contemplate his next move. Whatever the case, he certainly had the time to think upon Mary's situation, and though she may have been alone in her dilemma, she was not the only person considering their next move.[44] Much like Warwick, who was by this time the Duke of Northumberland, and the king, William was happy to sacrifice the two Tudor sisters for the sake of the new Common Prayer, and likely to save his position, which he would unlikely retain if Mary succeeded Edward. Mary would likely remember William's part in the late protector's accusations of her involvement in the uprisings. In his favour for a *de facto* Dudley succession, he was also betraying his pupil and friend, Princess Elizabeth.[45]

William not only had his position, wealth and many houses to consider but also the religious reform he had aided to bring about. He also had to consider the safety of his young family and the future of his own dynasty. Mildred had not yet given William another child, yet she would have acted as a mother figure for Thomas. William was cunning enough to know that if he became somewhat neutral in whatever was to come, his family and his political career may survive. His hand may have been plainly written on the king's device, but he could easily have protested that he was ordered to do so (which he likely was), in the event of a Catholic succession. The men who signed the king's device may well have done so under royal command, but the following suspense of what would come next must have been agonising for William. Whatever his reservations, he had given his signature and had to face the consequences.

Lady Jane Grey had less than a month to settle into her marriage before learning of her fate. She knew of her place in the line of succession according to the will of Henry VIII, being a direct descendant of his sister, Mary. She had returned home to the Charterhouse for a brief time before moving on to her husband's family seat at Durham Place on the strand. Yet, by the time she began to settle herself into married life, she would have heard that the king was dying. Indeed, on 9 July 1553, Edward VI, not yet a man, died in the arms of his childhood friend, Henry Sidney.[46] Though they were all prepared for this eventuality, the group that had given their commitment to the Protestant succession must have felt grieved in two ways. The young king whom they had served was gone, and put the future of the Tudor dynasty in question. What kind of king would he have been if he had lived to adulthood? And what would his Reformation have brought? Wriothesley's *Chronicle* recorded that the Lord Mayor of London was called to court at Greenwich on 8 July. With him were eight aldermen, six merchant staplers and six merchant adventurers. The king's death was announced to the council in secret, for obvious reasons. The council were sworn to secrecy until the succession had been dealt with. Two days later on 10 July at 3.00 pm, Lady Jane Grey was summoned to Syon House by barge, where she was informed that she was the Queen of England.[47] That same day, a proclamation naming Jane as queen from the Tower of London, ordered the people's obedience to her as 'their lawful sovereign'. It also openly declared that Lady Mary and Lady Elizabeth were illegitimate.[48]

Any attempt made by Warwick, or rather Northumberland as he should henceforth be referred to as, due to his rise in rank and his daughter-in-law's position as queen, to obtain custody of Mary or Elizabeth, had failed. Jane could never have imagined that the king would leave his kingdom to her.

Indeed, her reaction to the news is unsurprising, considering that she had not been well, and was still coming to terms with her parents' choice of her husband and her relocating to his family home. She later reputedly described the reaction of the lords around her 'giving her so much homage, and not in keeping with my position, kneeling before me...' She added that this 'embarrassed' her.[49] Notable members present were Northumberland, her father Henry Grey, her mother Frances Grey, the Sidneys – for her brother was married to Mary Sidney, and as former secretary to the late king, and likely hoping to keep that title, William Cecil. Jane was said to have fallen to the floor, weeping. She denied the right to the crown immediately upon gaining her composure, and exclaimed 'The crown is not my right and pleases me not. The Lady Mary is the rightful heir.'[50] After much persuasion from the council, her father and father-in-law, she submitted to their will and accepted her fate:

> I greatly bewailed myself for the death of so noble a prince, and
> at the same time, turned myself to God, humbly praying and
> beseeching him, that if what was given to me was rightfully
> and lawfully mine, his divine Majesty would grant me such
> grace and spirit that I might govern it to his glory and service,
> and to the advantage of this realm.[51]

While the council were busying themselves with the new succession, Mary was in Norfolk, on her way to Kenninghall. She had likely been told of the king's death on the morning of 7 July, by her goldsmith, who had recently returned from London. Apparently, she did not believe the news, and barred it from being told in the area. This was a clever tact on Mary's part, for if she were to proclaim herself queen, and the king was in fact alive, she could have been tried for treason. When she reached Kenninghall the next day however, her physician, John Hughes, confirmed the king's demise. On 9 July, the day before Jane Grey was herself summoned to London, Mary proclaimed herself queen of England. However, that was easier said than done, for the day after, having sent a letter to the council, she realised that her right to the throne had been rejected in preference to her teenage cousin, Jane. However, if the council thought that Mary would accept the proclamation, and submit to their will, they were mistaken. Mary had a small, but deeply loyal force to serve her cause, and many proclamations in the area surrounding her residence demanded her ascension to the throne. Many Catholic nobles flocked to her, proclaiming their fealty. It is likely that she had known for some time what would come about after the king's death, for she was readily prepared. Northumberland, and indeed, William, underestimated Mary and the loyalty of the people. Clearly, William's hand in the late king's Reformation had not touched as many as he thought, for England's loyalty to the first princess went deeper than religion; the people were reminded of the will of the late Henry VIII, and his once revered first queen – Katherine of Aragon.[52]

When the council told Jane of her new position, they already knew that Mary had a large following. Her band of soldiers began to grow as she rode towards London, seeking her destiny. Three days later, the council became aware of the growing opposition to Jane's ascension. From then, Mary's victory was almost certain. Northumberland left London with a group of lords on the thirteenth day, but those who he felt he could rely on most had sided with Mary, such as the Earl of Oxford. If Mary was ready for a fight, she needn't have been. By 16 July, the council had met to discuss their options. Many believed that Mary would be merciful if they changed their loyalties to her. Indeed, it was even believed that she might spare her young cousin. Two days later, it was reported that she had around 30,000 men following her banner, loyal to her cause.[53]

By 19 July, it was all over. The council were split, with William, amongst many others, siding with Mary. He likely knew by this point that she would succeed, and so, to save his own skin, as well as that of his family's, not to mention his position, he had little choice. Mary was propelled to power, supplanting Jane easily by the stroke of a pen. This was the most popular succession since her great-grandfather Edward IV's defeat of Henry VI and Margaret of Anjou in the 1460s. William was not only one of many to celebrate the changing winds of succession in Mary's favour, but he was also, according to his own testimony, one of many on the council who argued in favour of the princess. He 'practiced with the Lord Treasurer to win the Lord Privy Seal that I might by the Lord Russell's means, cause Windsor Castle to serve the Queen [Mary].'[54] He was quick to show his loyalty to the new queen, and rode towards Ipswich where she was already moving towards London. This was a wise decision, one that may have influenced his survival. Mr Secretary would be given a pardon, but would he still be able to refer to himself as such for much longer...?

Chapter 3

Heretics and Martyrs

In his *Chronicle,* Wriothesley described the day of Mary's triumph. It appears that William was not the only member of the council to declare their loyalty to the new queen and quickly ride out to meet her. Indeed, William, the Lord Mayor of London, the Earl of Shrewsbury, a council clerk, Sir John Mason and likely more, met her on her way to London. They met her at the Earl of Pembroke's home, Baynard's Castle. There, they all rode into London, declaring Mary Tudor, the daughter of Henry VIII, as Queen of England. It was said that the people wept with joy.[1] On the evening of the 20th, the Earls of Arundel and Paget had also met Mary at her base at Baynard's, and thus also rode with her to London. It is interesting, that the men who had sworn fealty to Jane, could quickly turn against her when they knew Mary's victory was imminent. Indeed, Arundel, who had recently declared for Jane, stated in a speech when the council met, that:

> This Crown belongs rightfully, by direct succession, to My Lady Mary lawful and natural daughter of our King Henry VIII. Therefore, why should you let yourselves be corrupted and tolerate that anybody might unjustly possess what does not belong to him…?[2]

Most men who declared their loyalty to Mary were lucky, including William. She knew William well. Whether they were on the same terms as William and Elizabeth is another matter. But Mary, like her predecessors and eventual successor, saw the value in William's loyalty and service. She knew a lot about him, his abilities and his religious convictions. Two years earlier, during the council's inquisition of her religion, she read the king's letter handed to her and reputedly exclaimed 'Ah, good master Cecil took much pain here'. Here she suggested that it was William who drafted the letter and not the king himself. She pardoned him, likely much to his relief. In fact, the new queen was apparently very fond of him, and suggested that if he changed his religion, she would happily have him as her secretary and councillor.[3]

William probably made no such deal with the new queen, for he was not appointed to any office. He was eventually ordered to give up his seals of the Order of the Garter.

> After our hearty commendations. The Queen's Highness pleasure is, that you [William Cecil] shall immediately upon sight hereof send unto her highness all such seals as remaineth in your custody belonging to the Order of the Garter, sealed either in some bag or otherwise as the same may come most safely to her Majesty's hands. Whereof we pray you fail not. From St. James's 21st September 1553.[4]

This meant giving up his position as chancellor also, which is unsurprising. This reveals his true piety and staunch belief in the Protestant religion. Indeed, he would have been happy to serve the queen, but he served God first.

Mary, upon her ride to London on 3 August, was joined by her sister Elizabeth and members of the council. Elizabeth had previously written to her sister, congratulating her on her victory. It is unknown what Elizabeth thought about Jane's ascension in the first place. She likely disfavoured the notion, as it would have an effect on her own place in the line of succession, despite Jane's Protestant faith. Elizabeth had not played any part in Mary's success. Indeed, she may have had her reasons for laying low during Jane's nine days as queen, despite her own feelings regarding the rights of her sister's succession.[5] She only rallied behind Mary when she knew she would triumph, much like William had.

Despite the thirteen years between them, it is not difficult to dissect the similarities between Elizabeth's and William's minds. They were shrewd, tactful, and knew when to pledge their loyalty, and when to stay away. Where William could not accept Mary's proposition for his remaining as secretary if he were to denounce his faith, Elizabeth, despite her piety, was not so stubborn. Likely due to her place in the line of succession, and Mary's age. Elizabeth was given a position beside Mary, as appropriate for the next in line to the throne. This was a public statement, ensuring that it was known that she was Mary's heir, and that the House of Tudor was bountiful and secure.[6] At this time, the fact that they were both women mattered little, for all of Edward's heirs were female anyway.

Though not given an official position, William was far too important a figure to simply vanish into obscurity, like his family in the Welsh Marches. Indeed, he was far too cunning. Despite his staunch faith, in order to survive both literally and politically, he had to show his loyalty to the crown, and its new bearer in some fashion. He was a member of the commissions of the peace, and strangely, on the one that sought out heretics. He also served as a secretary and treasurer to a number of councilors, such as Paget. There were many instances where William was working behind the scenes of foreign, diplomatic affairs, yet he was simply not mentioned due to his lack of official position. He was not present in Mary's first three openings of Parliament. Interestingly, Gardiner, who was by this time Chancellor and no friend of William's, was likely the person responsible for appointing positions for occasions such as these.[7] Gardiner had risen high since Mary's accession and had even crowned her during her coronation on 1 October 1553.[8] However, by 1555, his health was declining, and whether this had an impact or not, William found a seat in Parliament once more, serving for Lincolnshire. By the time William was crawling out of the shadows, Mary, the queen, was sinking deep within their depths. Her marriage to her cousin, Prince Philip of Spain, later Philip II, was disastrous. She was in love with her husband, but was far older than him at thirty-seven. He was indifferent towards her. Despite two phantom pregnancies, also likely the symptoms of cancer, Mary never produced an heir for England. By 1555, after her failed 'pregnancy', many knew that Mary was ill and her reign would soon come to an end.[9]

This was in stark contrast to the depiction of Mary upon becoming queen. In 1554, she was described as 'the most serene Madame Mary... Defendress of the faith'. Yet, in her thirty-eighth year, she was also said to be low in stature, with a red and white complexion, very thin with large eyes and reddish hair. It was also said that if it were not for her age, 'she might be called handsome'.[10]

William's personal life on the other hand, despite the uncertainty of his career, was rather happy. His second wife, Mildred, after many years of marriage, gave birth to a baby girl in 1554, whom they named Frances. He recorded this is his memoranda/diary of dates.[11] This is another reason why he was willing to outwardly renounce his faith to an extent, but not in the name of royal service. It has been rarely suggested, if speculated, that William's loyalty during these years lay not with the crown, nor the job, but with his family. Now that he was a father of two, with a wife and extended family to think of, it must be considered that he remained subordinate to Mary for the safety of his own dynasty. While the queen herself concentrated on returning England to the Catholic faith and giving it a Catholic heir to cement that reversal, William already had a family to consider, and a family man he was. He was happy to attend mass, made generous offerings in his parish, had a priest serve in his household as his chaplain, and even strolled with his rosary beads in his hands.[12]

Many Protestants fled England upon Mary's succession, though those who were brave enough to stay were also careful not to flaunt their reformed faith. Those who did faced the dire consequences of inquisition, imprisonment or worse – we know how that went. As Smith mentions, William had options upon Mary's triumph, and at least three. One was to remain in England and conform to an extent, which he did. He could have fled to mainland Europe. There were many options, such as Germany and Geneva, for reformers like William to hang up their hats and wait through the storm. Both of William's fathers-in-law, Cooke and Cheke, fled. The final option that he could have taken was to have stayed and proclaimed his faith openly, and hope that he might survive.[13] But that was too much of a risk for William to take. He was sure that staying in England was the better option, rather than relocating his family, and likely a pregnant wife, to mainland Europe.

For the next several years, William was patient. He conformed outwardly, but observed, and was careful not to step out of line. This is where he mastered his skills in self-effacement, according to Smith.[14] He likely kept himself busy with his own estates and affairs, which luckily he was permitted to keep. With his growing family, it was a much safer and tactful option to stay at Wimbledon or Canon Row. His mother, now ageing herself and a widow after the death of William's father, remained at Burghley, yet they had a good relationship. This should not be seen as a form of retirement on William's part, but rather a time in which he took to reflect on his status, and the possibilities of the future. Indeed, though the five years of Mary's reign were chaotic and even bloody, they were no bloodier than Henry VIII's or the future Elizabeth's. However, it was the fates of Northumberland and Lady Jane, along with members of their families, that proved to William how dangerous it could be to be ambitious.

The surviving members of the council now had to conclude what was to be done with those who had dismissed Mary's claim to the throne and placed Jane in her stead. Many were arrested and interrogated between 23 and 26 July. William, however, was safe for now. But the Duke of Northumberland and his family were questioned, along with the Marquis of Southampton, the Duke of Suffolk, the Earl of Huntington, Jane Grey and a number of knights and members of the clergy.[15] Most blamed Northumberland, and Mary herself seems to have put most of the blame on him. Jane was the only woman later tried for treason for the whole affair. Northumberland was eventually executed in late August. All the Dudley sons were convicted. However, Jane's father, the Duke of Suffolk, was pardoned. Though Jane was imprisoned in the Tower, Mary was inclined to also pardon her, that is, if it were not for her father's foolish rebellion.[16] She too would be later executed in February 1554, at the Tower.

Though Gardiner was now at the head of Mary's government and court, there was another who wished to eradicate the Protestant religion on the behalf of the new queen, but in a less violent manner than Gardiner. Cardinal Pole, Mary's cousin, attempted to convert reformers back to the old faith rather than submit them to interrogation or worse. William had defied the queen in refusing to return to Catholicism and was spending much time on his estates, and was probably rather irritated by his non-existing position. However, as Mary's government in general began to crack down on Protestant households, he decided that a new course of action was needed. The House of Commons was resisting the new Marian sanguinary laws proposed by the government. As William was still a member of the parliament of Lincoln, he was amongst those who wholly opposed the proposed enactments. This was bold, daring and particularly dangerous, considering he had escaped death by the skin of his teeth and had witnessed the downfall of so many who were once close to him. This only led to further suspicion of Protestants on the outskirts of the newly formed court.[17]

It was by Mary's orders that the council requested the presence of 'dissenters'. However, he was saved, despite his open opposition to the government's new proposals. This was likely due to him being brought before his former colleagues, Paget and Petre. He asked to be heard first before being found guilty, and he was able to defend himself and his convictions, while avoiding accusations of treason. Loades states that though this version of events cannot be fully validated, it was likely true. William's diary is scant of anything in particular to indicate this, besides stating that he was present for the debate and was 'at some risk', but that does not necessarily mean it did not occur. William kept in touch with those who had fled abroad, notably John Cheke, who settled himself in Strasburg. While he 'debated' with Parliament, his conformity in general cannot be dismissed. He may have felt some guilt for this, but in a letter in 1556, Cheke commended him for voicing his opposition to Parliament, which likely alleviated his conscience somewhat.[18]

By the beginning of 1556, William was hopeful for the succession of Elizabeth, and though Mary was slowly but surely reversing her brother's and father's reformations, the period of her reign was not a happy one, for herself, nor England. Many were unhappy with the brutality of the Marian government, and plots began in the attempt to place Elizabeth on the throne. Though by this time she was unlikely involved personally, Elizabeth would be punished simply for being unwillingly at the epicenter of conspiracy. Throughout these difficult times for Elizabeth and Protestants in general in England, William remained loyal to her in a sense, and continued in her service when necessary.[19] It was during this period that William may have been one of few reformers personally attached to the future queen. It is unknown how close they were at this point, but it is likely that their bond, which lasted most of their lifetimes, was established out of their mutual outward conformity, and underlying zeal for learning, reform and ultimately survival.

The queen herself had become unpopular. This was due to her unmovable position towards the punishment for heresy. However, it began out of her marriage to Philip. As the son of the emperor, with royal blood to better, if not to match that of Mary's distinguished heritage, Philip may have seemed a suitable contender to join Mary on the throne. Indeed, England had never before had a queen regnant in her own right. She was the first woman, besides the wobbly nine days of Jane's ascension, to rule England in her own right, and due to her own popularity. However, it was inconceivable at this time, as William would one day dispute with Elizabeth, that a woman, whether queen or not, should not have a husband. Mary understood this and was happy to conform to the expectations of her gender, despite her position. She chose Philip, but she ruffled a few feathers in the process. William, though arguably semi-retired, was occasionally given employment and thus was witness to the first of many poor decisions on Mary's part that overshadowed her reign as England's first queen regnant. From the shadows, he watched as Mary grew more and more unpopular, and with the opposition to her marriage and the revival of the heresy laws, not to mention the lack of an heir, William may have thought that it would only be a matter of time until Elizabeth's accession. He became braver too, opposing the threat of confiscation of properties belonging to fellow reformers abroad. He reputedly proclaimed that 'Although with danger to myself, I spoke my opinion freely and brought upon me some odium thereby; but it is better to serve God than man.' This was again, his tactful way of expressing his true faith and opposition to the Marian government without committing treason.[20]

William was lucky to have many connections at Mary's court. He was popular with the Bacons and Greys, the latter being the relations of the ill-fated Lady Jane. Jane, her father, husband and uncle had all been executed after the Greys' involvement in the Wyatt Rebellion, but some members of the family survived. However, William's influence could only go so far. His brother-in-law John Cheke was kidnapped and brought back to England after a series of what Smith refers to as 'vigorous campaigns with his pen'.[21] Though Cheke repented, conformed outwardly like William, and seemed to be a converted Catholic, he eventually died in 1557. Whatever the reason, for the year of 1557 in his memoranda, William did not make a recording, either for the death of his beloved friend Cheke, nor any other event. Whether this was because of his grief regarding the year is merely speculative, although it does evoke one to suspect such sentiments.

The question of Mary's position as queen remained unquestionable to most, whether or not they openly conformed to the heresy laws and inwardly opposed them. Mary was the eldest surviving child of Henry VIII and despite her religion, had every right to be queen. William did not dispute this, but like many repressed reformers, he must have feared the notion of her becoming pregnant and producing a Catholic male heir. We know in hindsight that Mary probably never became pregnant in the first place, despite twice believing that she was. By the time Mary sat firmly and confidently on the throne, and had settled into a marriage of political necessity and convenience rather than that of mutual affection or love, she was already approaching her fortieth year. As was the case for many if not most women over forty during this period, she was likely beyond her child-bearing years.[22] Not only this, but she had long suffered from menstrual conditions for much of her life which often made her 'melancholy' and brought her great pain. Indeed, her condition was referred to as the 'suffocation of the matrix [womb]' by Giovanni Michieli, the Venetian Ambassador in 1557, in his final report upon leaving England.[23] Soon after her marriage, Mary believed that she was pregnant, and that she could feel the child 'stir' inside of her. Indeed, her physicians soon confirmed her suspicions and it was soon proclaimed across the kingdom and Europe that 'The queen is with child'. Soon, she showed all the symptoms of a woman carrying a child. Her clothes no longer fit, her stomach grew, and she apparently continued to feel her child moving within her. It was predicted that she would give birth some time before 9 May 1555. As letters to announce the baby's arrival were prepared, William, Elizabeth, and many of England's underground Protestant population may have held their breath.[24] If Mary had a healthy baby, then they could entirely abandon any hopes for a Protestant succession.

Mary prepared for the usual confinement protocol and ceremonies. Philip was present in England during this time and they moved to Hampton Court prior to her lying-in. Elizabeth was at Woodstock at the time and was summoned to court. She arrived in late April, and had to endure Mary's lecturing regarding her involvement in the Wyatt Rebellion and her refusal to admit any wrong-doing. They were reconciled and as the country awaited the birth of an heir, Mary must have felt sure of her victory. On 30 April, bells rang announcing that Mary had delivered a baby safely. Not only that, but it was reported to be a boy. William's reaction to the news is unknown, but soon afterwards, it became clear that the reports of a son being born to the queen were merely rumour. The bells stopped ringing and the rejoicing ended.[25] There was no baby. There never would be. Whether this fiasco was the result of a phantom pregnancy or cancer of the womb, of which she may have died from in the end, one thing was certain, Elizabeth would one day succeed Mary as queen.

The evidence of Elizabeth's compliance in the Wyatt Rebellion is scant. Indeed, it may seem that the rumour of her involvement in movements to put her on the throne stemmed from Mary's (and much of her council's) paranoia. Gardiner in particular kept his eye on her during this traumatic time in her life. She was summoned, interrogated, imprisoned, released and put under house-arrest, and was continuously under the watchful eyes of Mary's supporters. Some have stated that it was Gardiner who came to Elizabeth's defence when it was proposed she be put on trial. Some also depict him as being her greatest enemy. Nares discusses the possibilities in depth and reveals that Gardiner was unlikely to have offered such lenity to the princess, he was also far from her worst enemy at the time. As Nares also points out, it is difficult to state whether there was any existing correspondence between William and Elizabeth during the period of her incarceration, house-arrest and the queen's 'pregnancy'. However, as he was the first she called upon to be by her side when she ascended the throne, it is likely that he had been in some way helpful to her during her time of peril. This is simply speculative but the 'Wyatt period' was one which undoubtedly remained embedded in Elizabeth's memory, as it did her then supporters.[26]

By the time Elizabeth was moved to Woodstock under house-arrest, the country was already stirring with political unrest and many were unsatisfied with the current queen's policy. She may have previously been given more power as a female sovereign by Parliament as a means of controlling the power of her husband, but all of these factors began to bubble over by the time it became clear that Mary was not pregnant. About ten months after Mary had married Philip, William accompanied Paget and Hastings to Brussels. This was to bring back Cardinal Pole, Mary and Elizabeth's cousin through their Plantagenet line. This was Mary's attempt to bring England back to the subjugation of Rome through the means of direct contact with her own blood. It is unsurprising that he accepted the commission to travel to Brussels, seeing as he had already declined the queen's offer as secretary. If anything, this shows that William remained in some favour with Mary, despite his loyalty to the Reformation and to the Princess Elizabeth. The queen herself was careful in trusting him completely, but neither did she allow any man to accuse him of treachery. After some time, William and his comrades were recalled back to England, and Pole remained on the continent.[27]

By 1556, Elizabeth had so-far managed to survive the wrath of Mary and her Catholic supporters, as had William by conforming to the best of his ability and to which his conscience could allow. It is clear that Mary and Elizabeth were not close sisters. In fact, they were likely more than unfond of one another. Mary had not given the kingdom an heir that was so desired, and Philip was becoming frustrated. The English would not crown him as king, and Mary would not give him the son he needed to secure his authority in England and in Spain. This is when the behaviour of the queen's husband became suspicious. It was clear to many that the heir to the throne was Elizabeth, not only by law or right, but by fact. She was the only legitimate contender, and the only acknowledged living child of Henry VIII after Mary. Philip was clever to lend a hand of friendship to Elizabeth, but it was evident to many that this olive branch suited his own agenda more than anything. Elizabeth spent the next two years keeping Philip at bay. The once obscure princess was now becoming more visible, as were those loyal to her. William had managed to keep his foot in the door of politics just enough to not become entirely invisible, and he was able to keep an eye on Elizabeth. He kept to his local duties and had connections abroad with men like Thomas Cornwallis for example, the Treasurer of Calais.[28]

One question is how William survived financially during Mary's five-year reign. By 1557, the Earl of Bedford, who had long been a thorn in Mary's side, had made his peace with her. He kept in contact with William while stationed abroad in Calais. It is notable that William had taken the Earl's wife and children into his care during this time, and this may account for his financial stability towards the end of the Marian reign. Indeed, William may have been lucky to have some financial stability after the death of his father as this only added to his wealth. But it helped to maintain relations both at home and abroad. William's services went beyond that of the Princess Elizabeth's and it was his ability to form close friendships with individuals of some means that reveals his shrewd, tactful nature and survival abilities. Indeed, he kept his family well-connected in general – his sister Elizabeth married well in 1555. His children were well-educated and no expense was spared during this time regarding their musical talents, as Loades states. [29]

By October 1558, it became clear that Queen Mary was not only seriously ill, but likely to die within weeks. Her health may have always been poor, but since her ascension it had fluctuated greatly. She would be well and merry for a period and then ill and down for months at a time. This may well have accounted for her poor treatment of Elizabeth in 1556. Mary was also left abandoned by Philip, and by the time she was at death's door, he was not by her side. Oddly, several months after he left for Spain, Mary again thought she was pregnant, but it was clear to all by this time that she was not. Nobody would take her seriously, and though her ladies seemingly humoured her, her mental state was also clearly affected by the physical strain on her body – likely caused by cancer and years of stress. Philip avoided returning to England; probably for the simple fact that he did not want to. Nor was he willing to claim the throne as Mary's spouse for fear of bringing about civil war. Mary was eventually convinced to acknowledge Elizabeth as her heir, and therefore, acknowledge that her life was coming to an end. Mary Tudor, England's first queen regnant, died at St James's on 17 November 1558, at around 6.00 am. She was forty-two years old. William recorded her parting in his memorandum, while also noting Elizabeth's accession.[30] Before Mary's body went cold, many had already flocked to Hatfield to pay their respects to the new queen. William was one of them and perhaps an instigator of the plan to quickly show allegiance to the new queen. Elizabeth was quick to assemble a new council for a new reign, and William was perhaps the wisest choice amongst the first.[31]

Wriothesley's *Chronicle* notes that on the same day, at 11.00 am, Lady Elizabeth, as Mary's heir to the crown, was proclaimed Queen of England, France and Ireland, and Defender of the Faith, in London, with heralds of arms and trumpeters. On the exact same day of her ascension, her cousin, and one of Mary's firm supporters, Cardinal Pole, Archbishop of Canterbury, also died at Christchurch. Only days later, on 23 November, after the flocking of her new subjects and courtiers had ceased, Elizabeth left Hatfield and made her way to the Charterhouse in London. She was met by the sheriffs of London in Middlesex, and by the 28th, made her way into London.[32]

Out of many who flocked to Elizabeth before she left Hatfield was Philip's adviser, Count Feria. He had been present when the former queen lay dying but had made his way to Elizabeth in the anticipation of her accession. This was Philip's way of keeping in with Elizabeth and England, in the hope that he could still wield some political influence. According to Feria, Elizabeth knew of her close proximity to power as Mary lay on her deathbed. The fact that she appeared to be conscious of this is a reflection of her own shrewd character. Those chosen for her skeleton council, William included, not only revered her, but already feared her.

One week after being proclaimed queen, Elizabeth was already showing signs of great promise. Feria reported to Philip:

> The kingdom is entirely in the hands of young folks, heretics and traitors, and the Queen does not favour a single man... who served her sister. ... The old people and the Catholics are dissatisfied, but dare not open their lips. She seems to me incomparably more feared than her sister, and gives her orders, and has her way, as absolutely as her father did. Her pre-sent Controller, Parry, and Secretary Cecil, govern the kingdom, and they tell me the Earl of Bedford has a good deal to say.[33]

She was every bit the daughter of the late king Henry, as she showed through her diligence, reservation and acumen regarding those she chose to serve her. William in particular, according to Feria, became one of her greatest favourites in the days even prior to Mary's death. She knew who to trust and who her friends were. Nobody more than William deserved her recognition, for without his loyalty to the Protestant cause, and indeed assistance to her regarding her estates, the new queen may well have found herself in a different position. William's ability to survive the severity of the Marian regime was proof enough of his capabilities, he had seen more than one Tudor reign. Notably, he was young – not as young as the twenty-five-year-old queen, but at thirty-seven, he was experienced, yet young enough to set a new reign and regime in motion.[34]

It was William who apparently, prior to the rest of the council's arrival at Hatfield, had informed the queen of her accession. On 20 November, she welcomed William to Hatfield:

> I give you this charge, that you shall be of my Privy Council and content yourself to take pains of me and my realm. This judgement I have of you, that you may not be corrupted of any manner of gift, and that you will be faithful to the state, and that without respect of my private will you give me that counsel that you think best, and if you show anything necessary to be declared to me as secrecy, you shall shew it to myself only. And assure yourself I will not fail to keep taciturnity therein, and therefore herewith I charge you.[35]

As Hume notes, William had drawn up a document aimed to guide the new sovereign. This provided her with in-depth detail of her role, what was expected, and what her initial duties were. Some of these details provided the suggestion that she move to the Tower prior to her coronation, and to secure herself there with her officers and council until further instructed, or rather, advised. She was also initially advised to consider the dangers of Scotland and France during this time of transition. And as she had witnessed the fall of Lady Jane Grey, she knew all too well the fragility of her position prior to being securely brought to the capital. The queen took William's council very seriously, as he took his newfound position. Indeed, within one week of Elizabeth's seemingly smooth ascension, all religious persecutions across the country had ceased, and those imprisoned for 'heresy' were released. All refugees who had fled their homeland five years previously began to flock back to England in droves. Neither William, nor Elizabeth, initially wished to adopt extreme measures towards Catholics, as Mary had done to Protestants. However, if William thought the struggle regarding England's religion was a thing of the past, he would soon find that his work towards securing the succession of Protestantism, in Elizabeth's name, had only just begun.[36]

Chapter 4

A New Regime

It is easy for us to compare the successes of Elizabeth's reign to the failures of her sister Mary's in retrospect. Indeed, it is often stated that without the men around her who offered wise council, such as William, that Elizabeth's reign may not now be referred to as England's 'Golden Age'. However, that is not to say that Elizabeth solely depended on her chosen council of advisors from the beginning of her reign. Nor should we be quick to judge the perils of Mary Tudor's short time of the throne. Indeed, for all the great men that these unprecedented rulers surrounded themselves with, they were well capable of knowing whose guidance to seek, who to keep close, and who to keep as far away from the throne as possible. Elizabeth's reign may well have been very different to that of Mary's, but it must also be considered that Elizabeth had Mary's reign to look back on, as did her council, made up entirely of men.

The men who flocked from the dying Mary's court to Hatfield in pursuit of the new queen were likely already reformers at heart. Indeed, William and Sir Nicholas Bacon for example, were only two of many who took advantage of Mary's death, and both ended up on Elizabeth's council because they had the wit to express their loyalty to her. Mary kept the council of men such as her husband Philip, or her cousin, Reginald Pole. She traditionally and willingly gave men offices such as lord chancellor and privy seal. However, Elizabeth kept such offices for herself, as had her father. Mary may well have felt it wise to keep to the traditions of her many predecessors, but Elizabeth, ever the Tudor propagandist, and perhaps due to the advice of her new council of which William was a member, chose to make her secretary her principal advisor. It is no surprise then, given that William was granted this office, that Elizabeth's reign remains one of the most celebrated to date.[1]

Within hours of Mary's death, the proclamation of Elizabeth's accession was read out in Westminster and London. She was proclaimed 'by the grace of God, Queen of England, France, and Ireland, defender of the faith...'. William, in his newfound position, took no moment of respite to take it all in. He acted quickly for this proclamation to be announced. It is likely that he even had it ready prior to Mary's death. The day after the proclamation, he wrote 'done, to Jugge', referring to Richard Jugge, who was the newly appointed royal printer. His workshop was conveniently located beside St Paul's Cathedral in London. Here William was already beginning to show his true ability, not just as the queen's head of council and her private secretary, but also as a man of true economic and political strategy. The proclamation was printed five-hundred times, and at the low price of twenty-two shillings and sixpence. This was to be paid for by the new government in the name of the new queen. This was one of William's first successes in office. Though it may seem like a mundane task, this is the William that should be remembered. He was concise, prepared, and knew exactly how to promote Elizabeth's reign in its earliest days, at no huge cost to a country that was not the economic powerhouse it had been during Henry VIII's early reign. Within a few short weeks, the world knew that England and Ireland had a new queen.[2]

It is often stated that Elizabeth's reign differed from Mary's due to her religious tolerance. However, though Elizabeth wished to show such leniency by discharging her subjects of all of their previous bonds and obligations, who now simply had to show their loyalty to her, the situation eventually became more complicated. Mary too, in many ways, showed tolerance to some extent. For if she was wholly opposed to religious reformers such as William, he would not have been alive to witness Elizabeth's triumph. Mary may have burned some 300 Protestants to return England to the old faith, but she evidently did not burn all 'heretics'. Indeed, Elizabeth herself, and their father Henry, were just as bloody as Mary when it came to supremacy and religion. So, what started out as a reign of tolerance and peace, would eventually mirror the Marian reign in many ways, due to the religious and political conflicts of the period. But for now, with the many copies of proclamations finding themselves in the hands of Elizabeth's new subjects, her people were happy to cry out 'God save the Queen'. Elizabeth herself however, was apparently saddened by the loss of her sister, despite their differences and difficult relationship. She also expressed that her reign was the work of God, and God's wish. William himself, despite all his efforts in making Elizabeth's accession popular and as smooth as possible, was also a man of God, and believed that Elizabeth's accession, and therefore his own newfound position, was the will of God. The new queen's intelligence, stamina and independence was clear for all to see. Yet, the new queen had a vanity about her, which was also noticed, mostly by Feria, even prior to her accession. It would be up to her new council and men like William Cecil, to now navigate through that vanity and independence, and to help mold a young woman into every bit the Tudor queen.[3]

Elizabeth's reign, despite her being the last of Henry VIII's legitimate children, was in no way more secure than her brother's, sister's, nor even Lady Jane Grey's, for she was not the only remaining contender for the throne. However, William and Elizabeth's council's choice of language used to proclaim her 'as the only right heir by blood, and lawful succession' gave Elizabeth's legitimacy and right to the crown that extra bit of zeal. Mary's reign began popular, but the people, whether Catholic or fearful Protestants, may have hoped that the young, beautiful and vivacious new queen would bring about change. Elizabeth's legitimacy and her right to the crown have long been debated upon and discussed. Indeed, few historians would dare argue against her legitimacy, and so, we can safely put any notions of bastardy to one side. However, it must be noted that both Elizabeth and Mary felt it necessary to pronounce the validity of their parents' marriages, but in different ways. Elizabeth's ability to quickly insist on her own legitimacy was either clever, or cleverly advised – it is difficult to say how often Elizabeth's decisions were made without the aid of some council, but most definitely she felt it necessary to proclaim her blood was stronger than that of her aunts' descendants' claims, such as Mary, Queen of Scots, or Frances Grey, Duchess of Suffolk, and her surviving daughters.[4] However, Mary's need to legally note the validity of her parents' marriage, was not because Queen Anne Boleyn was any more popular than Katherine of Aragon, but because under the order of her father and in fear of her life, she had agreed that Henry's and Katherine's marriage was incestuous. Elizabeth herself never proclaimed or agreed that her parents' marriage was unlawful, even despite her own dire predicament during Mary's reign. However, both queens had different experiences that cannot always be compared. However, though Elizabeth's mother was decapitated for trumped up charges of adultery and incest, her circumstances upon ascension, in terms of the people's support and affection, were far greater than Mary's. William's work on the proclamation of Elizabeth's reign only further strengthened the people's belief in legitimacy.

The queen's legitimacy and the religious direction that England would move towards, were two matters which William and the government had to contend with. Indeed, by the time the last Tudor came to the throne, England was not only in religious and social turmoil, but financial difficulty. Elizabeth found that most of her revenue was long spent. Not only that, but the kingdom was indebted by around four million pounds according to Nares, who points out that Mary I had bankrupted England though her 'madness'.[5] Whatever that meant. Nares also points out that the author of William's memoirs published in 1738 pointed out the mismanagement of Mary's financial affairs – '…the treasures of the Crown exhausted, the Crown itself in debt, and mightily dishonoured by the late feeble administration…'.[6] However, in truth, it seems that Henry VIII spent heavily during his reign, depleting much of the bursting treasury his father had left him. Indeed, though Mary's reign was in many ways a failure, particularly in that she was unable to provide a Catholic male heir, she did much of what she set out to do in her short tenure, and for that, she should be commended. Whoever was to blame for England's financial instability, William would find a way to manage the country's expenses – and the privy-purse.

It was clear from the onset, that the man who had the balance of power in his hands was William Cecil. It was he who had kept a link between the court, those who secretly favoured the new religion and Elizabeth when she was in Hatfield during Mary's short reign. Smith makes a comparison between William, Somerset and Northumberland by stating that William used the company of the queen, who was indeed rather vulnerable during the early days of her reign, the very same way the latter two used Edward VI.[7] However, though it is likely true that William saw Elizabeth's accession as the opportunity to continue the Reformation in England, and to secure the Protestant religion as the dominant faith, he was not as self-serving as the men that came before him. Elizabeth was no child, nor was she easily influenced, nor entirely trusting. She may have wished to rule through good counsel, but she was the queen.

Elizabeth may not have been the first queen regnant of England, but her reign was unique. The political situation in Europe was at boiling point, as was the religious fervour. Elizabeth was a young woman, never thought to rule. As a Protestant, she stood rather alone. She counted on the men she chose to lead her government out of absolute necessity of their talents. Elizabeth often had an imperious demeanor – at least, that's what we like to think. But her belief in William is evident from the very beginning of her reign, and he would be one of few who seldom disappointed her. It is important to note that in terms of Elizabeth's gender, that though she was queen, she was still a woman, thought to be weaker in both body and mind to that of men. Whether a woman had royal status or not, as Guy points out, she was still expected to be subordinate to a man.[8] The problem was however, that no man of higher status existed in England when she became queen. She had male relatives, but none that could match that of her own legitimacy. She had no husband – an issue which William would remind the queen of daily. Though Elizabeth may have been offered some honorary status above her male subjects, this is not to say that her position was seen as androgynous. It is also notable that though the queen would have many favourites or fancies during her reign, William was never one of them. Indeed, when she first came to the throne, William Cecil was distinguished, wealthy, powerful and only thirty-five years old. Yet, their relationship grew into something stronger than friendship, and more valuable to Elizabeth than romantic love.[9]

William may well have been the new queen's most trusted adviser, and he may have found himself at the pinnacle of his career, but there were others who attempted to give her advice in the early days of her reign. Elizabeth had known Nicholas Throckmorton from her youth, when she lived in her stepmother, Katherine Parr's household. Shortly after her accession, Throckmorton advised Elizabeth that 'neither the old or new councillors... should wholly understand what you mean, but [you should] ... use them as instruments to serve yourself with.'[10] The queen most definitely remembered this advice. She may have always listened to William's counsel, but he should never forget that it was her who gave him the position of which he wielded so much power. Later, as they both grew older, and Elizabeth grew stubborn and more complicated, William would have to adapt to her mood and favouritism.

William's creed, sense of duty and purpose, and his experience in governance during the reign of Edward VI and his survival during the reign of Mary I were all crucial factors during the first decade of Elizabeth's reign. Throckmorton's advice to Elizabeth may or may not have been aimed at William directly, but he also advised the queen to make use of William Honyng and Bernard Hampton, both clerks, to attend her and dispatch her letters. Alford states that though William and Elizabeth had a close bond, even prior to her reign, and that there existed a close bond between both monarch and the head of the council and principal secretary, his position was entirely political.[11] Where it may be true that by definition, William's close proximity to the queen and the level of his power was merely due to his abilities, there has to be more consideration for the nature of their friendship behind the politics, bureaucracy and formality.

William's loyalty to the queen and policy often gives the impression that he was a boring character. Indeed, perhaps he was even viewed in this way by the younger courtiers of Elizabeth's early reign. However, the interpretation of William as a miserly, old and politically obsessed and non-ambitious man likely comes from the depictions and accounts of him in his old age. Camden rightly observed that 'of all men of genius he was the most drudge...'. Whereas Camden's accounts can often be taken with a pinch of salt, it is important to note that he knew William. It also notable that he further stated that William '...of all men of business the most a genius'.[12]

This one comment reveals so much about the man who put the welfare and affairs of state over any worldly pleasure. Perhaps he even found some pleasure in his new position.

Much damage was done to the Reformation. The shocking state of the treasury meant that William likely had no time for fun, courtly games or gossip. Oftentimes, the affairs of state were interrupted by the necessity of his attendance to the queen when she either moved from one palace to another, held a banquet or indeed a masque. The young queen was initially not eager to attend every council meeting, and much of the responsibility of the daily running of the kingdom was left to William. The reason for his necessity to be constantly close to the queen may have either been due to her wishes, or to his. What matters most is that he had such strong influence over the queen that no fanciful male courtier could match.[13]

Smith notes that when the queen had a moment of intense emotional outburst, it was William, not her 'Robin'– Robert Dudley, or one of her ladies who could calm her. Where all others had to flatter her to and beyond, William was often given some privilege in this regard. No matter her course language or the abuse and varying insults she spat at him on more than one occasion, Elizabeth knew how far she could push her secretary, and in this he knew where he stood. Smith even goes as far as to state that she knew William was her master, and that she was secretly afraid.[14] This is not to imply that she was 'afraid' of William, but rather the overbearing responsibility of her position. Though it may be a far stretch to state that Elizabeth was subordinate to William and saw him as her 'master', for her era, she was well aware that her position as a female ruler was precarious and unstable. Thus, if she were to go too far with William regarding her temper, she risked losing the one man who she knew could keep her safe.

There were many matters that Elizabeth had to deal with early on in her reign beside the religious and financial. The resolution of the political conflict between Scotland and France, of which England found itself intertwined in (another legacy of Mary's reign) was absolutely necessary for the stability of the English realm, the religious situation and the protection of the new queen. Without William, Elizabeth would never have been able to deal with this conflict. Elizabeth was adamant that her reign would bring about a new regime. Loades states that the queen's priorities differed slightly to those of William's and although this is true to an extent, Elizabeth's priorities and her motives, such as purging her household, went deeper than that of her favouritism. Indeed, the dismissal of many Catholic factions at court was as much a part of Elizabeth's vision for her reign as was finding a solution to the political tensions between France and Scotland.[15]

The main priority for Elizabeth was to cut down the size of her council and give positions to those who were trustworthy and shared her vision for her reign. The queen herself could not have possibly gone through every commission alone, and to get through tasks such as knowing who could be trusted, who could not, who could make a difference, and who would rarely attend meetings could only be done with the counsel and experience of William Cecil. In the end, Catholics fared just as well as Protestants in terms of their positions. Those who can be referred to as 'Henrican Catholics' were mostly loyal to Elizabeth based on her father's last will and testament, and to the House of Tudor. Those who were zealous Protestants like William represented the future of England's established religion. This balance of tradition, loyalty and reform was mostly down to William's knowledge of the court, English politics, and an ability to demonstrate real influence over the young queen. This was absolutely necessary for the success of the reformation, bringing as little conflict and political strife as possible.

As early as January 1559, there were attempts to come to some form of reconciliation with France. William's papers, or rather the Cecil papers, are a rich source regarding the early Anglo-French negotiations towards peace. The relationship between England, Ireland, Scotland and France were all part of William's early policy-making process from June 1559. Two months previously, France, England and Spain had signed the two treaties of the Peace of Chateau-Cambrésis. This was a means of ending any political conflict in Western Europe. However, this would be one of the greatest political failures of the early Elizabethan era. Direct support of either Scotland or France could have spelt disaster for England, especially as Scotland and England were joined as one island. An attack on the North was a very serious threat to England. On the other hand, William was opposed to bringing on any full military mediation as he would much have preferred to maintain relations though a means of peace talks. It is also notable that he was prepared to support Scottish reformers. There was a method to William's approach. If England were to come down too hard on the Scots, the British Isles as a whole may not have been able to stand against the might of the Catholic continent. As early as 1560, the young Mary Stuart's claim on Elizabeth's throne through her grandmother, Margaret Tudor's line, became a real danger to Elizabeth's safety and the future of the Protestant religion in England.[16]

William was also quick to act on the financial situation in England within the first year of Elizabeth's reign. The queen was eager to have new coins minted, not only out of financial necessity, but as a political statement of her power and legitimacy. In a letter dated 30 January 1559, Lord Edward North wrote to William regarding the commission for coining of halfpennies and farthings. He advised that there was to be no delays in the commission and wished to know the queen's 'determination' – likely referring to her goals for the commission.[17] Another letter dated 3 February that same year, from William Paget to Thomas Parry (the treasurer of the queen's household) and William Cecil, offers two choices for the amendments of commissioned coins. The details in these letters may seem trivial, even mundane, yet it is letters like these that offer the most compelling information regarding William's character, and the work put into establishing Elizabeth's reign. These coins not only gave England a source of new wealth, but also depicted the queen's face. This gave her subjects a glimpse of who their sovereign was.[18]

It is also notable that by 1561, William's efforts to redeem the English treasury would be successful. By April of that year, around £70,000 worth of English coin would be recycled. This helped stabilise prices and brought the crown a profit of somewhere around £50,000. Unfortunately, William was not to know that this new era, and indeed new economic stability would encourage a population growth which slightly hindered the attempt to completely bring down prices.[19]

It is important to understand why William was so concerned with England's financial, political and religious situation in the late 1550s because it not only allows us to see his vision for Elizabeth's England, but his own fears for the future of his country, and his religion. Indeed, Elizabeth was the only surviving Tudor. Though at this time she may have been young, she was unmarried and childless. The succession crisis of England, along with its financial and religious plight, made continental Catholic Europe a real threat to England's national security. Mary's reign may have attempted to bring England back into the Catholic fold to an extent, but by the time Elizabeth had succeeded her sister, England was already well on its way to becoming a Protestant country anyway. The past five years had simply halted what was inevitable, and in many ways, had made men like William Cecil all the more determined to settle the question of England's official religion.

William's aims of settling English/continental politics would dominate the discussions of Elizabeth's Privy Council and Parliament for much of the 1560s, as well as the succession crisis and her lack of an heir. For now, there were many claimants to Elizabeth's throne, mostly female, but nonetheless a potential threat to William's plans for the new regime. The only way to secure Elizabeth's regime was to firstly direct the country towards a revival of the previous Edwardian Protestant Reformation, but more subtly.

William's view towards English religiosity is clear where he wrote in the summer of 1559:

> Papistes, Jesuittes, and Seminary Prestes do dayly increases, and do pervert the simple and wyn dayly many to ther faction.[20]

What William meant by this is that the root cause of trouble for the new Elizabethan government and the future of the English realm was not simply foreign powers and the Catholic Church, but the Catholics within England who remained loyal to Rome above any fealty or loyalty to the Crown. The biggest question is likely: why were Catholic countries such as Spain and France so concerned with England, its queen and her religion? What was it about Elizabeth and her Protestant men surrounding the throne that so threatened the might of such wealthy, large and highly militarised nations? During previous reigns, France and Spain may have decided to leave England and its religion alone. Mostly, the divide in religion not only affected England by the mid-sixteenth century, but also many other nations that were predominantly Catholic. Violence amongst divided factions of faith was the norm, and the ambitions of the new Spanish King Philip II were limitless. Mary Queen of Scots, as far away as she was and despite her ties to France, was also a real threat to the Protestant Elizabethan government. In Autumn 1559, the Franco-Stuart union between Mary and her husband Francis allowed for the couple to openly declare their claim to Elizabeth's throne. Commissions issued by Mary and Francis entitled *Franciscus et Maria Dei gratia Rx et Regina Franciae, Scotae, Angliae, et Hiberniae* were meant as an insult to Elizabeth's position, legitimacy and a reminder that Mary's marriage to France, the latter's ties to England and Mary's trickle of Tudor blood all posed a serious threat to the new Elizabethan establishment.[21] The French regency over Scotland in 1560 spelled disaster for England's Protestant vision, and William knew this. This is likely why he then began to press the queen, along with the help of other councillors, to support Scottish Protestants who opposed this regency.[22]

After the many wars that had incurred between Scotland, England and France over the centuries, peace seemed to be the way forward. William's ideal would have seen England exist safely as a Protestant country in a world of Catholic kingdoms, yet this was never going to be possible. But England could not afford another war, and as William believed that England and Scotland should be in some sense 'united' as one island, the 1559 Agreement *for observation of the truce between England and Scotland* meant that the British Isles could remain as a whole, united by the Catholic powers of Europe. This was more than necessary by this point as the French had drawn up the *Treaty of Cateau-Cambrésis* which removed England's right to the possession of any lands in France or the continent in general. Could an allied England and Scotland be the answer to the question of the French and/or Spanish threat? And would it be enough to keep Elizabeth's reign secure? These were the questions William must have pondered.[23]

William may have had some success initially with Scotland by July 1560, having pushed for the conclusion of the *Treaty of Edinburgh*, which removed French forces from Scotland. However, the death of Mary Stuart's husband, Francis II of France, that December would have definitive repercussions for Elizabeth and England in general. The Catholic Mary returned to Scotland to take her place as Queen in August of 1561. This caused enormous complications for Elizabeth's government and particularly for William. She was not only Elizabeth's kinswoman and a Catholic, she had a strong claim to Elizabeth's throne as she was a direct descendant of Elizabeth's grandfather, Henry VII of England, by his daughter, Margaret Tudor, Queen of Scots. From the moment she landed in the British Isles, Mary became a constant threat to Elizabeth's legitimacy, the stability of the Protestant religion, and a thorn in William's side.[24]

However, Mary Stuart was not Elizabeth's only rival to the throne. Indeed, William and Elizabeth had much greater problems regarding the threat to the stability of the new reign, and this was much closer to home than Scotland. In 1560, Catherine Grey, Elizabeth's cousin, secretly married Edward Seymour, Earl of Hertford, and son of the late traitor-protector. Elizabeth had not yet shown any inclination of marriage herself, and so the idea that her kinswoman could do so without royal consent was too much for the new queen to ignore. Catherine was of royal blood, and so any child produced from this marriage, especially a boy, could seriously threaten Elizabeth's position. Interestingly, all those involved, including the earl's mother Ann, the dowager duchess, Catherine's uncle Lord Grey, and his servant John Hales, were all friends of William's. Not only did this put him in a difficult position with the queen, but it tested his loyalties to those who had long championed him and his fealty to Elizabeth and the crown. Many favoured the marriage, despite the lack of royal approval, and this greatly undermined Elizabeth's power and government in general. Clearly, this situation had an effect on William as he later wrote to Thomas Smith of the 'troublesome, fond matter'. Luckily, his closeness to those disgraced and consequently imprisoned had little-to-no effect on his relationship with the queen.[25]

It would be too easy to state that Elizabeth's reaction to this clandestine marriage was understandably furious. Some have suggested that this was due to a jealousy and vanity within her that would appear on numerous occasions throughout her reign. However, though later clandestine marriages between her relatives and favourites would result in a similar if not more severe reaction of fury, it is important to note that Elizabeth was still young by 1560. The pursuit for her hand in marriage would rival if not topple that of her late sister Mary, her cousin Mary Stuart and many other marriageable princes of the period. Therefore, the severe punishment of a contender for the throne in this case was simply down to the delicate state of the monarchy, government and state religion during her early reign.

Hume states that during the early 1560s, Elizabeth was easily influenced by others around her, and blames her vanity for this. However, this seems in contradiction to her initial words spoken to William in 1558, where she clearly outlined the necessity of his guidance. It is likely that as she became more secure in her position during the first three years of her reign, William's attempts at what she may have regarded as dictations frustrated her, as did the tensions between England, Scotland and France. Many began to denounce William for his revived Protestant policy and how this affected the relationship between England and other foreign powers. It did not help his position that foreign diplomats from every corner of Europe swarmed Elizabeth's early court. If William's enemies thought him a danger to England's national welfare, they would be disappointed in all attempts to persuade the queen of this. It must be noted that William's success in Scotland and his return of this first diplomatic achievement in July of 1560 had cemented the queen's belief in him and his approach to policy. As Hume states:

> Thus the Scottish-French question, which had been a standing menace to England for centuries, was settled by the statesmanship of Cecil; and perhaps through the whole of his great career no achievement shows more clearly than this the consummate tact. Patience firmness, moderation, and foresight that characterized his policy.[26]

William was well aware that England was inevitably a part of the wider pattern of European politics. However, he continued to struggle between his personal convictions and his duty to the queen, who would often undermine his drafted notes concerning the continuous Scottish issue, its recently-arrived queen, and the mounting diplomatic tensions. When Elizabeth rejected the council's advice regarding the press for military action – for she disfavoured English intervention, William's frustration turned to desperation, and it is believed that at this point he seriously considered retiring from his position. A draft of his letter, assumed to be that of a resignation notice, still exists. This is an example of what Read refers to as 'both the recognition of ministerial responsibility and of the refusal of a minister to administer a policy with which he was in fundal disagreement'.[27]

However, MacCaffrey reads this letter differently. Instead of his resignation of his position as Elizabeth's Secretary of State and his position on her council, it is more likely that he was extremely discontent with the queen's lack of interest in military intervention in removing the French hold on Scotland, and wished only to be removed from the policy regarding Scotland.[28] Whichever way this is to be read, William did not resign from his position and continued to insist that France was a serious threat to the security of the realm, due to Mary, Queen of Scots' affiliation to the French royal family and her Tudor blood. At this point of 'crisis' in 1559, it is clear how tactful and manipulative William could be when it came to Elizabeth. Regardless of its true intent, the language he used such as: 'to serve Your Majesty in anything *that myself cannot allow* must needs be an unprofitable service', is an indication of his ability to coerce the queen into giving him his way, for without him, she could not manage her state of affairs and William knew it, as did she.[29]

William's early views of 'female power' during Elizabeth's early reign come into view when in 1560, he scolded Nicholas Throckmorton's secretary, Robert Jones, for discussing matters of religion with the queen in private. Jones reported that William '...wished I had not told the Queen's Majesty a matter of such weight...' as it '...being too much for a woman's knowledge....' Whether this means that William wholly followed the conventional view that women were incapable of equaling men in knowledge and education, or whether he simply disliked the notion of another courtier discussing the matter of religion with Elizabeth is speculative. However, as Guy states, though Elizabeth was an ardent Protestant, and had been from her teenage years under the probable influence of her stepmother, Katherine Parr, she was not 'zealous' enough for William. She rejected Calvinist ideology, whereas William began to seriously admire it.[30]

The most domineering discussion during the 1560s was the question of the succession. Indeed, this would take up most of William's time and likely occupied his mind daily. Technically, Henry VIII's will stated that the heirs of his youngest sister Mary Tudor, the dowager queen of France, would be granted to succeed his children in the event of none of them producing an heir. Therefore, it could have been that William and Elizabeth had little to worry about in terms of Mary Stuart succeeding her. But Lady Frances Grey had already remarried after her husband's rebellion and execution during Mary I's reign. Her daughter Jane's execution meant that her family were far beyond disgrace at this point. Catherine Grey's clandestine marriage did little to help the family's restoration – or what was left of the family anyway. Despite their disgrace however, it must be noted that for William, Catherine was a much more suitable heir to Elizabeth's throne than Mary. She was presumably a Protestant, but had conformed under the Marian regime like William himself, and would likely have been willing to be queen in the event of Elizabeth's death. This is not to say that Elizabeth was an ill woman at the beginning of her reign. Indeed, she was rather robust, much like her father. But the question of the succession weighed heavily on William's mind, and would become an obsession.[31]

It must also be noted that though Elizabeth openly expressed her opposition to the idea of marriage very early on in her reign, this did not stop William or the other members of her Privy Council from discussing the matter. The question was, however, who was the most suitable match? William was more or less anti-French, and the Wars of Religion that were to dominate European relations during the 1560s, and in fact, most of the Elizabethan reign, caused William to contemplate what it would mean for Elizabeth, and England, to marry into a foreign dynasty. We cannot say for sure whether Elizabeth herself really considered Mary Stuart as her best option as an heir. However, it seems that regardless of the queen's thoughts, the powerful men that surrounded her were not willing to accept another Catholic queen in the event of Elizabeth's demise. It is no surprise then that when some issues relating to the Franco-Scottish conflict and the question of England's religious settlement could be put to one side, the most important of William's duties was to ensure England avoided a succession crisis. In hindsight, it may seem perhaps odd that the question of England's succession lay in the hands of a man of relatively obscure origin, rather lowly birth and with no family ties or blood connection to the House of Tudor. Yet, for William, this was just a part of his job, and his duty to his queen, country, and religion.

One particular moment of crisis arose on 10 October 1562, when Elizabeth fell seriously ill. She was staying at Hampton Court and had taken a bath and then a long walk. She became weaker and weaker as the week went on and became less responsive the weaker she got. Many tried to bring her out from her illness, and it was determined by German-born Dr Burcot, that the queen had smallpox. Elizabeth had found some consciousness at this point and when told of her diagnosis, ordered the doctor to leave her presence. Nobody knew quite how to handle the situation, and as the queen was barely into the fourth year of her reign, without a husband, child or Tudor heir to the throne, a panic ensued over who would, or rather should, succeed her. We can almost certainly state that William's vote was with Catherine Grey, yet the council as a whole were split between her and Margaret Douglas, and some wished to see Henry Hastings, Lord Huntingdon as her heir. Obviously, nobody voted in favour of Mary, Queen of Scots, who was likely anticipating the outcome of her cousin's illness. Margaret Douglas, though a Catholic, had two healthy sons at this point, and so discussions continued as to who was most suitable. Elizabeth refused to name a successor, but when she was at her most ill, William and the other members of the council came to her supposed 'deathbed' to ask her to dictate the succession to which she replied that her favourite – Lord Robert Dudley, be the protector of the realm. She then became so delirious and ill that the council had no choice but to adhere to her wishes.[32] Elizabeth would survive this bout of severe illness, and the panic was averted. However, this not only changed her outlook of her position and indeed made her incredibly insecure, it also made William pursue his career's greatest goal, to see the queen marry and to settle the succession – a Protestant succession.

We know how William and the rest of the council felt about the idea of Mary Stuart's possible succession. Conflicting debates state that Mary was either deluded in staking her claims to Elizabeth's throne, or that Elizabeth secretly preferred Mary as her successor despite her religion and given the fact that she disfavoured Catherine Grey. However, some would state that despite Henry VIII's ban on a foreigner inheriting the English throne, Mary was not in fact delusional and that Elizabeth, as Mary's cousin, would have been happy to verify her as her successor, had it not been for the anti-Catholic sentiment within her government. Indeed, Antonia Fraser states that if Mary was willing to enter an acceptable marriage, ally herself with England and convert to Protestantism, then she may well have been more favourable to those surrounding, or rather, protecting Elizabeth's throne.[33] The conversion condition may be questionable, but the idea that Mary would willingly transition from a Papist to a reformer is not so far-fetched as many would believe. Indeed, Elizabeth and William had both conformed (in their own ways) to the Marian regime only some years previously.

Both queens at this point had long been in contact by means of letter and though Elizabeth seemed to favour Mary, despite the hiccups of the past, it seems that Elizabeth felt she could not trust her cousin entirely. William was also evidently weary of the Scottish queen. Elizabeth and Mary had a lot in common. They were both queens, considered rulers yet members of the 'weaker sex'. They were both extremely well-educated, spoke multiple languages, were cultured and inquisitive, and most notably, had to find ways of navigating their way through a man's world. Mary needed Elizabeth's full confidence, and yet the one person who held that much regard in the English queen's favour was William. If Mary were to meet Elizabeth, she likely would have charmed her and put her at ease in naming her as her heir. This not only indicates that Mary was sure of her claim to the English throne, but that she was just as capable of the level of political strategy as her cousin-queen. William Maitland, who would eventually become Mary's Secretary of State, kept up correspondence with William, which was suggested by Elizabeth.[34]

Ultimately, William and the council managed to dissuade the queen from meeting her cousin in person, due to the growing tensions between the Catholic and Huguenot factions in Europe. However, this is not to say that William did not see some benefit in the two queens meeting. He may have hoped that if it ever went ahead, Mary would either agree to convert to Protestantism, or bring an end to the Franco-Scottish alliance that posed a threat to England. Either way, the two queens would never meet, and much to the benefit of William. Though Elizabeth and Mary may have been in many ways more rivals than friends, William and Mary would become sworn enemies, their enmity much deeper than that of the French and Scottish or the Scottish and the English. Elizabeth's possible heir and Secretary of State would embark on a personal war that could only end with one outcome – death.

By 1563, William would begin to come up with an ingenious way of forcing the queen to marry and secure the succession crisis. He would even threaten to deny her necessary funds from taxes if she did not agree to the council's advice that she marry. He also began to construct a Parliamentary plan to exclude all Catholics from the succession of the English Crown. However, what William did not expect was Elizabeth's defiance. He may well have been able to manipulate the queen in many instances, but when it came to marriage, his pleas and threats would mostly fall on deaf ears. Despite this, William's efforts to find a suitable husband for Elizabeth and therefore a suitable king for England would dominate the next twenty years of his career, and he had many candidates to choose from.[35]

Chapter 5

The Hunt for a King

With Mary Stuart now in Scotland, and ever confident in her claim to the English throne, a throne that would be vacant for her to take in the event of Elizabeth's death, which by now was deemed possible due to her pervious illness, William had work to do. He set about finding the queen a suitable husband to secure the succession of the Tudor dynasty and to solidify the Protestant religion. In July 1561, he was already aware of the seriousness of the situation. He wrote to Nicholas Throckmorton, half exclaiming, half praying 'God send our mistress a husband, and by him a son, that we may hope our posterity shall have a masculine succession.'[1]

It is important to remember that Elizabeth's reign brought more changes to the English realm than any previous reign. Yes, her sister Mary was England's first queen regnant (if we completely ignore Jane Grey's tenure and the Empress Matilda), and yes Mary had also 'failed' to produce an heir. However, where Mary Tudor conformed in marriage and tried to produce an heir, likely never once doubting that it was her duty to do so, Elizabeth was wholly opposed to the idea of marriage and more so having children – or was she?

Elizabeth had spent the last two years of her sister's reign trying to brush off marriage proposals and avoid marrying a candidate that her brother-in-law found suitable. Therefore, when she became queen, there can be no doubt that she wanted to bask in her independence for as long as possible. Whether she really believed that she could get away with avoiding marriage forever is debatable. William became more and more keen for his mistress to find a consort, one that would suit England politically, without affecting Elizabeth's power entirely, therefore securing William's own interests at her side. In many ways, William believed in the traditional ways of marriage, and his queen was to be no exception to this. However, as early as 1559, gossip began to spread regarding Elizabeth's relationship with Lord Robert Dudley, brother of Lady Jane Grey's husband, Guilford Dudley. Not only was this 'friendship' unsuitable in William's view because Robert was the son and brother of a traitor – indeed, his family had a long history of treachery, and he was a commoner in comparison to the queen and therefore, would bring no political gain to England as a suitor. Moreover, Robert Dudley was already married.[2] However, by 1560, Elizabeth remained 'disposed to marry'.[3]

From the moment she became queen, she was no longer simply Elizabeth Tudor. She now represented the very stability of her kingdom, and everything that it came with. It is no surprise that though William had much more to contend with at the beginning of Elizabeth's reign, he would always have had the question of her marriage and the succession in the back of his mind. For without a legitimate male heir from his queen, what would be the point of all his diplomacy and tiresome work towards re-establishing the Protestant religion? It is easy in hindsight to imagine William as a man who badgered Elizabeth to marry until it became apparent that it would no longer serve the realm. However, the reality is much more complex. Elizabeth, though now known for her virginity and famous for the very fact that she did not marry, never totally rejected the concept of marriage, despite her 1559 declaration that she 'have already joined myself in marriage to a husband, namely the kingdom of England'.[4]

It seems that from the beginning, everyone was concerned with Elizabeth's marriage. Some it appears, were more keen to see her married than William Cecil. Her brother-in-law Philip was initially the keenest to see her married, and if not to himself, which he did contemplate, someone that would be beneficial to Spain. Elizabeth saw right through this, and as the early months of her reign wore on, Philip's opinion, as her late sister's husband, mattered little. However, if William and Philip could not convince her to marry, then who would or could? The longer she reigned, the longer her list of suitors grew, and most to no advantage for the realm. Some of her privy councillors wished for an English match. Someone of noble stock and with a blood tie to the house of Tudor perhaps. This indeed would bring further stability to the new reign, and indeed secure the question of succession. However, some argued that a foreign match would bring an alliance that England was so desperately in need of. Apparently, Sir William Pickering stated that Elizabeth would die a maid and would laugh at them all.[5] However, nobody at this point believed that Elizabeth, for all her fortitude and stubbornness, would not marry. For William, the biggest obstacle in the matter of Elizabeth's marriage was not her stubborn nature, her opposition to the idea of childbirth, or even her vanity which was evidently emerging due to her number of suitors; it was Robert Dudley.

At the beginning, not many would have thought much of Elizabeth's fondness for Dudley, he was of good (albeit traitorous) noble stock, young, handsome and yet spoken for. Indeed, William himself, for all of his experience as a twice husband, had no inclination that any of the surfacing rumours of Elizabeth's relationship held any merit. In William's mind, he could not imagine that even if Elizabeth was attracted to Dudley, extramarital sex was an option. Though we cannot be certain that Elizabeth's relationship with Dudley was anything but platonic, there existed rumours of Elizabeth visiting Dudley in his chambers both day and night. However, as Loades questions, who were those who began such gossip?[6] It seems that much of the gossip preluding Elizabeth's indiscretion when it came to Robert Dudley, came from the reports of none other than the Count of Feria, the Spanish Ambassador.

William may not have initially minded Elizabeth's dalliance with Dudley, for he was initially intent on the Franco-Scottish situation. But when his success in Scotland went largely ignored by his queen, it became apparent to William that she was wholly distracted from the affairs of State. All that seemed to matter to Elizabeth, was how or when she could spend time with Robert Dudley. It was probably only the fact that Robert was married to Amy Robsart that kept William's suspicions at bay, for a time.

In 1560, all this would change. Another Spanish ambassador, Alvaro de la Quadra, Bishop of Avila, who was no Anglophile, wrote that William was (again) on the verge of resignation due to the queen's relationship with Dudley and the scandal that it brought. Quadra reported that William was by this time 'in disgrace' with the queen and that 'the Lord Robert had made himself master of the business of the state and of the person of the queen, to the extreme injury of the realm...'[7]

It is most likely the case that the ambassador was intent on creating scandal within the English court, for his hatred of the English and indeed, for the new Protestant queen was no secret. He was well aware that his reports would reach the many European courts and therefore blacken the name of the new queen. However, speckles of truth emerge through his report. Elizabeth's conduct with Dudley had done more than to raise a few eyebrows within the English court and abroad. He may well have been a good contender as a husband if he had not already been married, but the fact that he was, and indeed, the fact that his wife was reportedly very ill, portrayed enough of the character of Elizabeth's favourite. This only encouraged the public's disfavour towards the friendship. Amy Dudley was later found dead at Cumnor, at the end of her stairs just days after Quadra's letter. This would bring about such scandal that Elizabeth was forced to part with her favourite, and Robert swiftly left court for a time. It seems that Dudley was genuinely grievous for his wife's death and Elizabeth herself seems to have emerged from her delusions. Whatever the case, Dudley was mostly blamed for his wife's death and even the queen was not immune to accusations of murder. Though Dudley was evidently a terrible husband, and Elizabeth insensitive to a fellow woman, the circumstances of Amy's death did not make them murderers.[8]

It is interesting that though both Dudley and William had very little in common other than their devotion to the queen, that the former often found himself turning to the latter for guidance. It is important to note that while William and Dudley were very different, and were rivals for the queen's attention (albeit in differing ways), this does not mean that one wholly loathed the other, nor does it imply that one did not benefit from the other's favour when necessary.

De Quadra's letters to Spain discussing Elizabeth's and Dudley's conduct, stating that Dudley wished to be rid of his wife and marry the queen, just days before Amy's death, had a significant effect on Europe's view on their relationship. If Amy had died of her apparent illness, Robert Dudley may well have been capable of convincing the queen to marry him. Indeed, she may well have entered into a marriage with him willingly if circumstances were different. We can only speculate out of hindsight what may have been if it were not for the suspiciousness and tragedy of Amy's death. In *The Death of Amy Robsart* by R. Dudley, John Applyard and James Gairdner, it is discussed that the source of De Quadra's reports was none other than William Cecil. Indeed, it is further stated in some works that Elizabeth herself knew of the events to come. Dudley, Applyard and Gairdner also discuss the problems with blaming William and Elizabeth for the death or 'murder' of Amy Robsart.[9] However, it is also imperative that we should not completely let Dudley, Elizabeth nor William off the hook entirely.

Firstly, there is the argument that William, amongst others in government, feared that a foreign match would be a detriment to England. As Elizabeth was a woman, her marriage to a foreign prince could possibly make Protestant England significantly submissive to a more powerful, and notably Catholic foreign power. If this was indeed the case, then it would make sense for Elizabeth's subjects, her council, and William (who wished to preserve the Protestant faith in England and protect it from foreign influence) to approve of her relationship with and possible marriage to Robert Dudley. The evidence for this could also be interpreted from the grants bestowed upon Dudley at the queen's pleasure. On the other hand, it must be considered that the notion of the sovereign, woman or not, conspiring to kill an innocent in order to avoid marrying a foreigner, without facing any repercussions is a stretch too far. Elizabeth, Dudley, and William would have known that even condoning the murder of Amy Robsart would have seriously put Elizabeth's position as queen at risk. If Elizabeth were to lose her throne, then Dudley would lose all royal favour, and William would lose his position and thus his vision for Protestant England.[10]

The theory that Elizabeth, Dudley and William conspired or agreed upon harming Amy Robsart in any fashion, has been mostly dismissed by historians and authors. Some continue to argue that Dudley may have had some role in her demise, but most strictly dismiss Elizabeth's and William Cecil's taking part or approval of murder. Indeed, De Quadra's reports of Dudley's rise in favour and influence were nothing new, and it was no secret that William lamented this and the queen's snubs. It seems that perhaps William vented his frustration regarding the matter of Dudley to De Quadra, stating that he wished to retire to the country, have no more to do with the affairs of state, and would sooner 'commit him to the Tower sooner than let him go, and he besought the ambassador "for the love of God" to remonstrate with the queen that, she might not throw herself away as she seemed bent on doing.'[11] This also contradicts the theory that William favoured any match between the queen and her favourite. It must be noted that though William was at this time somewhat anti-French, he was not ignorant of the fact that England was alone, small and uniquely vulnerable. He was a shrewd diplomat, as evident in his attempts to bring about some peace and unity between England and Scotland, and to solve the Franco-Scottish tensions. A foreign match, despite the differences in religion, may well have served the queen and England well, and would provide much needed protection against another foreign invasion. It would also solve the issue of the succession and the problem that Mary, Queen of Scots was becoming. All in all, there is little-to-no evidence besides letters of rumour and scandal to suggest that Elizabeth or William definitively had anything to do with Amy Robsart's death. It is also difficult to definitively state that Amy was murdered in the first place.

Far from disapproving a foreign match, William encouraged most of Elizabeth's princely suitors in the 1560s and 1570s. Prior to the queen's accession, she had a suitor in another English man, Sir William Pickering. Though they were old friends and she favoured him dearly, she never considered marrying him, despite his pursuit of her. The Earl of Arundel was another contender for Elizabeth's hand, but he too would be sorely disappointed by Elizabeth's lack of sincere romantic interest. Indeed, in late 1558, Pickering and Arundel engaged in a physical quarrel over Elizabeth's favour. Elizabeth's favour of these men and their attempts to woo her, was all a part of her growing cult of love in the new court. The queen engaged in numerous flirtatious conversations with seemingly love-struck male courtiers, but it was all a façade in the end.[12]

William may well have been Elizabeth's most trusted advisor, perhaps even her 'greatest friend', as Hilton remarks. Certainly in hindsight, he was the most loyal person at her side. She may have thought that the one person she could trust most was Robert Dudley, but with his poor reputation after the death of his wife, it is no surprise that the queen gave her favourite a wide berth for some time afterwards. However, there was another man in Elizabeth's life, who, if he cannot be described as the most dangerous to her reign, was certainly the most curious of her suitors. Philip of Spain was Elizabeth's late sister Mary I's widower. He had become king of Spain in 1556, and though he was her one-time brother-in-law, he was only six years her senior and was one of the most powerful monarchs in Europe. After she became queen, Philip was generous enough to give Elizabeth some time to settle into her new role. However, he made sure to be her first official royal suitor and would be her most powerful. In early 1559, some months after her accession, Philip gave Feria authorisation to propose to Elizabeth on his behalf. He stated that he would not have proposed to her 'if it were not to serve God…' It seems that his vision was to return England to Catholicism, removing William's polices regarding the state's religion. Philip's proposal came at an important time in Elizabeth's early reign. Her first Parliament was about to meet, and her supremacy over the Church of England was about to be officially established. It is no surprise then, that though William wished his queen to marry and produce an heir for the stability of England, he was not prepared to advise his queen on entering a marriage with the most Catholic king in Christendom. He need not have worried however, as the queen never seriously contemplated marrying Philip.[13]

A marriage to her late brother-in-law may have made an attack from the French less likely. There was the possibility that Philip could have some influence regarding the Pope's views of Elizabeth's legitimacy and a marriage between a Protestant queen to a Catholic king could reduce the possibility of Catholic rebellions. However, as Elizabeth's sister had been married to the Spanish king, she felt she could not contemplate marrying him, amongst other reasons. Though a Papal dispensation would have been arguably possible, Elizabeth had to deny the Pope's authority, especially during this early period of her reign.[14]

Not only was there the condition that Elizabeth revert her country back under the authority of Rome as had her sister, undoing her secretary's work, but it would also mean that she, as a woman would have to relinquish a particular amount of personal power. For if she were to marry, her husband, whoever he may be, would become king. This actually may be the reason why Elizabeth chose to never marry. There is also the fact that France and Spain were negotiating towards the *Peace of Câteau-Cambrésis*, which meant that if England were to ally with Spain, any negotiations of peace between England and France would be seriously impacted upon. This mean that Elizabeth's and William's hopes to restore Calais under English rule would likely never come to fruition. Elizabeth and William knew the failings of Mary's reign in a similar regard, as her reputation plummeted after the loss of Calais in 1557 after over two centuries of English domination. Though negotiations over Calais would go on for another decade, William would be greatly disappointed, as it would never again be considered an English territory. Elizabeth was also aware (likely from the council of William), that her choice in husband would have serious consequences for the Protestant Reformation.[15]

The loss of Calais would also be a blow to Elizabeth, for she likely wanted to do good her sister's wrongs. However, Philip was also struggling to settle his own affairs. William went to-and-between both representatives of Spain and France. Though he was no fan of the French, Philip of Spain was a much bigger worry for him. This is likely why peace with France was absolutely necessary. If Spain could be left on the fringes, England may have been able to gain some benefit in an alliance with France. Though Feria was well aware of Elizabeth's need to keep Spain dangling, he was no match for William's cunning nature. The Huguenot faction in France was growing, and as Elizabeth was becoming more and more popular with her people, William's revival of the Protestant Reformation seemed to be gaining some substance.[16]

William never really believed that Elizabeth would marry without considering the consequences. Indeed, though Robert Dudley remained Elizabeth's favourite and most serious English suitor, the scandal of Amy Robsart's death may have put the secretary's mind at ease. Whatever the queen's feelings truly were, her council would never have agreed to allow a marriage between her and Dudley to take place, and she depended on good council in order to reign safely. The fact that William threatened to resign due to her relationship with Dudley and the fact that it got in the way of the daily governance of the kingdom, Elizabeth became, at least in pretense, somewhat more interested in the prospect of finding a husband. Interestingly, there were many candidates within Elizabeth's own court that may well have been her king. The Duke of Norfolk was one consideration. As were the Earls of Arundel and Westmorland. Arundel was particularly keen on the idea for a time. Again, here was also Sir William Pickering who Elizabeth seemed to favour somewhat. Yet these fancies never led to any serious level of matrimonial negotiation. The Scottish Earl of Arran was a serious contender as Mary Stuart's successor prior to the birth of her son. This would have suited William perfected as Arran was a Protestant and as Mary's potential heir, could easily have openly made his claim to her throne.[17]

Of all Elizabeth's suitors, many at court felt that the most suitable was Archduke Charles of Austria. The negotiations of marriage in 1564 were not the first to take place regarding a match between Elizabeth and Charles. In fact, he seemed most appropriate in terms of age and royal lineage. He would not bring any foreign territories, as Doran notes, but what he would bring was political stability and give England a real place on the European political stage. This marriage would allow some form of an alliance with Spain, therefore killing two birds with one stone. It would also provide protection in the event of any possible muck-up in the peace treaty with France. The papacy would be pacified and there was the possibility that Elizabeth would be able to hold onto some personal power. In terms of trade, it would broaden England's commercial horizon, expanding the queen's personal wealth and the kingdom's stability.[18]

Many knew that the problem of the Archduke's religion could have serious implications for the stability of the Protestant religion and Elizabeth's supremacy. Interestingly, Doran states that William chose to ignore this factor. It seems that when it came to the topic of religion when discussing the queen's marriage prospects, William tended to either wholly oppose a suitor due to his religion, or ignore this factor entirely. This depended on what England could gain politically and financially out of the situation. William felt that Charles would bend to the Elizabethan policy towards religion and perhaps could outwardly conform or even convert. Others argued that though conversion was unlikely, the Archduke would openly attend English church service, but attend Catholic mass privately. The problem was, William seriously overestimated the Habsburg's openness towards religious uniformity in this instance.[19]

Other suitors of the 1560s included Eric XIV of Sweden, although not even the queen seriously contemplated that marrying him would do England any good. In hindsight, her rejection of him was for the best, as he would later murder several of his nobles, be declared insane and was deposed, imprisoned and eventually poisoned to death. The French king and his brother were proposed, but they were at that time deemed too young. Any Protestant prince's hopes of securing Elizabeth's hand would be sorely disappointed. They may have held the same or similar religious principles, but they lacked the financial and political prowess that Elizabeth's realm needed in order to secure England's safety and political platform in Europe. The negotiations between Elizabeth and the Archduke were prolonged as long as possible, likely due to pressure from those who supported the match. In the end, Elizabeth herself had to let down the Archduke's imperial envoy, Adam Zwetkovic, and told him that 'owing to the religion everything would be in vain' and therefore it was useless to speak about it'. By this she meant that the marriage could not occur as an agreement on the obstacle of religion was impossible.[20]

Elizabeth was by this time under an enormous amount of strain. The pressure to marry, when she did not wish to do so, took its toll on her emotionally. She became prone to emotional outbursts and this was not helped by the news that her cousin, Mary, Queen of Scots, had married their mutual cousin, Lord Darnley, an Englishman, a noble, and a serious male contender for Elizabeth's throne as a direct descendant of Henry VII, albeit through a female line. This not only infuriated Elizabeth, but startled William and the council. This marriage not only increased Mary's threat to Elizabeth's rule, but any child it produced would be most likely to succeed Mary and even Elizabeth in the event of her dying without producing a male heir. All of this tension boiled over and the queen railed furiously at William and Dudley amongst others, that the pressure they put on her to marry would be the end of her.[21]

The eventual birth of Mary Stuart's son James had serious implications for England and thus, Elizabeth's worst nightmare began. The lack of an heir for Elizabeth's throne in comparison to Mary's plunged England into a serious crisis regarding the succession. William may well have understood his mistress's plight and was likely sympathetic, but he knew that the only way to secure her safety and the Protestant state was for the queen to marry and produce a legitimate heir. The second session of Elizabeth's second Parliament commenced in September of 1566, and this is where the debate over her marriage really began to reach a climax. The many speeches and debates lasted until November. The prospect of Elizabeth's marriage was the easiest of discussions. The talk on the succession however, was not. Without the queen's consent to marry, whoever that may be, there could be no further discussion on who would succeed her in the event of her death. The naming of an adult heir within close proximity to the throne could have dire consequences such as rebellion. William worked on many of the drafts of petition put to the queen, encouraging her to act on her marriage and the succession as her duty to her realm as the monarch. All were met with Elizabeth's fury and rejection. William's own diaries record the queen's displeasure with the Earl of Pembroke and even Lord Robert Dudley also for further discussing the matter of her marriage and the importance of her consent regarding the succession.[22]

By November 1566, many suitors had come and gone, and Elizabeth's stubbornness began to put a serious strain on her government. It now seemed that the Privy Council and Parliament may have been able to apply enough pressure to convince the queen that the succession had to be settled one way or another. The meeting of thirty lords and forty commoners had taken place over a period of months. Despite this, Elizabeth rejected Parliament's request. When William read out the queen's reply to the lords and committees, it was recorded that the whole house fell silent. However, not only is this evidence that the queen's council were seriously concerned about the succession at this point, but that William, despite his own determination to see his mistress marry and produce an heir for the kingdom, ultimately understood Elizabeth's concerns. The queen believed that the settlement of the succession was not only detrimental to her personally, but would also cause division. Whereas, the council believed that it would have the opposite effect. As Alford points out, William's draft notes taken during this time not only relay the pressure on the queen and her council in general to settle the succession question, but also his attention to detail. William came back to these notes, edited them carefully and made changes where he felt necessary. Language mattered to William, and the finer details of each line were important to him. This reveals the true perfectionist that he really was, as Alford states: 'The petition had a strong political purpose and Cecil reinforced this by detailed editing.'[23]

If we are to believe that William was subordinate to his queen in all matters, only willing to serve her interests in the interest of the state, then there exists a serious misunderstanding of who William Cecil was as a man. The queen was the queen, and her Parliament and commons knew that. Elizabeth expressed command that debate over the succession was to be prohibited. Yet, days later, William was confident in his position enough to remind all involved of Parliament's 'ancient right to free discussion and counsel'. In other words, Elizabeth was free to reject Parliament's petition, but they, as her government body, were free to discuss her marriage and the succession as they so desired, due to the position that she herself bestowed upon them. William may have simply been emphasising his freedom of speech, but this kind of politics was radical for the time. He, as her secretary of state and most trusted counsellor, was comfortable enough to disobey his queen when it came to the protection and succession of the English State. Elizabeth may have been ordained by God, but William was able to clearly and concisely argue that Parliament had the right to play a role in the affairs of state, and to discuss the succession.[24]

William's frustrations with the queen are evident in his memorandum of 1566, as McLaren mentions. Where the queen was able to find ways of avoiding marriage by rejecting the suitors and petitions, it seems that William could never comprehend this. He felt that:

> To urge both marriage and establishing of succession is the uttermost that can be desired. To deny both is the uttermost that can be denied. To require marriage is the most natural, most easy, most plausible to the queen's majesty. To require certainty of succession is the most plausible to all the people. To require succession is the hardest to be obtained both for the difficulty to discuss the right and for the loathsomeness in the Queen's Majesty to consent thereto...The loathsomeness to grant it is by reason of natural suspicion against a successor that hath right by law to succeed.[25]

In many ways, William sympathised with Elizabeth's plight. At this point in her life, she was enjoying exercising her own personal rule. Despite everything, she had survived the abuse of her time with her stepfather, Thomas Seymour. She had survived imprisonment during the reign of her sister Mary, and she had survived smallpox, a disease which had taken many lives – both common and royal. However, we must remember that hindsight has a role in how we usually interpret Elizabeth's reign, and therefore her relationship with William. Yes, both were of the same period, both were like-minded, both well-educated and may have had more in common than William did with his own wife. However, Elizabeth was a woman, and living on an island of two kingdoms. The other kingdom was ruled by another woman who had already produced one healthy male child. Both Mary and James had a claim to Elizabeth's throne and while she remained childless, her reign would never be totally secure. Therefore, William could not understand why a woman, whose most natural duty was to marry and produce children, could display behaviour divergent to that of the era's expectations.

The reason for William's severity when it came to the queen's marriage must also be understood by the attitudes of the day towards marriage. Women were not considered capable of ruling, never mind alone. So, the only reasonable solution to all of William's problems – the succession, the political stability and safety of the realm, the protection of the Protestant religion against the Catholic Mary Stuart, was to find a suitable husband for the queen, and for the queen to bear a (preferably male) child. It is true, that if Elizabeth were to marry, this would open a discussion on whether her husband's title was to be considered greater than hers. William's argument that the succession was the most important matter to settle despite the queen's fears, fell on deaf ears, but plagued Elizabeth for the rest of her life. It was only when it became clear that she could no longer have children, that her 'spirit' would relent somewhat in his quest, and allow her respite from the discussion.[26]

King Philip eventually married Elisabeth of France, daughter of Henry II and Catherine de Medici; the latter being one of Elizabeth's correspondents.[27] Despite this, the Spanish and English remained amicably connected for some time. Elizabeth's and Philip's friendship meant that some form of a political alliance could be possible. We now know that this was for nothing, as this veil of friendship could not last, and became a power struggle that would lead to war on an unprecedented scale. But for now, Elizabeth maintained the image of a loyal sister and friend. Philip kept a keen interest in Elizabeth's political and personal affairs, and it seems that everyone had an opinion on who she should marry. The queen maintained that she could not marry a man without seeing him first. This seemed reasonable enough, and on a number of occasions it was suggested that those who wished to court her should visit her in secret at the English court. The reason why the queen found flirtations and the romance of being pursued so invigorating is perplexing, considering that she stated she preferred to remain in the state of virginity from so early on in her reign. It can only be suggested that this in some way made up for the lack of sexual fulfilment in her life. Even her deadly relationship with Dudley, which irked William so greatly, almost definitely went unconsummated.

Elizabeth's responses to Parliament's petitions for her to marry infuriated her, and she wrote again and again, outwardly accusing them of prejudice and asked them if she had done any ill in reigning over her kingdom thus far alone. She expressed that she had the liberties of all other princes:

> God forbid that your liberty should make my bondage or that
> your lawful liberties should any ways have been infringed.[28]

Elizabeth's reign may have been different in that the men of her day held greater influence and power because their sovereign was a woman, but she was still their queen and a queen-regnant and therefore technically had the liberty of a king. If the queen did not wish to marry, her council and Parliament could only beg, plead and petition. But here, in her replies to the petitions that she should marry, the queen was explicitly reminding them that she held the power.

By 1567, any notions of a match between Elizabeth and the Archduke Charles had also been abandoned for good. Though he did make attempts in many ways to pacify Elizabeth's Privy Council, it simply came down to the fact that she did not love him, nor did she love the idea of sharing her power with him. However, the greatest obstacle, as ever was the fact that the Archduke was as staunchly Catholic as Philip of Spain. Though William was concerned at this time that his queen had still not yet accepted a suitor, and that the long list of men willing to take the queen's hand in marriage could not go on forever, he had other issues to worry about. In that same year of 1567, civil war broke out in Scotland. The Scottish nobles rebelled against Mary after the suspicious death of her second husband Lord Darnley. Mary then married her third husband, the Earl of Bothwell, who possibly raped her and forced her into marriage not long after Darnley had been removed. Though the Scottish queen may have believed that she had the support of her nobles, tensions had been growing for some time and her new husband was likely worse than her last. That July, Mary was forced to abdicate the throne in favour of her infant son. This outraged the English queen, who had been shocked by Darnley's death, but was more concerned that a queen could be removed from her position so easily. If Scottish nobles were capable of forcing their queen to abdicate, who was to say the same could not happen to her. William saw multiple opportunities in Mary's downfall however. She crossed the border into England after escaping her imprisonment in May 1568. Her presence caused a flux of panic. Yet for William, this meant that he could now regain some influence in Scottish affairs such as he had in 1559, prior to Mary's return to Scotland from France.[29]

Finally, after almost a decade of claiming her right to Elizabeth's crown, Mary Stuart was in English hands, and thus, in William Cecil's hands. Though Elizabeth would have insisted that her cousin queen was treated and revered with the respect owed to her position, she could not have been able to deny that the situation was beneficial for the safety of her reign as well as a threat to the concept of female rule. Mary was a Catholic, but her country was mainly Protestant. This meant that a new friendship between Scotland and England was possible. Though the *de facto* imprisonment of the Scottish queen on English soil meant that William could regain some serious political influence, he was not ignorant to the fact that Catholic Europe looked on in horror. Indeed, it seemed to most English Protestants at this point that there existed a serious threat of Catholic conspiracy against England. The biggest threat at this time was the French, for not only was Mary their former queen-consort, her mother Mary of Guise was also French, and the two countries had a long-standing familial link. This is why Mary's stay in England had to be dealt with most carefully. She was technically a prisoner, yet she was also in a sense a refugee, and therefore was treated with the dignity of a queen. England had to be seen to treat her in accordance to her station, for if she were to be harmed in any way, it would bring about a war on England. Yet, as Alford states, we must remember how William saw England's position in general on the British Isles. Though of Welsh heritage, William viewed England as the dominant power over the whole Island. The fact that Scotland too was also a Protestant country and had strong ties to other European countries could also have been beneficial. The biggest question of the day besides who the queen should marry, was: how could Britain as a Protestant island nation, be used in a way to mould England into a European political powerhouse? It seems that William Cecil now had the answer.[30]

If Elizabeth thought that the scandals of Mary Stuart would put a pause on her council's pressure for her to marry, she was wrong. On the contrary, as Elizabeth's reign wore on, more and more suitors came and went. The most notable of royal suitors towards the end of the 1560s and 1570s were the French brothers. Attempts to negotiate a match between Elizabeth and a French prince had long been in existence and the queen had always managed to avoid it going any further. However, with the tensions in Scotland and the relationship between the Protestant Scots and the Catholic French, it appears that a marriage of sorts may have been the logical answer. Mary Stuart was at this point a political prisoner and beyond consideration of a matrimonial alliance. Now, Elizabeth seemed appealing as a potential bride more than ever.

Back in 1564, Catherine de Medici, the French queen-mother, was curious of the English queen's unmarried status. This curiosity would lead to almost two decades of marital negotiations between France and England. In 1564, Catherine proposed her son the then king Charles IX as a possible candidate for Elizabeth's hand. This was likely genuine as Catherine longed for peace in France between Catholics and Protestants and a general peace within Europe. William seemed genuinely interested in the prospect at the time, for this alliance would most definitely bring security to the English realm, and hopefully an heir. But at that time, Catherine was in need of support and so a marriage to her son with the English queen would have had to take place almost immediately. Elizabeth at that time was not interested and continued to remain happily in her state of virginity.[31]

With the rebellion against Mary Stuart in Scotland and the civil war ensuing in France, England was finally standing strong on its own. Yet, that did not mean the safety of the British Isles was permanent. Elizabeth was brave enough to demand the return of Calais in 1567 and Catherine knew that at this point, there was a serious possibility of further war. Indeed, though both women were more rivals for influence on the European stage, they were not total enemies, and had a mutual respect for one another. In 1569, Catherine's son, the sixteen-year-old Duke of Anjou, became the hero of the battle of Jarnac. The Catholics had won the battle with the Huguenots, yet Catherine was well aware that the stability of her country was more than fragile. Again, proposal of marriage between a Protestant queen and a French Prince could prove useful in terms of settling the tensions and divisions of religion in France and Europe in general. This was Catherine's second attempt to woo Elizabeth on behalf of one of her sons.[32]

Though the proposal may have come as a surprise to Elizabeth, her thoughts on the match may have been even more surprising for William. This was mostly due to the presence of her likely successor, Mary, being present in England. As long as Elizabeth remained unmarried and childless, her Catholic cousin was a potential heir. Every moment that went by without an English, Protestant heir, the more danger the queen's life was in, and everyone knew it. Even by 1570, Elizabeth may have been seriously regretting her refusals to marry and produce an heir, for the Catholic threat and tensions in Europe, mainly the defeat of the Huguenots, proposed serious danger for the security of the Protestant religion in England, and those who governed it. It didn't help that the Pope had excommunicated Elizabeth and released all her Catholic subjects from their obedience to her. The queen seriously contemplated the French match despite everything, as she knew she needed allies. William, for whatever reason, was convinced of his mistress's genuine interest in marriage at this point and wrote: 'if I be not much deceived, her majesty is earnest in this'.[33]

It is interesting that Elizabeth once rejected the proposal by Charles IX mostly due to his young age, yet his brother, the then Duke of Anjou was only sixteen when the negotiations began again in the 1570s. The young Duke Henry seemed uninterested in marrying a much older woman at first. Yet, when it was discussed that the Duke could practice his religion in private, the prince was soon convinced that the match may be prosperous. However, Elizabeth soon doubted the probable success of the match and Henry soon became disinterested again and moved on. These negotiations led to nothing. William later wrote to Walsingham in despair:

> I see the imminent perils to this state...that I cannot but persist
> in seeking marriage for her Majesty.[34]

The French negotiations would end here for some time. However, this would not be the end of Elizabeth's many suitors. Later on in her reign, the third French brother, Francis, Duke of Alençon and later of Anjou upon the death of his brother Henry, would come the closest to marrying the virgin queen than all other suitor of her reign. In this instance, much of their courtship would take place either by letter, and then later in person when Anjou visited Elizabeth in England twice during the marriage negotiations. Their affection for each other seemed genuine, and though there were serious doubts by the 1580s that the queen could produce an heir, William was convinced that the marriage would benefit England, at least politically. However, despite Elizabeth's seemingly genuine intentions to marry the duke, with the support of the most powerful man in the kingdom, there was a great divide within the Privy Council. Dudley and Walsingham for example opposed the match, while William and the Earl of Sussex were all for it. In the end, though William was supportive of his queen, he knew that the duke's religion was too much for the English people to bear. Elizabeth herself seemed happy enough by this point to take her council's earlier advice to marry, and was therefore shocked at the divide in opinion and the level of hostility and opposition to the match. In the end, an agreement could not be obtained after many months of negotiations and waiting. Therefore, they informed the queen that ultimately the decision was hers. Much to her despair, she herself felt that without the full support of her Privy Council and her subjects, that she could not marry the Duke of Anjou. William's support for the match is evident in a letter written in 1579. Here he outlines his support for the queen's decision:

> If then I have proved it as necessary your majesty have content and pleasure as rule and treasure; if I have showed where it is not and where it is, and now prove plainly you may take it is you please, I have then ended my desire, though to no effect beside.

He continued by insinuating that as she was queen, and had previously stated that it was her liberty to remain unmarried, so too was it her decision to marry now:

> ...doubt not Lady, for when lions make a leap, the bears and other beasts lie down.[35]

This would be Elizabeth's final courtship and suitor. Though William never gave up in trying to find a suitable husband for his queen and to secure the Protestant kingdom he had worked so hard to re-establish and protect, he would never put pressure on Elizabeth to marry again. The marriage negotiations soon ended and Anjou left England and returned to France. He later died in 1584, still only in his twenties and unmarried. This would have serious implications for European politics. Not only did his death plunge the queen into a depression for some time, but it meant without the duke's influence in the Netherlands, not to mention the assassination of William of Orange, that England was now alone and had no protection from the might of Spain. If the Dutch were to be defeated, England would be put in a dangerous situation. By August 1585, after much negotiation, William and Elizabeth were in agreement that England had to intervene in the war. The times when marital negotiations could prevent conflict were well and truly over by the mid-1580s. William would have to come up with new political tactics. [36]

Chapter 6

The Secretary's Circle

It is difficult to ascertain how exactly William perceived himself and his position on the council and at court. In one sense he was inferior of birth in comparison to many other male courtiers and advisors. His wealth and status depended on his abilities as the queen's secretary and his good counsel. His father was a mere gentleman in comparison to the father of Robert Dudley, who was a duke. During the 1560s, he would have been acutely aware of his position, where he ranked and perhaps, where he wanted to go. Though he was not yet entitled, he was proud of his close circle of friends, confidantes and fellow advisors. Loades goes as far as to describe William as somewhat of a 'snob' in his pride for his aristocratic colleagues. But is this a fair assumption? Was William Cecil really just as hungry for power, privilege and position as Robert Dudley for example? Who was his circle of friends? And how was his rising star perceived amongst his courtly contemporaries?

William was ever the pragmatist. Many of his connections at court and afar gave him a sense of pride. For example, in the 1560s, he invested in an Anglo-German metallurgical company. He went into this with Robert Dudley, by then Earl of Leicester and the Earl of Pembroke. By 1568, he and his counterparts held four and a quarter of the twenty-four shares in the Mines Royal Company, according to Loades. It is thought that William entered into these business ventures with men of such stature out of pride for the mere association with them, rather than for any financial gain. He had similar investments in other companies which though brought him no financial benefit, did not ruin his finances either as they had done to the earl's. This is further evidence of William's shrewd nature as a businessman and his outstanding abilities in comparison to men who were 'born better' than him.[1]

It has often been insinuated that William and Elizabeth had some kind of partnership and unspoken understanding whereby the kingdom of England could be ruled by both of them, but in complimentary ways. Often, there is the view of William wielding much more political power than he should have been permitted. It is true that he was bold enough on occasion to push Elizabeth regarding the succession. However, the idea that William sought to

74

rule England in any manner is to insult the man that he was. Elizabeth ruled, William advised. The relationship between the queen and her secretary was not only worlds apart in terms of their station, but political approach. It has been long suggested that Elizabeth's forty-five-year reign would not have been as successful as it was without William by her side, and likewise, William would never have risen the way he did without his queen's favour and trust. To pair these two very different, yet strong characters together and suggest that if they were to part, the kingdom of England would have fallen to ruin, is perhaps a stretch too far. There is much more to William Cecil as a man – as a genius, than his association with Elizabeth.[2]

But what of William's other contemporaries? It is safe to say that though William was a shrewd politician, and was careful in who he trusted; he formed many close friendships that would last a lifetime. This is the William that is often denied to us. The close friendship between William and John Cheke, who became his brother-in-law from his first marriage to Mary Cheke is well-known and documented. In his early years at Cambridge, he had many friends such as John Redman, George Day, Robert Horne and James Pilkington, two of which would eventually become ardent Catholics. Despite this, William seemed to always have an ability for forming close and meaningful friendships.[3] During his time in the service of Somerset, William made friends with other members of the household such as Sir Thomas Smith, and Sir John Thynne. Thomas Smith remained one of William's lifelong correspondents, whether friend or foe. During the negotiations of marriage between the Archduke Charles and the French brothers in the 1560s, William trusted Thomas enough to discuss his thoughts and frustrations regarding the queen's marriage discussions:

> One great obstacle is that the queen's majesty will needs see
> before she marry. And how that device may be performed, if
> she should assent either to the French king of the Archduke,
> will prove hard…what shall follow, God knoweth.[4]

Another contemporary of William's was Sir Nicholas Throckmorton, who was also involved in the queen's marital negotiations. Both Throckmorton and Smith worked on William's behalf during this period, either as envoys or ambassadors in France when necessary. This was likely a great help to William who could not undertake these many trips himself when he was needed in England, at the queen's side. William knew most of his close confidantes prior to his rise in status upon Elizabeth's ascension to the throne. For example, both Smith and Ralph Sadler had to navigate the murky waters of Mary I's reign alongside William. The many thousands of letters and documents within the Cecil Papers reveal that many men, despite their rank at court and in society in general, sought the advice and favour of William Cecil. It is not difficult to understand why it was important to be on the queen's 'spirit's' good side. Yet, though friendly and conscientious towards many, the secretary was often cautious, and kept his circle of friends small and manageable. To gain an understanding of why William favoured and trusted particular men and women, it is important to understand their origins, careers, and positions at court.

Thomas Smith was educated at Queen's College at Cambridge. He, like William, came from a good family. However, Smith's background was somewhat more interesting than that of William Cecil's. The Smiths of Essex were reputedly descendants of Sir Roger de Clarendon, who was the illegitimate son of Edward of Woodstock, the 'Black Prince' – eldest son of King Edward III of England. If this were true, Smith's trickle of royal blood may have made him an interesting man, even during his own era. He was a part of William's small group of young men at Cambridge who studied Greek, and he was a good friend of Sir John Cheke, William's brother-in-law and close confidante. He lost all of his offices upon Mary I's ascension but when Elizabeth's reign came around, he was quickly re-elevated and returned to public office. Due to his acquaintance with William, and due to the favour of the queen, he also rose in popularity at court and in Parliament.

Smith's relationship with William is important as he was one of the most prolific writers of the period. His many letters to William reveal their friendship was complicated, as was his relationship with the queen. When he served as Ambassador to France in the 1560s and 1670s, his recordings of intrigues, scandals, rumours and political observations made him an invaluable source for the Tudor court and government. His writings are also an invaluable source of information regarding William's life, as he wrote to him almost daily.[5] William was able to carve out a career which allowed him the greatest power of the state after the queen. This was not unprecedented. Both Thomas Wolsey and Thomas Cromwell had manipulated Elizabeth's father to grant them power and further influence. Under Elizabeth Tudor, William was able to move up in the world and reap the financial benefits, but without losing his head. Smith likewise used his connections from Cambridge to further his career; not quite on par with William, but he wielded considerable power in politics and at court nonetheless.[6] However, at the beginning of the reign, when he offered his services of counsel to the new queen, he was not selected of the six to do so.

This was when William's star began to rise and so, it seems that he forgot about Smith. Smith was enraged by this snub and the pair quarrelled for a time. William was initially cautious to send Smith to France in the early 1560s, even though his good friend and advisor to the queen, Throckmorton, felt it was appropriate. William felt that Smith did not possess the necessary level of French, despite the fact that he had been a negotiator in the French embassy in 1551. Eventually, his complaints to William and Elizabeth in letters made them relent. Smith was also notably an ardent supporter or Robert Dudley's pursuit of the queen and genuinely counselled her to take him as her husband. Though William and Smith were on good terms again by the mid-1560s, his favour of the Dudley faction at court put some further strain on the pair's relationship.[7]

Sir Nicholas Throckmorton was another contemporary and a great friend of William's. Their correspondence is also vast and like William and Smith, he struggled during the reign of Mary I. He was imprisoned for some time in the Tower, but was released and rose rapidly in Elizabeth's favour when she became queen. Like William and Smith, Throckmorton was eager to see the queen marry and secure the succession. In the 1560s, he was also sent as an ambassador to France, though under Thomas Smith. Throckmorton's friendship with William cannot be overlooked. However, he also formed a close friendship with Mary, Queen of Scots, when he was sent as an ambassador in 1565 to try to prevent the marriage of the Scottish queen to Lord Darnley. His failure to do so was humiliating for William, Elizabeth and England. However, he was also sent in 1567, after the death of Lord Darnley. His friendship with the Scottish queen, may have created tension between Throckmorton and William, but it is likely that he supported Mary merely out of his fondness for her, as he favoured the reformed religion and William's approach to politics and governance.[8]

Throckmorton's daughter Elizabeth or 'Bess' became a lady-in-waiting to Elizabeth I and eventually, albeit scandalously, married Sir Walter Raleigh. When Throckmorton fell under suspicion during the Duke of Norfolk's conspiracy to place Mary Stuart on Elizabeth's throne in 1569, he was imprisoned for some time. However, his close friendship with William and the queen's favour may have been the reason why he was eventually released. He died in early 1571, just weeks before William's elevation to a peerage. It must have been a bitter-sweet moment for the now Lord Burghley, who valued his friends and colleagues as much as he did his duty at the queen's side.[9]

Among William's most trusted colleagues was Sir Francis Walsingham. Walsingham was born sometime around 1532 and though was around twelve years William's junior, this mattered little by the time both men were working together under a new regime.[10] In fact, it was these two men, who together, made the Elizabethan era, certainly by a political perspective, what we now understand it to have been. Walsingham was born to a well-connected gentile family – like many of William's friends and colleagues. Like William, he was also well educated and attended Cambridge. At the age of around twenty, he took to travelling in Europe and embarked on a career in law.[11] These years abroad had a profound effect on Walsingham's later understanding and workings of European/continental politics. He was a believer in the reformed faith and therefore, shared William's vision for a Protestant Elizabethan state. During the reign of Mary I, Walsingham, unlike his later companion, joined many in exile in Switzerland and Italy until Elizabeth's succession. Though he possessed a will similar to that of William Cecil's and indeed, possessed his own sense of genius in his later position as Elizabeth's principal secretary, he nevertheless owed his rise to none other than William. He would later be nicknamed 'Elizabeth's Spymaster'.

When Walsingham returned to England, it was likely through his connections with William, Nicholas Throckmorton, who was also an old friend, and Sir Francis Russell, that he was elected to Elizabeth's first Parliament in 1559.[12] It was William who would first bring Walsingham into 'public service' as Read refers to it. His work would have initially gone under William's direction who was at the beginning of Elizabeth's reign, the new queen's shining star. By 1570, Walsingham was appointed as an ambassador in France. This may have been due to William's influence that he got such a notable position. Nonetheless, it was also due to his own abilities, intelligence and determination, that his time abroad was so successful. This may have been the point where William really felt that he could entirely trust his new colleague. Not trust in the sense that there was any possibility of foul play of Walsingham's part, but rather, that he possessed the ability to help bring William's vision for England into effect. Historians generally mark the beginning of Walsingham's career as 1570.[13] However, the reality was much more complicated than that, and it is likely that both secretary Cecil and Walsingham would have interpreted the beginnings of their political careers much earlier on in Elizabeth's reign.

Interestingly, where William struggled with his opinion of Lord Robert Dudley in the early years of Elizabeth's reign, Walsingham seemed to win over his colleague's foe. The fact that they corresponded regularly was no secret. However, there is no evidence to suggest that he was in any way involved in the quarrels between the queen's secretary and favourite. While he was aboard on mission in the early 1570s, Walsingham wrote to William often of the goings-on at the French court, the political situation, and any rumours that could be of some use to England. He was not ignorant of the fact that without William as his friend, he may never have risen so high as to be chosen as an ambassador on behalf of Elizabeth. He wrote to William in the summer of 1572 for example: 'I can say no more, but that I owe myself and all that I have to your Lordship'.[14]

Walsingham's time abroad served him well. Not only did he have a greater understanding of foreign politics and the foreign view of Protestant England, but he also understood more fundamentally than William of the threat to England from those who opposed its Protestant queen's right to rule. Indeed, though we may view William as the Elizabethan genius of his time, Elizabeth's spymaster offered something to the Protestant regime that William simply could not, a bird's eye view of the enemy, the foe, and the ally. In terms of his religiosity, Walsingham was much stauncher and extremist than William, and indeed, many of his English contemporaries. By the time he was in his mid-forties, his position as Elizabeth's secretary, with William's own further rise in status and power, made him one of the most powerful men in England, perhaps even Europe – at least in terms of foreign policy. He was described by the Spanish as perhaps the 'worst heretic' of them all. His radicalism regarding the Protestant faith was not really representative of the Elizabethan State, yet this seemed to matter little to the queen and William. He was not the most learned man, and in terms of his religiosity, he was more Puritan than Anglican. According to Read, Walsingham's religion influenced his position to, and understanding of, foreign policy. When it came to diplomacy for example, the religion of the state, kingdom or sovereign that he dealt with, had a role in how he approached negotiations. For example, when it came to foreign policy with Spain, Walsingham left little room for negotiation at all, and wholly disregarded any form of reconciliation between Elizabeth and Philip. He often persuaded the queen, likely without William's opposition, to rally behind her Protestant contemporaries in France and the low countries. He differed greatly from William however, in that he viewed the safety and endurance of his religion as more important than sound foreign policy. This was likely due to his different views towards Protestantism to that of William. For William, the Protestant state was in fact the representation of the Elizabethan regime, and therefore one could not endure without the other. Though some believe that Walsingham also believed both to be of the same value, the fact that he was unmovable in his opposition to marital foreign alliances with Catholic powers such as Spain and France speaks volumes.[15]

This is likely why Walsingham would have viewed any notion of Elizabeth marrying a Catholic prince as abhorrent. For example, during the Anjou negotiations in the late 1570s and early 1580s, Walsingham, like his friend and the favourite, Lord Robert Dudley, was wholly opposed to the match. He felt it a danger to the stability of the Protestant faith in England. For him, no Catholic would do. William was much more interested in supporting his queen in this matter, as it was his biggest wish to ensure the security of the succession and not see the crown pass to Mary Stuart, despite the suggestion of the late 1560s to allow Parliament to decide the successor in the event of Elizabeth's death if she did not name an heir. In the end, Walsingham remained one of Elizabeth's most loyal servants and advisors, and his relationship with William was even stronger. Despite the relationship between these two men and how they worked alongside each other with the same goal, to protect Elizabeth and the Protestant faith in England, there has been little attention paid to their friendship in itself. This could most definitely be an interesting study on its own, and the correspondence between these two men would certainly provide the basis for such an endeavour. Walsingham died in 1590, almost a decade before his friend, who he believed he owed so much to.

It is no surprise that the men who William befriended, and the queen trusted, had much more in common than their time at Cambridge, their philosophy or their religiosity and political aspirations. William and Elizabeth's generation had lived through one of England's most chaotic periods. The mid-Tudor period was represented by intense political, social and religious crises. Since William's birth, there had been four Tudor monarchs on the throne, each with their own virtues, flaws, aspirations and brilliance. By the time Elizabeth came to power, the men that made up her council and court had lived through such turbulence that it is no surprise that Elizabethan domestic and it can be said, foreign policy, was rather tranquil than that of her father's or brother's reigns. But this was not due to Elizabeth herself, for despite all her virtues, naturally inherited grace and intelligence, she was not wholly responsible for the 'Elizabethan regime' herself, but merely the vessel which allowed it to be born. William's friends and foes also contributed to how the Elizabethan State was fashioned and this can certainly be said for Sir Philip Sidney.[16]

Philip Sidney was the son of Sir Henry Sidney, a life-long friend of William's. He was of an aristocratic background. He is now known as one of the most brilliant men of the Elizabethan period. He was a courtier, soldier, famous poet and scholar. His mother was interestingly, Lady Mary Dudley, the sister of Lord Robert Dudley, the queen's favourite and the bane of William's life during the 1560 negotiations regarding Elizabeth's marriage. Sidney's sister Mary was married to Henry Herbert, Earl of Pembroke, also a friend of William's, and so the familial connections throughout court created the foundation for William's network of friends, confidantes and spies.[17]

By the time he was eighteen in 1572, still rather young, even for the period; he was elected to Parliament. This coincided with one of the most important years of his friend William Cecil's life. By the year 1570, William was in his fiftieth year. His position as the queen's secretary and man of the day seemed absolutely secure – and it was. However, there was still room to grow for this great man, whose leadership had pushed Elizabeth's England into a brave new period. Therefore, his reward by this time was well overdue. By February 1571, William was given the title of Baron Cecil of Burghley. He was vested in his robe by the queen herself. Interestingly, it seems that Dudley was in support of William's elevation to a peerage. Why the queen chose this moment to reward William is unclear, for he seemed very happy and settled in his position as it was. However, this did not mean that his duties wholly changed with his new title and he was now needed more than ever. In fact, the only initial difference in his career due to his change of title was that he sat in the Lords instead of the Commons in April that year during Parliament.[18]

As William aged, and his star continued to rise, there was a younger generation of men, the sons of some of his closest friends, who wanted a taste of politics and power. Philip Sidney was one of the younger men at court who contributed to its ever-changing culture through his talent as a poet. He had a very generous patronage, and even during his own lifetime was mythologised as Montrose states. However, Sidney's education meant that he was also to expected to embark on a successful career in politics. In the same year as his election to Parliament, Sidney was sent to France as a part of the earlier negotiations of marriage between the queen and the then Duke of Alençon, later the Duke of Anjou. It was during his time on the continent that he met many notable European scholars. However, it was Sidney's opposition to the queen's proposed marriage to the French duke that landed him in hot waters. Though he was favoured at court by Elizabeth and William, his opinions on the match and his open and written chastisation of his sovereign led to his disfavour, ostracisation and eventual retirement from the Elizabethan court.[19]

Notably, Sidney was arranged to marry Anne, William's daughter. However, this fell through in 1571. Sidney then went on to marry Frances Walsingham, the daughter of Francis Walsingham, William's great friend and colleague.

Sidney eventually died, rather young at the age of thirty-one, in 1586. This was after he was shot during the Battle of Zutphen in the Netherlands against the Catholic Spanish. He was remembered as a hero and a well-learned man. Though he was a staunch Protestant and opposed the queen's match to Anjou, he was not as extreme as his father-in-law Walsingham, and his many letters of correspondence with William Cecil show that he was a man that William felt he could trust, despite their differences.

It is from William's many surviving letters to his friends and colleagues that we gain an insight into his network of trusted confidantes. Despite many of Cecil's writings being lost, the sheer number that have survived is exceptional, considering sixteenth and seventeenth century archival methods. His letters to Smith for example, are so many in number that we can safely say that the pair were great friends despite their differences. Other letters reveal his friendships with aforementioned Nicholas Throckmorton, Robert Dudley, Sir William Petre and Sir Ralph Sadler. Much of William's time was taken up by letter-writing when he was not in the company of the queen or with his family. The weight of his duty obviously took its toll and though he never complained, the secretary often expressed the magnitude of his administrative duties to his colleagues and friends. In June 1565 for example, he wrote to Smith stating that this letter was already his twentieth written that day. Despite there being gaps during William's career that we cannot account for due to the lack of paperwork, that does not mean that it did not once exist and this may be due to some portions of Cecil's papers being lost or destroyed. It is also notable that though all of his paperwork has not survived, the sheer amount that does, indicates that he not only had a vast number of duties to perform, but that his network of trusted friends was the very basis for the success of his career.[20] Ironically, though a family man and devoted husband, the letters written between William and his wife Mildred are few. This, however, is likely due to the fact that they were hardly ever apart.

One character of particular note, and who William deemed a close and trustworthy friend was Sir Ralph Sadler. When Elizabeth became queen, and William rose to become her secretary and chief minister, many of his close friends benefitted from his close proximity to the queen. However, Sadler had already carved out a career as a statesman by the time William, thirteen years his junior, began his own career in politics. He served Henry VIII as a Privy Councillor, Secretary of State, and was even an ambassador to Scotland. Sadler found his way to prominence due to his family's close ties with Thomas Cromwell, a lawyer who became infamous for his service to Henry VIII as his chief minister and engineered the king's divorce from Katherine of Aragon, so that Henry could marry Elizabeth's mother, Anne Boleyn. When Sadler was still only a child, he found a place in Cromwell's household and from there, he was able to navigate, survive and create a prominent and powerful position for himself at court and in later Elizabethan politics.[21]

It was obviously Sadler's favour with Cromwell that brought him to Henry VIII's attention. It is believed that Sadler officially entered into public service in 1518, two years prior to William's birth. So, by the time of William's first breath, there were already men of his abilities working towards securing a steady, wealthy and influential career under the Tudor regime. By the time Henry was into his thirtieth year on the throne, Sadler was a Principal Secretary of State.[22] His influence and abilities brought him so far into Tudor politics, that despite the fall of his patron Cromwell in 1540, he could not escape a life in service to the Crown and State, however precarious that position could be. It is not entirely clear when William and Sadler became friends, but as Sadler was already a prominent member of the Tudor court and Privy Council, it is likely that they met by chance as William began his career in the service of the Lord Protector, Edward Seymour. Like William, Sadler was valuable to whoever wore the crown, or who wielded the power behind the throne. Like, William, Sadler signed the young king's *device for the succession,* which meant that upon Edward VI's death, the crown would bypass Mary and Elizabeth, and go to Lady Jane Grey. He also survived this hiccup when Mary came to the throne. Again, like William, Sadler retired to his estates during Mary's reign and did not return to royal favour until Elizabeth's accession.

Sadler was a man that William could trust. He was far more experienced than William in his service to the state. However, he clearly lacked any close tie or bond to the young queen which saw William's elevation to secretary ahead of men who had served the Tudors for decades. Interestingly, Sadler may have been responsible for reuniting the new queen with the memory of her late, and disgraced, mother. We know the story of Anne Boleyn's tragic downfall. But it is interesting to find that her memory and written word may have found its way to her daughter through a vast web of statesmen such as William Cecil and Ralph Sadler.

Many believe that the letter referred to as 'Anne Boleyn's letter from the tower' or 'the tower letter' is genuine. Though there have been many copies made over the past centuries, it is likely that the original letter would have been written for the queen, perhaps by a scribe or secretary. At the time of the queen's imprisonment, Sadler was Cromwell's secretary, or at least in service in his household. As Sadler was the executor of Cromwell's will and delivered the latter's own ironic letter begging for the king's mercy in

1540, it could be possible that Sadler not only delivered the queen's letter to Cromwell, who did not pass it on to Henry, but it may have been Sadler who wrote the queen's last words meant for her husband. Sandra Vasoli has studied the Tower Letter in great detail, and believes that Sadler may not only have been the letter's author on behalf of the queen, but that he knew the whereabouts of the letter after the queen's death and Cromwell's downfall. Therefore, it is likely that through his close friendship with the new secretary, that at some point after 1540, the letter was passed from Sadler to William. Though Elizabeth did not publicly speak of her mother, there exists a flicker of evidence suggesting that she kept her mother's memory alive. Vasoli states that it is highly likely that William shared the letter with Elizabeth when she became queen, and that the queen may have wished her mother's words to be preserved, and therefore, the copies that we are left with today, are the result of William's commission to preserve the original contents. This may also be the reason why we cannot know for sure who the original author was.[23]

William may well have trusted Sadler as a friend, but his opinions on matters of state and the queen's personal life, which both men would have viewed as one and the same, often irritated Elizabeth. Many historians debate the authenticity of the 'Tower Letter' and there is no definitive evidence of who its author may be. The possibility that Anne Boleyn dictated her letter to a scribe should not be dismissed. However, if the author was indeed Sadler, and if he did deliver the letter to William who may have given it to Elizabeth, there is also no evidence to suggest her reaction to it. Nor did she particularly favour Sadler or hold him to a high regard as William did. Indeed, when Parliament met in 1563 and 1566, he was just as concerned with the succession crisis as the secretary. He was also opposed to any notion of Mary Stuart's claim to the English throne, stating that though she was the queen's kin, her foreignness was a threat to the English nation.[24]

Sadler was also opposed to Elizabeth's proposed marriage with the Duke of Anjou in the late 1570s/early 1580s, despite his good friend William's approval of the match, or any match at that point in the succession crisis. The queen's disfavour for him is evident in that he only ever received one high office during Elizabeth's reign, that being the Chancellorship of the Duchy of Lancaster. This increased his income and lands considerably and many of his family members benefitted from this. In the late 1560s he was sent to the north to act as a member of the commission assembled to negotiate between Mary and Elizabeth. It is evident that William trusted Sadler enough that he entrusted him with the care of his first-born son, Thomas, who was to serve in Sussex's army in 1569. Sadler evidently did his duty, but when he was re-called in 1570, he had had enough and retired for some time to Standon. By the time Mary was incarcerated on English soil, the position of her custodian was given to Sadler. Elizabeth had avoided ever meeting her cousin, and therefore never fell under her charms. This cannot be said for Sadler however, and he became a most lenient gaoler; allowing her to take hawking trips. He became so friendly with her that he was eventually given discharge in 1586. Interestingly, he died less than a month after Mary's execution in 1587, aged eighty. His life, work and legacy live on in what are now referred to as the *Sadler Papers.*[25]

William Cecil's circle was unsurprisingly made up mostly of men, due to the lack of authority and political position granted to women of the day. However, as the monarch was a woman, women were afforded important roles at court. But then again, they always had been. Elizabeth's women were never far from her side, and many of them had been there since her childhood. Besides her beloved Kat Ashley, there was another who gained Elizabeth's affections. Blanche Parry was William's cousin and the pair became good friends. The queen also greatly favoured her Welsh servant. Blanche was one of few women who had served the queen from birth, and had even rocked her cradle.[26] She likely knew Elizabeth more than anyone by the time William became her secretary in her early reign. Whether or not Blanche's position had anything to do with William's first encounters with the queen when she was a princess, or his elevation above many other men who had served the Tudors for decades before his career even began, we cannot be sure. Blanche worked closely with William, and she may well have attempted to appease the queen on a number of occasions on William's behalf. Blanche's influence is evident in the fact that she became a Chief Gentlewoman of Elizabeth's Privy Chamber and Keeper of the Queen's Jewels. She not only helped choose the queen's clothes, but contributed to her wardrobe with many gifts. This is not only evidence of her influence on the queen, but her vast wealth in her ability to buy Elizabeth some of the most expensive gifts she would ever receive. William needed Blanche in many ways. She was familiar with the queen, could put her at ease, and knew exactly what she wanted and when she wanted it. William's close relationship with his cousin not only reveals him as a family man, but that he was willing to use his familial ties when affairs of state called for it, however small a matter may have been.[27]

One of William's most unlikely and unusual of friends was an Irishman named Nicholas White. White was a lawyer, judge and later Privy Councillor to Elizabeth I under William's direction. Nicholas was the son of James White, a steward of the Earl of Ormond during the reign of Henry VIII.

In 1546, James was poisoned alongside the Earl. Nicholas was able to attend Lincoln's Inn in 1552. During this period of study, he became tutor to William's children. Eventually, during Elizabeth's first year as queen, White was elected as a member of the Irish Parliament for the county of Kilkenny. He would eventually go on to buy Leixlip Castle and have a family of his own.[28] Despite the distance, William and Nicholas stayed in contact. William may well have considered White a close friend, and often wrote to him concerning the succession and problems presented by Mary Stuart. White himself interviewed Mary in 1569. White was elevated to many positions throughout his career, no doubt due to his friendship with William and the queen's favour for him. He was even knighted 1584, but by 1589 he was implicated in a treasonous controversy in Dublin whereby the queen's authority over Ireland was being questioned. Whether or not White was guilty of the charges, he was dismissed from the Irish council and was arrested in 1590, despite his old age and ailing health, and placed in the Tower of London by 1591. He had died by 1592, but it is unclear whether he died in the Tower or not. William withdrew from his correspondence from his long-time friend. It is uncertain whether this was due to his belief in White's guilt or his wish to stay clear of any scandal. It may have been due to William's influence however that White's son Thomas was permitted by the council to take his father's body back to Ireland from London upon his death. [29]

William made many connections and friendships throughout his life and career that lasted decades. Though he was evidently a man of good character, a generous and loyal friend, it cannot be doubted that he often used his web of colleagues and confidantes to his own personal advantage and to the advantage of the Elizabethan state. Though he was not one who enjoyed courtly gossip or intrigues, he no doubt benefitted from the reports of those at home and abroad, whom he kept correspondence with. The Cecil Papers are made up of many differing documents that reflect William's hard work and his influence on the formation and stability of the Elizabethan state. But it is notable that a very large portion of these papers are made up of his personal correspondence with friends and colleagues. By this it can be suggested that though he took on much of the governing of England on his own – a task that would no doubt contribute to his later poor health and decline, his circle of friends contributed to the decisions that he made and the actions that he took. Without many of his colleagues abroad, and his web of informants, William may well have struggled to maintain his grip on power and therefore protect the England that he worked so tirelessly to create.

Chapter 7

Patronage, Influence and Intrigue

The 1560s were some of the most difficult and yet successful years of William's life. The tensions in Europe and in the low countries in particular, were causing a complete deterioration of any diplomacy between Catholics and Protestants. As tensions were beginning to boil over, and would eventually become something much more catastrophic and dangerous for England's national security, neither Elizabeth or William wished to get involved in the drudgery of what they suspected would end up in all-out war. Elizabeth may have been weary, and indeed William may have wished to appear neutral on a political front, but it was certainly a shared reluctance to involve England in matters that it could for some time, avoid.

William and Elizabeth had formed a close friendship since her ascension. Though they fundamentally disagreed on many matters of state and on the sensitive topic of the queen's marriage, it cannot be doubted that he became her most trusted and loyal councillor. The reason for William's success was down to two factors. His staunch Protestantism, and the future of the Protestant English State were at the core of every domestic and foreign policy. He felt that the unity of Protestants, particularly on the British Isles, would bring about a new age for England. And in hindsight, he was right. Secondly, Elizabeth was less inclined towards extremism. In fact, as Loades states, the queen's religiosity was much subtler than that of her advisors. However, as William was happy for the queen to marry a Catholic once that said man's Catholicism could be deemed as non-threatening, it is evident that both queen and secretary understood the importance of diplomacy and the need for European allies.[1]

It is no surprise then that William was granted the peerage of Baron Burghley. A lavish ceremony was conducted in the presence chamber at Westminster. After a short speech by the new Lord Burghley, a dinner would have been held in celebration. Again, the reasons for this elevation at this time are uncertain. But, perhaps it was due to his years of loyalty, his close bond with the queen and notably, his poor health, that Elizabeth decided he deserved some further reward. Loades also takes this perspective.[2]

If we go by the Letters Patent, it can certainly be assured that the queen felt that William's elevation was deserving due to his service:

> As well for the long services in the time of our progenitors, kings of England, as also for the faithful and acceptable duty and observance which he hath always performed from the very beginning of our reign, and ceaseth not daily to perform many ways, not only in the great and mighty affairs of the Council but generally also in all other enterprises for the realm, and also for his circumspection, stoutness, wisdom, dexterity, integrity of life, providence, care and faithfulness.[3]

Read states that these words were hardly extravagant. However, eloquent they may not be, they reveal that the queen knew that her first decade (and then some) on the throne may not have been as successful or indeed safe, without the wisdom and advice of William. Even Dudley later wrote to Walsingham regarding William's peerage and how this would affect his position on the council, further suggesting that though William would remain as secretary for some time, he would soon be given the office of Lord Privy Seal.[4] However, this never happened. Sir Thomas Smith was appointed to help William in his duties as secretary until further notice. William as ever, was dedicated to whatever work he pursued himself and Smith was not sworn in as secretary or onto the council until William then succeeded as the Lord Treasurer sometime later in July of 1572. But how did this change William's status, what affect did it have on his family and what were his own views of his elevation in status?

William was grateful for his new title, but he played it humbly. He held many other offices and his wealth had vastly expanded, as had his influence on court life and foreign diplomacy, prior to his peerage. He described himself soon after his elevation as 'the poorest Lord in England'. However, this was far from the truth, and his many enterprises and offices had proven more than lucrative. William had always held a special position on the Privy Council and in the queen's esteem, and he was not unaware of this. His elevation only cemented his power, influence and expanded his already vast wealth. Yet, if we are to believe that Elizabeth gave William the title of Baron as a reward for his poor health, likely brought on by the pressures of his position as secretary, this is a total misconception of what it meant to be a peer of the realm. In fact, William's offices, and therefore his duties to perform only expanded, making it much more difficult for him to get away from the affairs of state and spend time on his own estates in the country with his family.[5] His wife in particular, though happy for her husband's success and likely for her new styling as 'Lady Burghley', did not favour court life. Nor do we know of her having any degree of interest in the affairs of state. It would appear that she played the diligent and dutiful role as the wife of an English statesman, for now that her husband was Lord Burghley, he was no longer simply the administrator, he was the statesman of his day.

Though he did not appear a man of ambition in the sense of wealth and title, he nonetheless gained both for his duties. He may not have performed his duties for reward other than that of the preservation of Elizabeth's reign, but to claim that he was a man of poverty or little means was untrue. Indeed, William was evidently proud of his elevation, writing to his friend Nicholas White in Ireland at the time, that:

> My style is Lord Burghley, if you mean to know it for your writing, and if you list to write, truly the poorest Lord in England.[6]

In another letter written to Walsingham, dated soon after he was made Lord Burghley, dated 14 April 1571, he first signed off as 'Your assured loving friend, William Cecil'. He then rather humorously added afterwards: 'I forgot my new word, William Burleigh'. As William's star continued to rise, his health continued to plummet.[7]

By this time, he was in his fifty-first year, and gout plagued him. His letters, especially those to Walsingham reveal the severity of his illness and how it affected his work. He even apologised in advance for a lack of replies to Walsingham's letters. It is also around this time that Sir Nicholas Throckmorton died. William recorded this in his diary and mentions his thoughts on the cause of death as pleurisy and pneumonia. There were rumours of poisoning, but there is no evidence other than a scant mention of rumour and hearsay. Even Robert Dudley mentioned in a letter to Walsingham, that Throckmorton's 'lungs were perished'.[8] It is hard to conclude how close as friends William and Throckmorton actually were. His time abroad in France and Scotland certainly owed to his close proximity to William, and both men had come up in the world around the same time during their service to the Seymours. To say that his death had no effect on William would be incorrect, as he himself would have noted his own mortality. He had a family of his own to think of, sons yet too young to inherit the burden which he carried, and a queen and kingdom in limbo, until his mistress either married, or Mary Stuart was silenced. If the death of Throckmorton did not bring about a tinge of sadness for the new

Lord Burghley, then it certainly would have reminded him that men lived on borrowed time.

As Willian's responsibilities grew, despite his ill health and the death of a presumably close confidante if not friend, so too did the never-ending problem of Mary Stuart. The de-throned queen may not have seemed as large a threat to many after being forced to abdicate the throne of Scotland in favour of her infant son and being implemented in the death of her husband. But once she remained alive, she gave Catholic conspirators motivation. Darnley had proven to be a bad match in the end. He may have given Mary what William wanted most for Elizabeth – a son, but by the time Scotland's heir had arrived, he had proven himself to be an unsatisfactory consort and a drunk. In the end, he was assassinated at Kirk o' Field in 1567, and the blame was put on his wife. After fleeing Scotland in 1568, Mary felt sure that Elizabeth would provide her with refuge. Though she was given permission to stay in England, her presence startled the council, and nobody was more worried than William. By the time William was made Lord Burghley, Mary had *de facto* been a prisoner – finding herself at the will and charity of Elizabeth and the Privy Council, and was often moved from one location to another. Whether we interpret her time in England as imprisonment or refuge, the fact was that her presence at all presented a threat to Elizabeth's position and the preservation of the Protestant State. While in Scotland, she was a distant figure, still dangerous nonetheless, but technically in another land. As a 'guest' in England, she became a solid representative to Catholics of the old faith, the old ties with Rome and this, therefore, made her more dangerous than ever.

Indeed, by 1571, Mary's Catholic supporters in Scotland began to request that their queen should be released from her state of imprisonment in England and restored as the Queen of Scots. Of course, this would never have happened. The political relations between Scotland and England had healed somewhat since the crowning of the infant king James VI. This was the vision of a Protestant union that William had worked so long to bring about, and though tensions were far from resolved, he likely hoped that in time, his vision would prevail. He was opposed to granting Mary any liberty within England or to leave England and was vehemently opposed to any notion of her restoration as Queen of Scots. As long as England had Mary in custody, she was as much a threat as she was a catch. She had stirred up tensions in her own country, encouraged treason and had been forced to abdicate in favour of a baby. If she had failed in her duties once, William could only have imagined what could come about if she was given a second chance, or some leniency in England. It may seem illogical that Mary would continue to proclaim herself as the rightful queen of England or as Elizabeth's heir, considering that she was little more than England's prisoner. However, William knew that the threat was more serious than ever because she had lost her kingdom, her power, her son and her liberty. Now that she had nothing, she had nothing to lose, and everything to gain.[9]

The decision of freeing Mary may have technically lay with Elizabeth, but William argued that 'If the Queen's Majesty shall put her [Mary] to liberty, whereby she must needs come to government, she shall ten, by implication, discharge her of her heinous crime [that being her assistance in the rebellion of the earls in the rising in the north], whereof she was accused before her majesty and to the which she never did make any plain answer for her acquittal. For after she be restored to government, the Queen's Majesty shall never have opportunity to denounce her former faults and crimes.'[10] The language here is striking. Not only does it reveal that William, in the early stages of his new status, was able to execute another level of power, but it also reveals that he was in many ways willing to contradict the queen if necessary. If Elizabeth were to agree to the terms of Mary's representatives and free the former Queen of Scots, possibly restoring her titles and powers, then she could never again take the opportunity to use her apparent former crimes to the advantage and for the safety of the English State.[11] In a way, William was stating that he knew best for the Elizabethan state, and that the queen needed to heed the words of her council. Indeed, she had just elevated her most trusted advisor to that of a Lord, granting him even more influence and power. This was his duty. However, If William thought that the queen would be more eager to heed his advice on 'dealing' with the problem of Mary Stuart, he was wrong and Elizabeth, as she did with everything else, procrastinated for years on the question of what to do with her cousin queen.

Not only did William's work continue to expand, and the worry of Mary Stuart remain, there also remained the question of the succession and Elizabeth's marriage. The queen was ageing, and as she was now in her thirty-eighth year, the chances of her finding a willing, suitable husband and producing a male heir were slim. Now, with the growing tensions in Europe between Protestants and Catholics and the continuous threat of Mary's supporters, there was never a better time for Elizabeth to produce a legitimate heir. But with the chaos in mainland Europe, who was the most suitable candidate for the queen's husband? What man would willingly accept her authority over his (the example of Mary and Lord Darnley's marriage was nothing to go by)? What Catholic prince would willingly denounce his faith to marry an ageing Protestant queen? Negotiations between Elizabeth and the Valois princes had begun in 1570, but it was really in 1571, that due to the many political factors, William once again began to press Elizabeth towards marriage, and the queen herself felt obliged to at least entertain the notion.

If the 1560s were an education for William and the men of Elizabeth's council, the 1570s were even more so. By the end of 1572, tensions in Europe had completely boiled over. On 23 August, a scene of violence broke out in Paris after King Charles IX had ordered the assassination of Admiral Gaspard de Coligny, a French nobleman and the leader of the Huguenots. He was once close to the king, but as peace between Catholics and Protestants became impossible, the assassination of Coligny was attempted on 22 August. He survived with minor wounds. However, the attempted assassination only triggered further violence and slaughter of thousands of Protestants, not only in Paris, but throughout much of the surrounding townlands and countryside. This event, now known as the Saint Bartholomew's Day Massacre, crippled the faction of French Aristocratic Protestants. It also further radicalised those Huguenots that survived, and caused Protestants afar to justify their suspicions of their own Catholic subjects. This way by no means a unique event, but it was certainly the worst example of slaughter *en masse* in the sixteenth century due to religious conflict. For those who witnessed and survived the event, though deplorable, the massacre would not have been entirely surprising. But it also gave Protestants in France, England and beyond, martyrs.[12]

Walsingham had been sent to France in 1571 to negotiate an alliance in matrimony between France and England. William's hope was that if he were to convince his queen to enter into a union with France, whatever duke she married would renounce his Catholicism. It was now necessary more than ever, for William to convince Elizabeth to marry, produce an heir and protect England with a strong political alliance.[13] However, Elizabeth's concerns by late 1571 had shifted again towards Scotland, and she wished to quash the civil war that had been ongoing in Scotland between Mary's supporters, mostly Catholics, and those who supported the regency of her son, James VI. Elizabeth promised to protect the Marian faction, if they yielded to the regency, and stated that she would encourage the preservation of their lives, lands and some influence in government. They declined the offer however, and as these supporters had many friends in France, the English and French commissioners struggled to bring about peace between the three states.[14]

The then Duke of Alençon, not yet the Duke of Anjou as he would be known later during the second negotiations of marriage with Elizabeth, due to the later death of his elder brother, was at this point still very young.

Elizabeth was well aware of the severity of the situation in Europe, and the advantages of a marital alliance with France were too great to ignore. On the matter of the marriage negotiations, William required information about the young man that may one day be his king. However, it is also likely that that queen asked William to do a little digging on the man that was proposed to become her husband. William used his connections and wrote to Walsingham: 'I am willed to require you to use all good means possibly to understand what you can of the Duke of Alençon, of his age in certainty, of his stature, of his condition, his inclination to religion. His devotion this way, the devotion of his followers and servitors. Hereof her Majesty seeketh speedily to be advertised that she may be resolved before the month.'[15]

This is interesting as it reveals that Elizabeth was somewhat interested in negotiating the possibility of an alliance with France through marriage. Or perhaps she at least wished to appear as if interested. William was more than happy to find all the necessary information about the duke that the queen needed, for he himself would not have been personally interested in the duke's appearance or stature.

It is clear however, that William was interested in the duke's religion; believing that the matter could go no further without a resolution to the said suitor's faith and attitude towards Protestantism. It is also notable that William believed Elizabeth would turn down the offer of marriage yet again, stating that: 'If somewhat be not devised to recompense the opinion that her majesty conceiveth, as that she should be misliked to make the choice of so young a prince, I doubt the end.'[16] Walsingham surprisingly sent back a glowing report of Anjou, that was likely over-exaggerated, and the queen seemed more interested in the eldest brother. Her interest in Alençon would come years later. By the time St Bartholomew's had shocked the world, the English began to feel unsettled with any notion of an alliance with the French, and a royal family that many felt were responsible for the massacre. Elizabeth herself did not wish to doubt the French king, and as many differing reports of those responsible for the bloodbath circulated, the possibility of an alliance by marriage became a shaky topic. The French wished to keep the possibility open, and Elizabeth was aware that she needed a strong ally, but William was cautious. His own feelings regarding the massacre and who he felt was responsible, are insinuated in a letter he wrote to the Earl of Shrewsbury sometime later:

> These French tragedies…and ending of unlucky marriage with
> blood and vile murders, cannot be expressed with tongue to
> declare the cruelties, whereof now it is said that the king taketh

repentance and that he was abused to cause it to be committed
by the duke of Guise [Mary Stuart's maternal uncle] and the
faction of the papists.[17]

In the presence of William and other members of the Privy Council, and a
hoard of the queen's ladies, the French ambassador was received by Elizabeth
some days later. He was greeted with a frigid silence. He attempted to explain
the French king played no part in the matter, and that he hoped the proposed
alliance would not be affected by the event. Elizabeth however, expressed
her doubts on the matter, questioning the French king's integrity and his
ability to protect his own subjects. At the point where the English needed
the French the most, they now distrusted them the most. As negotiations
wore on, the danger to Elizabeth's position grew. It is evident that though
William was no longer secretary, he put his hand on almost everything.
He himself kept the negotiations going on in the background, despite the
horrors of the massacre; for what mattered most was the preservation of
the Elizabethan State and Protestant religion by the means of the queen's
marriage and providing an heir. Title and influence simply meant more work
for William, and though the position of secretary had by then been filled, it
is clear that the new secretary was no match for the original.[18]

William's new position meant that he was also responsible for the
management of Parliament. A Parliament that he had once sat on when
he was a young man. Recently, historians have delved into the running of
the Elizabethan Parliament – who was responsible for what, and how local
government's ran their districts and with what varying levels of power.
Many have argued that the level of authority was made up of a hierarchy,
of which William was at the peak. The idea that the country was organised
by a series of 'local power grids' seems to stand with many scholars of the
topic. It appears that William and Elizabeth worked together, and with many
people of differing levels in this 'power grid' in order to create a functioning
government. Technically, the monarch owned the land on which English
nobles lived. This inevitably created both good relations and tensions
between the crown and landowners. It is no surprise then, that William's rise
to a peerage, and granting of the office of Lord High Treasurer meant that
besides that of the queen, he was the most powerful person in the country.
He oversaw the finances, security, religion and governance of the realm. Of
course, as every landowner owed fealty to the crown, so too did the Lord
Treasurer owe his position entirely to the queen.

Sir Thomas Smith even spoke of the purpose of the Tudor form of
government, stating that 'For no man holds land simply free in England, but

he or she that holds the Crown of England: all others holde their land in fee, that is upon faith or trust, and some service to be done…[19]

He further referred to England as *'re publica'* or 'common wealth', defining Elizabeth's government as something new for the period, a number of people from differing backgrounds, classes and levels of society, coming together in common interest to create something new. Therefore, Elizabeth's government under William can be seen as a mish-mash of formal and informal networks, some individuals being officials, and some not. William's role in this network of both formal and informal service was of utmost importance; as without the connections that he formed both at home and abroad, the web of individuals both official and unofficial in their service to the Elizabeth an state could not have existed. It was during this perilous time, where England lay alone in an ocean of discontent, civil war and massacre, that a man like William was needed. For his 'spidery hand', as Jones states, presents the weakness of the crown at this time, rather than its strength.[20]

Powerful men like William could not simply rise due to their abilities, however. Though Elizabeth's father Henry VIII has placed men far beyond their station than their beginnings in life should have allowed (men like Thomas Wolsey and Thomas Cromwell), Elizabeth disfavoured such notions. Yes, William did rise in rank to Baron Burghley due to his service to the Crown and his friendship with the queen, but he would never have been able to rise to such prominence without his family's previous proximity to the royal family. On that note, in many ways, William was also a historian and genealogist, and was particularly interested in his own family's genealogy, as evident from the Cecil Papers. William felt that good breeding as the basis for one's station in life and also one's virtue. He felt that a family's history could say much about an individual of that name. Therefore, the preservation of the Elizabethan state in his mind would have depended on the history of the families that ran it, as their history and genealogy impacted on their virtue. It is no surprise then that he was inclined to enjoy the favour of men who were above him in title and rank. Nor that he disfavoured the rise of men such as Robert Dudley, who came from a family of traitors to the crown. William was well read, and had a love for the history of royal families. He was also particularly interested in the writings of Cicero, for it was the latter's philosophy that politics allowed an individual to express their inner virtue. This does not mean that William's interest in his family history was a way of legitimising his own rise on the social ladder, but rather his understanding of how society should work to preserve order. Though seemingly humble, he may have felt that his elevation was deserved, due to his own morals, virtue and his family's genealogy, history and patronage under the Tudors.[21]

William was not the only person who had a network of individuals willing to aid him in running the kingdom. Mary Stuart, though technically a prisoner, also had her own web of petitioners, spies and supporters. It appears that even before the Massacre, coinciding with William's ever-growing mountain of work, the Queen of Scots was playing a very real-life version of chess. She had a network of supporters from Spain to Florence, Scotland and even some men based in the centre of power in London. This network of individuals made it their mission to depose Elizabeth and replace her with Mary. However, this web was quickly unwound as her messenger for her representative in England, that being the Bishop of Ross, was detained in Dover in April 1571. A bundle of letters was discovered on his person, which were sent to William. They revealed that Mary was part of a great conspiracy, which also involved Philip of Spain, some Florentine bankers, and the Pope. The Duke of Norfolk had already attempted to rebel against Elizabeth, free and then marry Mary some two years earlier, without success. He was kept alive for the time being, and Elizabeth even visited him on progress. However, Mary's influence and network were no match for that of William's. As her web began to break, so too was it revealed that Norfolk was again plotting against Elizabeth. The duke was sending funds directly to Scotland to Mary's supporters. These funds came from the Florentine banker Roberto Ridolfi. Norfolk's secretary was arrested, brought to the Tower and likely interrogated, or rather, tortured. By mid-1572, Norfolk had been tried and executed for treason and Mary Stuart had lost any lasting respect from her cousin. She was now more than a threat to the crown. She was a total liability. Even her presence and incarceration in England was not enough to quash her plotting.[22]

It was no surprise that Walsingham was sent to discuss an alliance with France, as both Parliaments of 1571 and 1572 were trying for William, to say the least. The queen had not yet agreed to marry and time was running out. Elizabeth was ageing, and the question of who would succeed her again became the main topic of discussion in Parliament. The queen herself had banned such discussions, but the commons went further than just marriage discussions. This time, they also wished to explore further reforms in the Church of England, and the future of Mary Stuart. The commons cried out for the death of an anointed, albeit deposed queen, but the House of Lords held the real power, and at the top was William Cecil. William could only go so far at this point in terms of putting pressure on the queen to find a solution. William himself had not been well for some time. Many from the Lords wished Mary to be formally barred from succession. This, to an extent may have been to Elizabeth's advantage, but as Mary was not an English subject, it was tricky. William, however, was hell-bent on bringing this bar to fruition, and with the backing of the Lords and Commons, he felt he could succeed in at least that. A bill was drawn up, signed by all members, passed, but it made the queen extremely uncomfortable. William later wrote to Walsingham: 'All that we laboured for and had with full consent brought to fashion…was by her majesty neither assented nor rejected, but deferred…'[23]

Mary Stuart was the kin of the queen, but gave William and Elizabeth anxiety during the 1570s. She may well have had her eye on Elizabeth's crown, but there was something perhaps even more precious to Elizabeth. Something that she would lose to another kinswoman. Robert Dudley had not remarried since the scandalous death of his wife, Amy Robsart, in 1560. If he had hoped that by biding his time, he could convince the queen, and perhaps her council that he was the best choice of husband for her, he was mistaken. The queen favoured Dudley above all other men at court, and though she may well have had other companions, Dudley was never far from her side. Therefore, he was often in William's presence, much to the latter's dismay. Elizabeth had long given Dudley professions of her love for him. Though she may or may not have been actually in love with him, her words gave him hope, for a time. The queen had many favourite ladies too. One of many was her cousin Lettice Knollys, whose mother, Catherine Carey, had also served the queen and was a daughter of her maternal aunt, Mary Boleyn. It is no surprise that the queen favoured her mother's family, and though Lettice's younger sister Elizabeth had married Sir Thomas Leighton in 1578, she was a young widow, with a son.[24]

It is unclear when exactly Lettice and Dudley began a secret liaison right under Elizabeth's nose. But it most likely began no later than the beginning of 1578. This is believed to have been a love match, or at least a lust match at the beginning. Whatever the origins of their union, Lettice and Dudley agreed to marry in secret. Both would have been aware of the consequences. But both also understood the benefits of such a match. Robert Dudley was the queen's favourite; he was wealthy, charming, cultured and influential. Lettice on the other hand was a favourite cousin of the queen's. She provided a minor royal connection through marriage. She had also proven herself capable of producing a male heir, something that by this time, Dudley may have been thinking of. Both were aware of the risks, and both knew that Elizabeth would never have given her consent. Therefore, the irrational became the only possible means of them being together. A secret marriage. There exist many examples of Elizabeth's favourites or family marrying without royal consent, and the consequences of such a betrayal were not desirable. Both

Mary and Catherine Grey had married without the queen's permission and the consequences were tragic. By the late 1570s, the negotiations of an alliance through marriage between England and France had been revived. They were unofficially put 'on hold' for some time after St Bartholomew's Day Massacre had caused tension and mistrust between both parties, and particularly due to the death of Charles IX in 1574. Elizabeth may well have been interested in rekindling the negotiations of an alliance with France, especially now that Alençon was somewhat older and was now the Duke of Anjou. But the revelation of Dudley's and Lettice's marriage may have pushed her further towards the duke, creating a distance between her and Dudley. The connection between William and Lettice was not a personal one. However, before the scandalous marriage took place, Lettice's son, Robert Devereux, spent some time in William's household, before beginning his studies at Trinity College in Cambridge. Throughout his life, William was dedicated to aiding a number of young noble individuals. Young Robert was in need of clothing by the next summer and it was William who as his tutor requested the necessary funding.[25]

Negotiations of a marital alliance between France and England may have been halted for a large proportion of the 1570s. However, this was not after numerous attempts to negotiate matters of religion, power and authority had come into discussion. A visit from Alençon to England had even been arranged for 1573, but the French became wary and nothing came of it. By the time Charles IX had died, the queen mother had run out of promises, and Elizabeth had run out of excuses. With no marriage for the queen in sight, William had much to contend with. Mary Stuart may have remained incarcerated, but news and gossip travelled far, and Elizabeth's failure to conclude a match in matrimony would only have given the exiled Scottish queen further hope. William's influence on matters may have been less intense in 1574 as he was again suffering with gout and was unable to conduct much of his heavy duties without the help of a clerk or servant. His writing, however, was not affected by this bout of ill health. It is evident from Smith's letters to William, that his incapacity had a dire effect on the running of the state, and the daily tasks that needed his presence and attention. Smith wrote: 'We have great want of you here dispatching matters'. The queen also, not doubt, missed the presence and advice of her most trusted councillor.[26]

Many thought that William Cecil was on his last legs, quite literally. However, rumours seem to have exaggerated his condition and though he needed time to recover, he was not dying just yet. Indeed, though gout was a physical ailment – one which there was no real understanding of, treatment for or cure, William's condition may well have been due to stress. Again, his duties had expanded, the French marriage proposal had been all but ended, and with the death of Charles IX, the accession of France's new king, Henry III, the former Duke of Anjou, meant that the French civil war raged on. The Duke of Alençon became the Duke of Anjou in 1576, and Henry III was eager to get him out of the way, and also bring about an alliance with England. Elizabeth was again deemed an ideal choice of bride despite her age.[27] This was due to the ongoing rebellion in the Netherlands. An alliance with Protestant England, may well have been the key to smoothing things over. Unfortunately, it would not be simple as that, and by 1578, with the scandal of Lettice's and Dudley's betrayal revealed, William saw an opportunity to re-address the marriage negotiations to find the queen a husband.

The queen's reaction to Dudley's betrayal of her trust may not have been down to her own burning love for him as so many would believe. Though she may well have once thought herself to be in love with him, and may have even considered marrying him herself; if not forcing him upon Mary Stuart to help ease the tensions between Scotland and England, his secret marriage to Lettice would have angered the queen due to the lack of respect for royal authority. As both Robert and Lettice were close to the queen, this made the betrayal even worse in her eyes. In her spite, Elizabeth was pushed towards the match with the new Duke of Anjou by the late 1570s. However, it was also down to William's influence and ability to see an opportunity to persuade the queen towards a marriage herself. With Robert Dudley being at the centre of the scandal himself, William did not need to battle with the favourite for now – as it was known that Dudley opposed the match with France, and that the queen often heeded his counsel.

It was also the Earl of Sussex's suggestion by 1578, that the negotiations of a marital alliance between England and France should be revived. Up until this point, the question of the English succession, the civil war in France, the rebellions in the Netherlands and the tensions in Europe in general had changed the political stability on the continent. Many at the English court were happy for Elizabeth to marry the Catholic prince if it meant that some form of peace would come about. Though many treaties had been drafted and signed throughout the 1570s, no real peace had come about. Catherine, Anjou's mother, was again interested in negotiating with Elizabeth on behalf of her son, and William was at this stage pondering on the future of the Elizabethan state that he had worked so hard to stabilise and protect. If all parties involved, including William, thought that the answer to the many political tensions in Europe could be answered by the duke's and queen's marriage, they were wrong, yet negotiations once again commenced. By August 1578, William was well into the negotiations of the marriage, and the duke in turn sent an envoy, Jean de Simier, to England. This was his way of wooing the queen with de Simier's charm and gifts, and it seemed to work. By 1579, Elizabeth became seriously interested in marrying Anjou, and though many historians state that this was the queen's way of keeping France happy, and any further political tensions at bay, there is sufficient evidence to suggest that the pair formed a unique bond. Their letters are evidently emotional and romantic, suggesting their true feelings. Whatever the true nature of their relationship, Elizabeth declared that she was interested in marrying Anjou, and this would have brought William relief. By this time, William held many offices, and was one of the most influential and richest men in England. However, despite his support for the queen's marriage to Anjou, members of the Privy Council were divided on the match with Walsingham and Dudley again opposing it.

The duke would visit England twice during the period of negotiations. Elizabeth's emotional state went up and down during this time. She would appear to be in love at one point, and then unsure of her feelings at another. Though there were many opponents to the Anjou match, William supported his queen. In a letter, he wrote to her expressing his support, but urging caution as always. Interestingly, though he certainly felt the need for the queen's marriage in terms of forming a political alliance and the succession question, his support also seems genuine on a personal front. William was in his mid-to-late fifties at this point, and was himself a family man who found much joy in his marriage and family life. Therefore, it is unsurprising that he wished the same for Elizabeth. In his letter he mentioned that the queen was in need of 'some partner' to give her 'delight, honour', and, most interestingly, 'pleasure'.[28] Clearly, the queen was impatient for an answer, but he suggested that she have patience. In the end, by 1580, it was clear that an agreement could not be met on the Anjou match, and though Elizabeth was given the final choice, she felt she could not continue the courtship without the full support of her council and all of the people. The duke would stay on in England during his second visit, but would ultimately end up just as disappointed as the queen.

The question of why William was so supportive of Elizabeth's possible marriage to the Duke of Anjou has many answers. The Succession would appear as the most appropriate answer, and yet, by the end of the Anjou courtship, Elizabeth was forty-nine years old, and it was unlikely that she should by then produce an heir, despite her physician's diagnosis. Indeed,

William may have favoured the match simply due to his support of the queen on a personal level. The pair had become close friends and it would make sense that he wished the queen to find happiness. Yet, the most prominent reason for his support of the Anjou match, despite the duke's Catholicism, young age, and apparent hunger for power, was due to his real worry about the threat of Spain.[29] An alliance with a militarily powerful nation like France was extremely desirable, considering the tensions between Catholics and Protestants in Europe. By 1581, it was clear to William and Elizabeth that no marriage would come about, and so she let the duke down. William's influence only went so far when it came to the queen's final decision. As a new decade dawned, he would have to put all of his energy into national security as England remained alone, and without a Protestant heir.

William's ascendency to power and privilege not only came with numerous offices and titles and influence on political affairs, but with great wealth and personal gain. He did not squander his own personal wealth, but used it to the advantage of his own family, and dynasty – a matter which greatly took much of his time when he was not immersed in state affairs. The many properties that William owned are not only evidence of his wealth and influence, but his need to establish a legacy for his family and name. Burghley House, for example, remains one of the most poignant physical memories of William's power. Construction began in 1555, some years before Elizabeth's ascension to the throne. This is evidence of William's early plans to carve out a physical legacy and inheritance for his children and descendants. By the time William and his wife had several children, and he was granted a peerage and the office of Lord High Treasurer, Burghley House at Stamford was the home of his mother, yet he began further renovations to the property later on. The Cecil family would eventually reside mainly at Cecil House on the Strand as it was closer to the centre of power. William therefore would have access to his family and the queen, with a lesser distance of travel needed. Another house was situated at Canon Row which was convenient when the court moved to Whitehall. Wimbledon was also another seat in Hertfordshire. The numerous properties acquired by William throughout his life not only came at a great expense, but they were also expensive in terms of their upkeep and staff. For example, the household on the Strand, where his family mostly resided, would have numbered at least eighty people. Therefore, William's power and influence was not only represented by his elevation in status, but by his ever-growing wealth and construction of properties.

William Cecil had risen high. He was ennobled, wealthy, and could entertain in and retreat to a number of wealthy properties across the kingdom. He was Chancellor of Cambridge University, and helped a number of smaller offices across the English countryside. His power, wealth and influence expanded far, and his close relationship with the queen and the latter's dependence on his counsel were the reason for this. William was much more than a statesman. He was a man of innovation, and a builder of great houses. His support for the queen's wish to marry the Duke of Anjou reveals another side to William's personality that is often overlooked. William not only supported the match due to the political necessity, but out of support for Elizabeth as a friend. The way in which the political situation played out in England and Europe during the 1570s, may well have been very different without William's influence and web of informants. The relationships that William formed at court and afar are further evidence of his influence. All of these factors of the 1570s combined indicate that William wished to carve out a legacy to preserve the Cecil name forever. His letters or correspondence with colleagues, friends and the queen, and the architecture of Burghley House, further indicate the important role the Cecil name and reputation held in Elizabethan governance and policy.

Chapter 8

A Family Man

William's second marriage, and the family life, routine and comfort it gave him, are an interesting part of his life that is rarely discussed in depth. Though his son Thomas was the son of William's first wife, Mary Cheke, it appears that Mildred did her best as a stepmother. After the death of Mary Cheke, Thomas Cecil seems to have remained in the household of his maternal grandmother, Agnes Cheke, for some time. As Mildred was deemed a more suitable match by the remaining Cecil family, notably William's mother Jane, whom he was very close to, it is unsurprising that the marriage was celebrated and successful. Upon marrying in 1545, Mildred brought a substantial dowry, and the couple set up home in London. This may not have been as grand as their future homes would be, as Elizabeth wasn't even thought to ever inherit the throne at this point. But it was a start. Once William became a member of Somerset's household in around 1549, the couple moved to Wimbledon, but had already acquired their home at Canon Row at Westminster. Interestingly, during their time at Wimbledon, William and Mildred shared the home with William's sister Mary and Mildred's sister Elizabeth. There were also a number of wards staying at the Cecil home during this time, which will be discussed in depth later.[1]

While the Cecil's were 'semi-retired' at Wimbledon during Mary I's early reign, their first child, Anne, was born in December 1556. There had been a previous daughter born in 1554, named Frances, yet the child only lived a few hours and William later wrote in his commonplace book:

> Between 11 and 12 this night my wife gave birth to a daughter called Frances but after a few hours the tiny girl departed this mortal life and was buried at Wimbledon.[2]

These first few years in retirement were particularly important to the Cecil couple and their growing family. Though William remained as active in his work as possible, he had a particular freedom regarding his family life during Mary I's reign that ironically, he would never have during Elizabeth's reign. The couple embarked on a number of family visits during this time of 'freedom' – to the Cecils and members of Mildred's family. Mildred had connections that interested the ambitious William during the 1550s. Her brother married a cousin of Lady Jane Grey. Though it would appear that William was later cautious in the naming of Jane as Edward VI's heir, it was his familial connections that saved him in the end, along with his unique capabilities.[3]

It is not known why, but as the couple married in 1545, and there is no record of Mildred giving birth until 1554 and 1556, it would appear that the couple had some difficulty in conceiving a child. As the human body was not understood as it is today, and indeed, infant mortality was extremely high during the Tudor period, it could be that Mildred suffered a number of miscarriages and/or stillbirths prior to the birth of the couple's first known ill-fated baby, Frances. Whatever the circumstances, when Anne was born in 1556, there was much to celebrate. She may have been a girl, but the couple were still relatively young, and William already had a male heir for his dynasty. We know that William's relationships with his children from Mildred were close, but what of that with his first-born son Thomas? When the couple moved into Wimbledon, it seems that they eventually sent for Thomas to join them. However, all was not well in terms of the relationship between father and son. William either took little interest in his first-born son, or he spent much of his time criticising young Thomas. This is something that would continue throughout his life, and the pair struggled to get along. There may not have been severe tension or even volatile argument between them, but neither was there a particular warmth or show of affection. This is not to say that William did not love his son, but he certainly struggled to understand him. Alan Gordon Smith commented on Thomas and William's relationship:

> He [Thomas] had grown into an unpromising lout, and a source
> of great anxiety to his parent.[4]

William's second son, protégé and apparently favourite, Robert, was born in 1563, during Elizabeth's reign, and into much more secure and lavish surroundings. Elizabeth Cecil followed in 1564. She was born at Cecil House, and Elizabeth I stood as her godmother – the little girl was likely named for the queen.[5] Robert Cecil is by far the most fascinating of William's children, and yet, his life and personality, much like his father's, are shrouded by myth and misinterpretation. By the time Robert was born, William and Mildred had been married for eighteen years, and as William was not particularly fond of his first-born son, it must have seemed like a miracle. Thomas was sent to France when he was nineteen, under the jurisdiction and protection of a secretary, Thomas Windebank. By this point, William had abandoned any hope that Thomas may reach his levels of expectations, but it was a given that he would one day inherit the family seat as the first-born son. Mildred had also given birth prior to the delivery of Robert, to a son named William, but as with their first daughter Frances, the boy did not live long. Robert was not the healthiest infant by any means, and indeed, he was the smallest of all the Cecil children, but he would survive, and most importantly – reach his father's expectations. During the first years of Robert's life, though the Cecil family was generally a happy one, William had much to contend with in terms of his duties to the queen – and his endeavours to see her married and produce a son of her own.[6]

William had a good relationship with all his children with Mildred, and early family life was particularly calm when Thomas was not present. Robert would become his father's favourite son. He was also likely born at Cecil House. By the time Mildred gave birth to Elizabeth, the baby of the family, she was almost forty years old. This may have been the reason for William's optimism in the queen's fertility later on, but we cannot be sure. He may not have been given a peerage by the time Robert and Elizabeth were born, but as he was the most powerful man in the kingdom and the closest to the queen, the family's status meant that Mildred most likely did not nurse her own children. There was a stigma attached to aristocratic women nursing their own offspring, and therefore there would have been a wet and dry nurse present for the menial tasks needed. Robert suffered from Spinal Scoliosis, which would also have carried stigma, but despite this, he was the apple of his parents' eyes, and likely even more precious to them. It was said that his condition was due to his nurse dropping him as an infant, but this was likely concocted to protect the integrity and reputation of the family, and the Cecils as a couple. Whatever the reason for Robert's condition, he was cherished in the family, which likely made the mockery of his 'deformity' at court later on in his life, extremely hurtful. In terms of the relationship between the two brothers, Thomas was already an adult by the time Robert was born, and had married by the time he had reached his first year. Therefore, an attachment between the two, certainly in Robert's early years, would have been unlikely, and Robert would have been brought up in the Cecil household as the only boy.

Yet, he was not the heir. How he felt about inheritance in his youth is not clear. Yet he may have been irked by it. The Cecil children grew up in relative harmony with one another, Robert spending much of his youth in the company of his sisters, Anne and Elizabeth. Robert and his sisters would have been taught at home as was the custom for aristocratic children. He had a number of tutors such as Michael Hicks and Richard Howland – praised scholars in their own right. Thomas Cartwright also tutored Robert in Latin and Greek. Robert made much progress as a student and this pleased his father. Though the attitude towards educating girls was different in Tudor society, despite the monarch being a woman – and a well-educated woman at that, the Cecil sisters would have received a grand enough education due to their position. Though attention would have been paid to the expectations that they would marry well and execute their family duty to perfection as Tudor ladies.[7]

Though the Cecil family was close-knit, it would be a mistake to think that they were without their flaws, internal issues and differences. Indeed, it could even be said that despite William's position, his family brought him as much comfort as they did discomfort. Robert may have been the apple of his father's eye, but the other Cecil children proved to be a challenge on a number of occasions. Thomas Cecil was not only a cause for anxiety because he was not as astute and duty-bound as his father had hoped. William had paid for Thomas to be as educated as possible for his limited academic abilities. His tutors were of Cambridge standard, but the pupil himself was not. In fact, there is no record of him ever attending Cambridge. He, as had all the Cecil children, learnt the necessary courtly etiquette required by his station. William thought that sending his eldest son to Paris in the early 1560s would polish him off. Unfortunately, the opposite occurred and Thomas indulged himself, perhaps getting a little carried away in the Parisian lifestyle.[8]

As Thomas was accompanied by Windebank, who had in his possession all the necessary money, William likely thought that Thomas could be controlled and perhaps prove useful. At this time, Sir Nicholas Throckmorton was staying at the French court as an ambassador. The Earl of Hertford who had been embroiled in scandal due to his secret marriage to Lady Catherine Grey was also present in Paris, but William warned Thomas not to keep his company, for fear of scandal.[9] In many ways, it is unsurprising that Thomas misbehaved in Paris. Though William Cecil loved all his children despite their differences, he was no doubt a domineering and controlling presence in their lives. For Thomas, as a young man of sufficient means and a good family background, Paris offered a sense of freedom. However, he was frivolous and quickly spent his way through his allowance offered by his father. William wrote to Windebank, chiding him for allowing his son to spend so whimsically, and stating that he [Thomas] would return 'like a spending sot, meet only to keep a tennis court', implying that his son would become a frivolous drunkard.[10]

Thomas caused William such anxiety, that he wrote to him, asking him to change his ways and to 'banish his wanton lusts'. He added that he would rather 'have him lost by an honourable death than be troubled with him in this way'.[11] This language may seem harsh to the modern parent, but in the sixteenth century, a large enough scandal could be the ruin of a respectable family, as it had done with the Grey sisters, and Mary Stuart. At this point, the Cecils had not even risen to a peerage, and William was only in his first years of power. Any notion of misbehaviour and scandal could ruin the Cecil name, therefore equalling to that of a tragic death. Despite Thomas's behaviour in Paris, he eventually married well in 1564, to Dorothy Neville, who was the daughter of John Neville, Lord Latimer, the stepson of the late queen Katherine Parr. This marriage proved to be a success and evidently a happy one, for the couple went on to have thirteen children.

If gaining their father's approval could be achieved by a successful marriage, it was Anne Cecil who, in the end, was the most disappointing of her father's children in that regard. As the eldest daughter of the most important and powerful man in the kingdom, Anne's marriage prospects offered much more than happiness for the young woman, or a means of ensuring that she followed the expectations of Tudor society. A marriage between Anne and a man from an influential noble family could bring about domestic political alliances which the successful governance of the kingdom relied upon. It could be stated that Anne was William's favourite child. A poem written by William himself for his daughter, dated 1 January 1567, along with a spinning-wheel, which she had likely wanted, is evidence of his affection for her:

> As yeres do growe, so cared encreasse
> And tyme will move to loke to thrifte,
> Thogh yeres in me worke nothing lesse
> Yet for your yeres, and new yeres gifte
> This huswifes toy is now my shifte.
> Tose you on woorke some thrifte to feele
> I send you now a spynneng wheele.
>
> But oon thing firste, I wisshe and pray
> Leste thirste of thryfte might soon you tyre.
> only to speynne oon pounde a daye.
> And play the reste, as tyme require.

Sweat not (oh fy) fling rock in fyre
God sende who sendth all thrifte & welth
You long yeres & your father helth.[12]

William's poem, and the gift that accompanied it, cannot only be seen as a gift from a doting father, but can be seen as William's realisation that his daughter was growing up, and would one day have to marry well, and exemplify the expectations of a Tudor lady. Whether one finds a hint of sorrow between the lines or not is subjective. Behind the sensitivity of this poem, is an ardent sense of sensibility, implying that Anne was expected to fit within the domestic expectations of the day. Anne was originally meant to marry Philip Sidney, the son of Sir Henry Sidney, a good friend of William's. However, nothing came of this and as noted previously, Philip married Frances Walsingham. By the time William had been given the title of Lord Burghley, his daughter was contracted to marry someone much grander – Edward de Vere, the young and handsome Earl of Oxford.[13] But why? How did this marriage come about? And what was William's level of influence on this match?

Oxford was not only a practical choice in husband due to his title and high standing, as William was very happy for his children to marry into influential and noble families. He had also been William's ward since the age of around thirteen. By the time he was on the rise to becoming a lord of the land, William's family and household was made up of much more than just the immediate Cecil family. Due to William's prominent position, many nobles entrusted the care of their eldest sons with the Lord Treasurer. A number of young noble men therefore became William's wards. Therefore, many young men on the rise by the end of Elizabeth's reign owed their success to William and Mildred, who cared for, nurtured and educated them. There were a number of reasons why William chose to take on the sons and daughters of noble Englishmen. Firstly, he was interested in forming political domestic alliances with English noble families. Secondly, he had a keen interest in the education of young Englishmen and likely enjoyed directing their future careers in politics. Thirdly, and lastly, William saw the possibilities that his influence over these young noble men could bring about in the future. His vision for England's future as a European power, wealthy and Protestant nation could be realised not only through his own children but through the boys whom he educated and cared for.

Indeed, William's household was deemed one of the best places to train England's young nobles. It is unclear how many youths came and went through the Cecil household, but there were certainly many. It was his noble wards in particular, which seems to have numbered at around eight at one point, that represented William's prestige and power amongst England's elite. Though Philip Sidney was one of these, in the end, Anne Cecil became the Countess of Oxford, for which her father was very proud. However, William's pride was not to last, and by the time the couple had been married two years, more than a few cracks began to appear. Though they grew up in the same household, and indeed would have known one another [although to what extent can only be speculated], the marriage was not technically arranged by William himself, who had likely wished his daughter to marry elsewhere. Whether or not this was a marriage that began out of mutual affection or lust, it is clear that this did not last. William begrudgingly gave his consent to the marriage, as did the queen.[14]

At this point, Anne was only fifteen, and though it was not unusual for women of the Tudor period to marry at such a young age, or even younger, William was surprised by the idea of his daughter's choice. William was very close to Anne and he seems to have shown her great affection. She, in turn, was a good and obedient daughter. Oxford may have been enamoured with her for some time, and when he approached the topic, the young woman was flattered. Whatever the case may be, William's reaction is unusual and yet, telling. On the topic, he wrote to the young Earl of Rutland, who had written to William regarding the said match:

> I think it doth seem strange that your Lordship to hear of a purposed determination in my Lord of Oxford to marry with my daughter...I could not well imagine what to think, considering I never meant to seek it nor hoped for it...[15]

Though William was happy to marry his daughter to a man of pedigree, wealth and good standing, his first choice, or even second choice of man was not Edward de Vere. William also mentions that he was much more comfortable with the idea of Anne marrying into the Sidney family:

> Truly, my Lord, after I was acquainted of the former intention of a marriage with Master Philip Sidney, whom I always loved and esteemed, I was fully determined to have of myself moved no marriage for my daughter until she should have been near sixteen.[16]

Not only is this evidence of William's high regard for a young Philip Sidney at the time, but it is also an indication that he had a fondness for his daughter and had hoped not to let her leave the family until at least sixteen years old. This shows a different side to William, as here, he is not thinking of how he can use his daughter as simply a pawn, which many have interpreted from the marriage, but that he was truly concerned for her welfare and happiness. He was evidently wary to see her leave the family home and marry at a young age.

Though William expressed anxiety regarding the idea that his favourite daughter might marry the Earl of Oxford, another line of the letter reveals much more about William's views on Oxford as a man, and as a son:

> Now that the matter is determined betwixt my lord of Oxford and me, I confess to your Lordship I do honour him so dearly from my heart as I do my own son, and in any case that may touch him for his honour and weal I shall think him mine own interest therein.[17]

This letter, and what it reveals, is fascinating. Not only does William express in his own hand the anxieties of a father who truly cares for his daughter's well-being, but he also openly displays his affection for Oxford, who he refers to as like his own son. This reveals that despite William's hectic schedule, he took the time to form real relationships not only with his children, but with the many wards that he took into his household. The fact that he is writing to Rutland, another ward, at all regarding this matter, shows that the Cecil household was one of respect, love and warmth, with open doors. Read warns that the reader of this letter should regard William's words of affection regarding Oxford as a son-in-law with less enthusiasm than his anxiety regarding the proposed marriage between his daughter and his ward. However, the fact that William expressed such emotion in a letter to another ward at all, and that he later gave his blessing for the marriage must also be taken into account.[18]

If William though that his eldest son Thomas had become a 'spending sot', he may have eventually had a much harsher term to describe his son-in-law. The marriage between Anne and Oxford was initially a happy one, or so it would seem. No children were recorded to have been born between 1571 and 1573, however, this may have been due to Anne's young age. Edward de Vere was a favourite of the queen. He was of noble birth, despite his close ties to his cousin Norfolk, who at this time was imprisoned in the Tower for his treason. He was ambitious and handsome, and now, he was officially a member of one of the most powerful families in the kingdom. But Oxford's desires went beyond the ambitions of a typical Tudor courtier.

He was hungry. But not for royal favouritism, dynastic power or courtly influence. He was hungry for adventure. The queen disapproved of Oxford's wish to be so often away from England. William may have regretted his decision to allow Anne to marry his ward, as by January 1573, Oxford was granted permission to leave England and travel abroad, and took no time in arranging his financial affairs before embarking for Paris. According to Read, it was William who urged Oxford to sort out his finances prior to leaving. It was good advice, for it would be a long time until the pair would meet again.[19]

It was understood that Oxford would heed William's advice while abroad, and keep him informed of his duties and actions. However, William would remain long-suffering when it came to his son-in-law. His patience may well have had more to do with the respect and love he had for his daughter than that of Oxford, although Smith also implies that it was down to his reverence for noble men in general that was to answer for his patience.[20] By March 1573, William wrote to Oxford to inform him that Anne was expecting her first child. Oxford responded expressing his joy at the idea of becoming a father, yet it was his requests for more money for his ventures abroad and refusal to return to England which reveals his true character. Oxford did write to his wife while abroad, and upon hearing the news of her pregnancy, sent a letter and a gift of his portrait. By the time his daughter was born in July, who Anne named Elizabeth, either for her sister or in honour of the queen, Oxford was running out of funds, and upon hearing the news of his daughter's birth in September, he seemed more concerned with securing the queen's approval to continue travelling, and receiving more funds from his father-in-law. Not only this, but he also informed William that he had borrowed some money, and needed him to pay the debt. Whatever Oxford was spending such copious amounts of money on is unclear. But what is clear is that at twenty-six years old, a husband and father, Edward's attitude, manner and disregard for his duty did not match the expectations for a man of his status, a status that William Cecil had so long respected. As Read puts it plainly: 'To Oxford the only thing which really mattered was Oxford'. By 1576, Oxford has burnt some serious bridges. His wife remained in her parents' household, his daughter had never met him, and the rumours of his debauchery abroad had shamed the Cecil name so greatly, that even the queen refused to allow his travels abroad to continue.[21]

But there was much more to the situation than Oxford's dismissal of his daughter, love of excess and desire for adventure. A glint of scandal loomed over the Cecil family, that if revealed to the world, it could cause shockwaves that would result in irreparable damage to the Cecil name. It appears that

Oxford was dismissive of his daughter's birth, and his wife's devotion, because he believed that the child was actually not his at all. William had written in his memorandum of the situation, stating his grievances. William stated that Oxford knew that Anne was in fact pregnant before his departure to Paris, and that there was no known reason for any unhappiness until April: 'where he [Oxford] wrote somewhat that, by reason of a man of his, his receiver, he had conceived some unkindness, but he prayed me to let pass the same for it did grow by the doubleness of servants...'

William then sent his son Thomas to where Oxford was staying, who reported back that there seemed no reason for a rift between the couple and that he gave his wife's commendations. William did not specify in his writings, but it appears that Oxford was suggesting that Anne had committed adultery, and that Elizabeth was not his child. There is no evidence to suggest that Anne committed adultery, or that Elizabeth was not Oxford's daughter, but only this hint. But the very fact that Oxford hinted at this, and openly rejected his wife and child in writing to her father, could have a serious impact on Anne's reputation if it were to become public.[22]

Few historians have paid attention to this particularly tense period within the Cecil family. However, Read presents an in-depth study of the troublesome Oxford marriage. Some days after William had written of Thomas's visit to Oxford in a bid to know his mind, de Vere himself wrote to William, in a shockingly disrespectful and disillusioned tone. To be honest, the letter reveals Oxford to be more problematic than his wife. His explanation to his father-in-law can be interpreted in more than one way:

> I have forborne in some respect, which should [be] private to myself, either to write or to come to your Lordship...I must let your Lordship understand this much, that is, until I can better satisfy or advertise myself of some mislikes I am not determined, as touching my wife, to accompany her. What they are, because some are not to be spoken of or written upon as imperfections...Some that discontented me I will not blazon or publish until it please me.

He continued that he wished to have no more 'troubles and molestations' in his life, and that 'nor will I, to please your Lordship only, discontent myself'.

He also mentioned that he would not expose Anne publicly, but that he recommended that she stay with her parents in their residence. So, he was willing to be rid of his wife entirely, but not willing to expose her publicly, only to disgrace himself and his own prospects. He would not reveal exactly what the reason for his rejection of Anne and Elizabeth was, but his insistence of 'molestations' and 'mislikes' have led to differing conclusions. The first obviously being that Anne had indeed committed adultery, as according to Lord Howard, when Oxford returned from his travels two years later, he stated that Elizabeth could not have been his child, for when she was born he had 'not lain with her for nearly a year before'. If what Howard mentioned had some truth to it, it would be entirely scandalous for the Cecil family. However, would it really have been likely or possible even, that the daughter of the most powerful man in the kingdom, and a woman of such great upbringing with more Christian zeal than the queen herself, would risk disgracing herself and her family by having an extra-marital affair? The lack of evidence suggests not. The Cecil family's support for their daughter and insistence that Oxford return to her also implies that they believed her to be virtuous, whatever the reason for her husband's 'mislikes'.

There is also the overwhelming suggestion that Oxford was in fact homosexual, and that his mislike for his wife, therefore, was the fact that she was not to his sexual preference. It seems a step too far to suggest that Oxford would marry Anne, knowing that he would likely have to consummate the marriage and sire children, if he was entirely disgusted by her physically. Also, there is the fact that the pair apparently married due to their genuine desire for one another. Where the physical intimacy between the married couple went wrong is not clear. Nor can it be ruled out however, despite Read's objections, that Edward de Vere had homosexual or at least bisexual tendencies. William himself later wrote in his memorandum of Oxford's 'inhumanity' towards his wife [Anne]. Yet any notion of homosexuality or 'sodomy' was not remarked upon until some ten years later when Charles Arundel, an enemy of Oxford's referred to the latter as 'A buggering of a boy that his cook and many other boys'.[23]

Both Howard and Arundel associated Oxford with the scandal of 'buggery' or 'sodomy'. But did this actually imply that they believed him to be homosexual? For Tudor language of the time, to refer to a man as perverse, a sodomite, or of buggary, was no light accusation. Indeed, Oxford's affiliation with the playwright and poet Christopher Marlowe, who would himself later become embroiled in homosexual intrigue, only gave his contemporaries fuel for the flame of accusation. However, it must be remembered that during the Elizabethan period, terms such as buggery, perversion and sodomite referred to sexual acts themselves rather than exclusively coining an individual's sexuality or identity. Therefore, the accusation that Oxford was guilty of buggery implied that there was some notion of an act having taken place. Many scholars insist that there is no evidence for both Oxford's or Marlowe's homosexuality at all. Whatever the case may be, William himself made no comment on his son-in-law's behaviour besides that of his drunkenness and blasphemy, with no mention of any notion of sodomy or buggery. Arundel also suggested that Oxford suffered from syphilis. Although this malady was more associated with heterosexual rather than homosexual acts.[24]

If Oxford had homosexual tendencies, he was most likely bisexual, for he and Anne eventually did reconcile for a time, and evidently had a sexual relationship. Anne went on to give birth to a son, who died soon after. She also went on to give birth to three more daughters, Bridget, Frances and Susan. Sadly, Anne died young aged thirty-one, at the Queen's court at Greenwich in 1588. It is not known what she died from. William, by that time an old man, was utterly heartbroken. Though the rift between William and his son-in-law had healed over the past few years, it never became as affectionate as it once had been. After Anne's death, it is likely that William and Oxford drifted further apart, although, he remained close to all his grandchildren. Much of Anne Cecil's married life was unhappy, but her relationship with her father, her duty to her family name and the effect that her unhappiness and eventual death had on her family as a whole, suggests that she is a character of much greater importance in the Cecil family legacy. Her burial at Westminster Abbey, was surely a testament to that.[25]

William's second daughter, Elizabeth, also had her own fascinating story, and a generally good relationship with her father. Anne may have been William's favourite daughter, but Elizabeth would end up much happier than her sister. Elizabeth was born in 1564, at a time when William himself was trying to convince the queen to marry a prince and settle the succession. The fact that his family was growing and that he had a successful and happy marriage, in his mind at least, was evidence that marriage and family were necessary for living a good, Christian life. The queen clearly disagreed, but William still named his daughter in honour of her anyway. Elizabeth was born on 1 July at Cecil House on the Strand in London. Her baptism was particularly lavish, and both the queen and Countess of Lennox stood as her godmothers. That night, the queen herself dined with the Cecil family on the Strand, to celebrate their joy. However, as it goes with Tudor daughters, the celebration of her birth was likely much more to do with William's virility and position than it was to do with the baby Elizabeth herself. As Loades states, not much is known of her early childhood other than that. She was, like all of her siblings, well-educated, mannerly, dutiful – a product of the times. Notably, it is likely that she was educated alongside Robert Devereux, the son of Lettice Knollys and her first husband Walter Devereux. In 1575, when Elizabeth was but eleven years old, the Earl of Shrewsbury suggested a match between his son and Elizabeth. Though flattered, William kindly declined the proposal, stating that if she were to marry, it would not be until she was at least fifteen years old. Perhaps William's experience with his first daughter's horrendous match with the Earl of Oxford made him think twice about pairing Elizabeth with the first noble family that offered one. She may have received other offers over a period of years, but we cannot be sure. What we do know is that William thereafter became cautious when it came to his children's marriages. Where Anne was quiet, demure and said to be a beauty, it is unclear whether Elizabeth had a different temperament or appearance. If she was anything like her namesake, demure would not have been the word to describe her. However, as the daughter of the Lord Treasurer, it is likely that she followed her sister's example and mannerisms.[26]

When Elizabeth turned eighteen, she was much more suitable for marriage, and perhaps the decision to let her remain in the family home for longer than her elder sister was William's repentance for the disaster that Anne's marriage became. Elizabeth caught the eye of William Wentworth, the son of Lord Thomas Wentworth. The family were barons, and therefore respectable, wealthy enough and favoured by the queen. It would appear that young William himself approached his father on the matter of marrying Elizabeth, and indeed, Thomas wrote to William telling him of his son's interest. William seemed genuinely happy with the proposal. Young Wentworth was not a ward of the crown and had not lived in the Cecil residence, but he would have been familiar enough with the family for his interest in Elizabeth to not be random. We do not know for example, if the pair had caught one another's eye some time before the proposal, but as there is no evidence of William's hesitancy nor Elizabeth's objection, we can safely say that the marriage was also one of mutual agreement between the couple. By this stage, William would not have forced his daughter into a marriage, if he felt that it would end up like her sister's. The wedding was not as lavish as Anne's, but perhaps this was rightly so. Nor did the queen attend. But it went ahead anyway in February 1582. The celebrations lasted some days. Though the marriage seemed to be a happy one, this is likely due to how short-lived it was. William Wentworth died of plague just months after the marriage in November. Elizabeth followed her husband to the grave only months later in April 1583. She was barely twenty years old. This devastated William and Mildred, and as there is no record of any child belonging to Elizabeth living with them thereafter, it can be safely said that she did not have time to get pregnant, and if she did, perhaps she died in childbirth, along with the child. Although, it seems unlikely that William would make no mention of this in his writings.[27]

Elizabeth's death had a profound effect on William's state of mind. He was already in a stressed state after the queen's final marital negotiations with the Duke of Anjou had ended. Mary Stuart was also of great concern, and even more so now that it was clear the queen would never marry or produce an heir. His daughter's death made something inside William break. The usually calm and in control Lord Burghley became a shell of his former self. He became depressed, so such so that everyone noticed, and the queen had to ask Walsingham to intervene, but to no effect. The queen needed William more than ever, but William did not seem to care. When he did return to court and to his duties, he remained outwardly melancholic. He became extremely sensitive, emotional and as Read mentions 'quick to take offence to any criticism'. It is even possible that he was muddling over resigning from his position entirely. But the queen would not allow this and wrote to him:

> Sir Spirit, I doubt I do misname you. For those of your kind (they say) have no sense. But I have of late seen an *ecce signum*, that if an ass kick you, you feel it too soon. I will recant you from being my *Spirit*, if ever I perceive that you distain not such a feeling...Let never care appear in you for such a rumour; but let them well know, that you rather desire the righting of such wrongs, by making known their error, than you to be so silly a soul...[28]

William's relationship with his eldest son Thomas did improve during the 1580s. Thomas's marriage to Dorothy seemed to change him. He had been given multiple offices since the mid-to-late 1570s such as a position in the Commission of the Peace for Lincolnshire and the office of bailiff of the lordship of Collyweston. However, it was his seat at Parliament on a number of occasions which reveals he was trusted by his father and had some capacity when it came to politics. By 1585, Thomas has been knighted, and later served as deputy lieutenant of Lincolnshire, his father being the Lord Lieutenant. Not only was it important that the rift between father and son healed to some capacity due to Thomas being the heir to the Barony, but it would also serve a purpose later on when William died, as Robert Cecil needed support to take on his father's political vision for England. Thomas, as will be discussed later, was perhaps the most unlikely of William's children to impress his father. Yet, the great Lord Burghley certainly underestimated his first-born son, as it was he who nurtured the Cecil name, fortune and material legacy that we see today in their homes and objects.[29]

Thomas Cecil had been a somewhat unruly youth. His sisters, despite their best efforts to please their father, had suffered greatly by either one tragedy in their marriage or another. Both daughters died relatively young, and this wounded their father deeply. But Robert Cecil would be different. He was born when his parents' marriage had long settled. Again, as the Cecil's had been married for almost two decades by the time their prodigal son arrived, he was perhaps a surprise, but nonetheless, proved to be everything his father dreamed of in a son. Though his physical health was fragile – something that may or may not have caused anxiety for his parents, his mind was razor sharp, like his father's. Robert had a unique upbringing, not only because he was the son of the most powerful man in the kingdom, but because he was raised alongside his father's wards and others who came and went from the Cecil household. By the time Robert's studies at home were well underway, he had mastered Greek, Latin, French and Italian. However, he was also educated in cosmology and of course Protestant theology.[30]

Robert would also make a good marriage in 1586 at the age of twenty-two, to Elizabeth Brooke, the daughter of Lord Cobham. The couple had a successful and happy marriage as had William and Mildred. Sadly, Elizabeth died in 1597. Unusually for the time, Robert chose not to re-marry, and although he continued in his affairs of state as his father would have, despite his grievance, he most definitely mourned her death for the rest of his life.[31] Robert's education under his father, his incredible ability as a man of politics, and the relationship he formed with Queen Elizabeth, will be discussed in depth later.

The years of 1587 and 1588 were perhaps the toughest of years in William's personal life as well as his career. Not only was 1588 the year of the Spanish Armada, which threatened England's queen, security, religion and independence – everything William had worked for, but it was a time of great sorrow for the whole Cecil family. William was progressively unwell during the 1580s. His long suffering from gout had taken its toll, and though he was able to take more time off from his duties with his family due to his son Robert's assistance, the security of the realm was never far from his mind. In March 1588, he lost his mother, Jane. William was unusually outward with his grief, and the queen herself commented that his reaction was excessive:

> She [Jane] was old...and you wise. And therefore, her
> death, happening according to natural course, is to be taken

moderately of you. To withdraw therefore your troubled mind from private grief to public cogitations...think upon the speedy dispatch of commissioners for Munster with all the haste you can.[32]

If one were to think of the queen as being dismissive of William's grief, she had reason to be, for the threat of the Spanish Armada at this time loomed, due to the execution of Mary Stuart the previous February. However, if Elizabeth felt that William's outpouring of grief was too much, she, and the whole court, would be in for a shock. As to what was to come, it was more devastating to William than anyone could have imagined. While William was trying to piece himself back together after the death of his mother in March, he lost his daughter. Ann died in June while at court. The only written reference to this of William's reaction was dated 24 June – 'And so I end *in Crepusculo*...a dark night afore a black morning for me and mine.'[33]

Amazingly, during this time, William was still working, as all-out war between England and Spain was now inevitable. We know in hindsight that the Spanish Armada was destroyed by Elizabeth's Navy, and that despite William's grief, he was able to continue in his duties and could function just enough to get through the attempted invasion in one piece. But, just months later in April 1589, William's wife Mildred died after forty-three years of marriage. To say that her death crushed him would be an understatement. The couple were very close, though they spent much time apart due to William's duties and Mildred preferred to remain at home, away from court intrigue and excessiveness. No letters between the couple over the final years of their marriage survive, if they existed at all. This may be due to the fact that William was able to visit home for breaks more often as he grew older, but perhaps they simply slipped into a comfortable understanding of their mutual affection, and did not need to write to one another. William later wrote upon her death:

> Thank Almighty God for his favour, in permitting her to live so many years together with me, and to have been given her grace to have had the true knowledge of her salvation...I ought to comfort myself with the remembrance of her many virtues and godly actions wherein she continued all her life.[34]

Mildred had run the Cecil household without complaint for decades. There is no doubt, whether she had political opinions of her own or not, that she contributed to the successes of her sons and daughters as much

Above left: William Cecil, Lord Burghley, attributed to the workshop of Marcus Gheeraerts the Younger, c.1580s. (*Wikimedia Commons*)

Above right: A pregnant Mildred Cecil by Hans Eworth, 1563. (*Wikimedia Commons*)

Thomas Cecil, 1st Earl of Exeter, eldest son of William Cecil, by an unknown artist, early seventeenth century. (*Wikimedia Commons*)

Left: Robert Cecil, 1st Earl of Salisbury, youngest son of William Cecil, attributed to John de Critz, 1599. (*Wikimedia Commons*)

Below: William Cecil, 1st Baron Burghley and Lord Treasurer with his son Robert Cecil, later 1st Earl of Salisbury, by an unknown artist, c. 1596. (*Wikimedia Commons*)

Above left: Mrs Jane Cecil, née Heckington, mother of William Cecil, attributed to Jacques Courtois, c. 1580. (*Courtesy of Burghley House Collections online*)

Above right: Sir Francis Walsingham, retract by John de Critz, c.1587. (*Wikimedia Commons*)

The Armada portrait of Elizabeth I, formerly attributed to George Gower, c. 1588. (*Wikimedia Commons*)

Above left: Mary, Queen of Scots by an unknown artist, c. 1578. (*Wikimedia Commons*)

Above right: William Cecil, 2nd Earl of Salisbury, son of Robert Cecil, 1st Earl of Salisbury, by George Geldorp, 1626. (*Wikimedia Commons*)

Left: Queen Mary I of England, by Antonis Mor, 1554. (*Wikimedia Commons*)

Above left: Edward Seymour, 1st Duke of Somerset, by an unknown artist, sixteenth century. (*Wikimedia Commons*)

Above right: Posthumous portrait of Sir Philip Sidney, possibly by Hieronimo Custodis, after an original attributed to Cornelis Ketel, 1578, c. 1586–1593. (*Wikimedia Commons*)

SIR THOMAS SMITH.

A line engraving of Sir Thomas Smith, after an unknown artist, c. early nineteenth century. (*Wikimedia Commons*)

The Hampden Portrait of Elizabeth I, now attributed to George Gower, c. 1567. (*Wikimedia Commons*)

Sir Nicholas Throckmorton
by an unknown artist, 1564.
(*Wikimedia Commons*)

Philip II of Spain by
Sofonisba Anguissola, 1573.
(*Wikimedia Commons*)

Above left: Portrait of a young gentleman, aged twenty-two, said to be Anthony Babington, 1616. (*Wikimedia Commons*)

Above right: Prince Hercule-François, Duke of Alençon, later Duke of Anjou, by François Clouet, 1572. (*Wikimedia Commons*)

Painting of James VI and I, wearing the jewel called the Three Brothers in his hat, after John de Critz (died 1641), c. 1605. (*Wikimedia Commons*)

as William. Though William would have been able to take more leisure at home from the mid-1570s, his work remained never ending and his grip on power only tightened. Mildred would not only have had to deal with the needs of her own children, but several young wards. On the topic of the Cecil's wards, we know that the Earl of Oxford, their future son-in-law was one of these wards, but what of the others? It is often thought that Philip Sidney was a permanent ward of the Cecils during his youth. However, though he was a proposed match for Ann, and William was a close friend of Philip's father, it is more likely that he simply spent a lot of time in the Cecil household, rather than being an actual ward. The young Earl of Rutland, as previously mentioned, was certainly a formal ward of the Cecils, as was Oxford, but there was also the young Philip Howard, son of the traitor, the late Duke of Norfolk, who himself would one day be arrested for his Roman Catholicism. The reason for his conversion was that he may not have remained in William's household for long. Another ward was Robert Devereux, 2nd Earl of Essex – son of Lettice Knollys by her first marriage. Essex would later become a favourite of the queen, but his lust for fame and power would also see him arrested and executed for treason under William's son Robert's regime. Henry Wriothesley, the young Earl of Southampton, was another ward. It is known that he spent some time at Cecil House on the Strand. Most of William's wards were generally good scholars. Rutland was particularly talented and almost became Lord Chancellor.[35]

Besides being an attentive husband, father, grandfather and a charitable man who took in several wards as well as educating many noble children in his household, William was also meticulously attentive to his household expenses and accounts. At Hatfield, there exists a book which includes the household finances of the Cecils. This includes expenses, receipts, and records of household inventory. Though this book only includes the accounts of a period of around two years from 1575–1577, it is an invaluable source when it comes to understanding why William's fortune grew, his income and expenses remained stable, and it explains how he was able to finance the education of his own children as well as multiple wards, whether permanent or not. The accounts were written by one of William's many stewards, Thomas Billot. As the most organised man in government, William was sure to have a staff within his household of clerks, stewards, scribes and other assistants. Many of the accounts in this book were made at Theobalds, one of William's many homes. Not only do these accounts allow for an insight into William's daily expenses during a period of two years, but they also clearly indicate that William did not visit Burghley House in Northamptonshire for the period of those two years. As Read mentions, despite the probability that William did not visit Burghley House for a long time, Billot's accounts for William's household would have followed him wherever he may have been. There are also existing summaries of Billot's accounts from 1566 to 1572, and from 1573 to 1578. Some are in William's own hand, and the rest are in Billot's.[36] This is evidence that though William trusted a number of household staff, the man of the house himself was never too far, keeping an eye on his expenses himself and taking account of what came in and what came out when he felt it necessary.

Billot, who remained in William's service until the latter's death, clearly outlines Lord Burghley's expanding income due to his new acquirement of land during the 1570s. This coincides with William's rise to a peerage, becoming the guardian of many noble young gentlemen, and the rise of the Cecil's prominence as one of England's great families. The rents from William's lands made up much of his income, but the sales of produce such as wood and farm products also contributed greatly to the great Lord Burghley's wealth, though farming was evidently not one of his greatest interests of life's pursuits. In terms of expenditure, the Cecils were not afraid to spend lavishly on food, drink, fine clothing or property. The money William spent on building his lavish homes, whether it be Burghley House, or Theobalds, is an important factor when considering the legacy which he wished to leave for his children, grandchildren and subsequent descendants of the Cecil family. Over the course of a single decade, William spent a thousand pounds a year, building and renovating the many homes and gardens where he and his beloved family could live and enjoy life comfortably. This would amount to millions by today's standards.

To understand William as a statesman, we cannot dismiss him as a family man. At the centre of Lord Burghley's world were his wife and children. Many historians tend to overlook the importance of William's family life when it comes to understanding him as a man. Even fewer scholars have attempted to mesh together the family man and the statesman, and yet, neither sides to William could have existed without the other. His love of life, his desire for knowledge, and his vision for England were not simply for the protection of his beloved queen or the future of the Elizabethan state, but for the future and security for his own family, dynasty and legacy. Therefore, when we dissect William Cecil the man, we should be careful not to separate the statesman from the father, son, brother and husband, because to do so dismisses the entire essence of who William Cecil was – a family man.

Chapter 9

Treachery and Victory

There can be no doubt that the decade of the 1580s was one of strife and heartbreak for William Cecil. He had reached the pinnacle of his power, and that power brought a mountain of responsibility. The higher William rose, the greater urgency he felt to protect his queen, country and religion. So far, William, Walsingham and others loyal to the regime had spared the crown from usurpation, the kingdom from invasion, and Protestantism from corruption. However, the Ridolfi Plot of 1571 proved that England was far from experiencing any sense of internal or external peace. The plot, which had involved the Pope, Philip of Spain, Mary Stuart, Roberto Ridolfi and none other than the Duke of Norfolk, was an example of the discontent amongst English Catholics, even those close to the crown. Though Norfolk was arrested and executed by mid-1572, the thought of executing a fellow anointed queen was still too much for Elizabeth to bear. Despite the threat of war with Spain, the French persecution of Protestants, and Saint Bartholomew's Day Massacre, Mary Stuart, though imprisoned, had endured. As had the threat she bore to the English crown. William wished to avoid any further threat from Mary, and as he aged, he became increasingly preoccupied with the question of what to do with her.

Since 1568, Mary had been Elizabeth and William's *de facto* prisoner. She may have been well looked after, even treated beyond what she deserved after the Ridolfi Plot and the aggravation that her presence presented to the English State. However, after almost two decades of captivity, with no power, freedom or purpose, it is no surprise that she became desperate to find a way out of her gilded cage. Whether or not one believes she actually unknowingly signed her own death warrant in a number of letters in the 1580s is at this moment irrelevant. What is important to note, is that England was suffering from a number of internal and external Catholic threats and conspiracies, of which Mary became an easy scapegoat and figurehead – whether involved personally or not. After such a long time of imprisonment, Mary may have thought that as Elizabeth's cousin, she was untouchable. Surely she was the only obstacle between the Catholic European powers and the British Isles? But she was not the only desperate individual. From the outside, William and Walsingham were working with a number of informants, spies, secretaries and foreign courtiers. Conspiracy was never far away. With at least one man spying from the corner of every enemy court, William could rest assured that Elizabeth's reign would remain safeguarded. Or so he thought.

The precursor to the eventuality of the destruction of Mary Stuart, her internal and external supporters and the intrigue that she attracted, was the Throckmorton Plot. By the 1580s, though William was at the head of Elizabeth's government, he needed ruthless men under him. Men like Francis Walsingham. The spymaster was by no means as subtle as Lord Burghley. A man who didn't mince his words and held little tolerance, if any, for Catholics, never mind their conspiring and plotting. Furthermore, where William felt Mary Stuart was a threat to England's security, Walsingham was more likely to absolutely despise her on every level. In 1583, Walsingham's agents discovered that Francis Throckmorton was at the head of a plot to dethrone Elizabeth, free Mary, and allow Spain to invade England. Throckmorton was arrested that November, and under torture, revealed the plot to overthrow the regime.[1] However, his personal letters and papers would have been damning enough on their own, to reveal him as a traitor and his plan to assist the imprisoned Queen of Scots. The plan was for the Duke of Guise to initially invade England from the south, free Mary, initiate a Spanish invasion with the approval of the Pope, and encourage the English people to rebel against their queen.[2]

All of this would have seemed pretty tidy, if it were not for Walsingham's ability to sense a plot before it had even been roused. William had little to do with this episode, but he was most certainly grateful to have Walsingham in his service. Furthermore, William had no part in Throckmorton's torture, though it should be noted that he knew of it. Throckmorton also confessed that the Spanish ambassador in England, Mendoza, knew of the plot, and yet failed to make any mention or report of it. Of course, this would have been expected. Mendoza, as a Spanish subject, was not tried or tortured, but he was expelled from England after a meeting with Walsingham and William. Throckmorton was tried for treason and executed at Tyburn.[3] William and Walsingham had every reason to come down hard on these plots, for the queen had just recently survived an assassination attempt by a 'madman'. But what of Mary Stuart? What was to be done with her? And what further internal treachery lurked within Elizabeth's circle? The Throckmorton plot confirmed English fears of Spanish invasion, and their wish to replace Elizabeth with Mary.

William may have had little to with the aftermath of the Throckmorton Plot, but he was certainly elbow deep in the next plot. By 1585, a number of attempts to take Elizabeth's life had failed, but the country lay uneasy. Throckmorton may have been a traitor, but he was no match for William Parry, who had worked for the English crown as a spy under William and Walsingham. Parry was the son of a Welsh gentleman, and much like William, had come from a line of Welsh men who served Elizabeth's grandfather, Henry VII. Parry was well received at court, and by the 1570s, entered into the queen's service, following in his father's footsteps. William may have trusted Parry, not only due to his Welsh origins, but due to the fact that his family had also dutifully served the Tudors. In this, we can see that William's ideology towards good breeding, genealogy, and family duty, often clouded the reality, and therefore could lead to poor judgement. While abroad in Venice and Paris in 1583, for whatever reason, Parry wrote to the Pope, offering his service to the Catholic cause in England. But at the same time, he was also reporting to William and Walsingham, and was one of their most trusted informants abroad. His time abroad had proven fruitful for his career. Yet, on returning to London in 1584, this still wasn't enough for the ambitious Parry. To him, it mattered little what the outcome of the clash between the English Protestant cause and the Roman Catholic cause would be, as long as he was on the winning side. Though his actions as a double agent were not only dangerous, but foolish, Parry was well aware by his return, that he could be discovered. This is likely why he exclaimed that he had 'intelligence' for the queen.[4]

Alford's remarks regarding Parry's loyalty sum up the situation perfectly. Parry was no doubt self-serving, going between two factions and playing one against the other. Neither side were aware of Parry's deceit, and neither expected him to have the ability for such treachery. However, while in Paris in 1582, Parry was most definitely reconciled with Catholicism, and therefore, we must consider that his loyalty as a Catholic superseded that of his loyalty as an Englishman – a thought wholly unbearable and incomprehensible to William Cecil. There is also the fact that as a subject of Elizabeth's, he was willing to later kill her in the name of the Catholic cause, despite the obvious consequences if he failed. Therefore, it can be suggested that he had embraced the financial prospects of killing England's heretic queen. By December 1583, he had met with Mary Stuart's own spy, who was gathering intelligence abroad – Thomas Morgan. It was with this meeting that Parry's fate was sealed, and another conspiracy to murder Elizabeth was realised. When he arrived back in England, he outwardly seemed the loyal subject. He himself was likely plagued by doubts and may have been split between his loyalties. He may have even been reconsidering his plan to assassinate Elizabeth. He was in financial difficulty, and William's patronage was a necessity.[5]

Parry conspired with a young man named Edmund Neville, and together they hatched the final plan for Elizabeth's murder. However, this very dealing with a man he himself did not entirely trust, brought on his destruction. The December of 1584 had seen Parliament pass a bill known as the Act for the Queen's Surety. This act made it legal for private subjects to kill anyone who threatened the life or throne of Elizabeth Tudor. Parry outwardly and shockingly opposed the bill, which promptly saw him arrested. Parry rushed to Neville on being released, realising that he had little time before Parliament made a decision on his open opposition to the bill. But Neville had reservations and was seriously doubting the plot. In the end, Neville gave himself up to the authorities, confessed to the plot to kill the queen, and of Parry's initiation of the plan. Parry was subsequently arrested and his trial began on 18 February 1585. Surprisingly, he pleaded guilty, then retracted his plea. He was found guilty and executed on 2 March 1585. His treason will forever be known as the 'Parry Plot'. Parry's plan is not only evidence for the financial instability of some of William's closest confidantes, but also that despite his patronage and support, there were internal individuals willing to destroy the Elizabethan state and risk the security of their own kingdom, in the name of religion, money and power.[6]

Between 1586 and 1587, an event so incredible would play out, that William Shakespeare himself may have struggled to dramatise it. The Parry plot served as a lesson for William and Walsingham, and encouraged them to pay closer attention not only to those within their own circle, but the English Catholic refugees abroad. Especially those in France where they could plot from afar, out of sight and interception. Mary maintained that she was innocent of any involvement in the many recurring conspiracies. Yet, though there was little proof of her involvement in earlier plots, it is the Babington Plot that would bring about her death. Mary was by this time well into secret correspondence with a man in France. Though she may have thought she was safe, every safely disguised letter was intercepted by William and Walsingham. Mary had already been transferred to Tutbury in 1585, but this did little to deter those plotting to put her on the English throne.[7]

Mary Stuart was now under twenty-four-hour surveillance. The man tasked to watch her was Sir Amyas Paulet, a no-nonsense man and once the English ambassador at the French court. Paulet was not one of William's, but Walsingham's men. Sadler had been Mary's 'gaoler' for some time.

Though, as we can safely say that Walsingham followed William's word, Paulet would have been an agreeable gaoler to all at this time. Walsingham knew what he was doing by using Paulet, who was known to be a staunch Puritan, despised Mary, Catholics and their cause. Mary was no longer to be treated as a queen, but as a dangerous criminal. She of course tried to charm Paulet, as she had with many others over the past two decades. But her attempts were met with contempt. Paulet even stripped her royal cloth of state from the wall, finding any notion of her queenship repulsive and offensive. Mary railed, but could do nothing. She was not permitted to receive letters, unless from the French ambassador, and those letters were read before they even reached her hand. She was permitted no other news, no private correspondence, no friendship and was not permitted to dine with others or ride out alone, or without permission. Thus, Paulet accomplished what William had wanted for some time – the isolation of Mary Stuart. She complained to Elizabeth, but her woes went ignored.[8]

Mary's secret letters with her supporters outside, such as Morgan, Gilbert Gifford and Charles Paget were initially halted. Yet, Walsingham had planned this for a specific reason – he was determined to once and for all, destroy Mary Stuart. Her desperation under Paulet, would be Walsingham's means of accomplishing this. The key to salvation from the threat of Catholic conspiracy was ironically found in a young, Catholic and foolish nobleman named Anthony Babington. This is why it is referred to as the 'Babington Plot'. However, it should be perhaps more appropriately named the 'Walsingham Plot', for Morgan, Paulet, Gifford, Paget and even Babington, were all mere pawns of a much greater scheme than their own. Mary had complained so bitterly of the conditions at Tutbury, that she was later moved to Chartley Manor. During Paulet's time as Mary's keeper, he not only reported to Walsingham, but to William Cecil directly. It was also due to Charles Paget's genuine fondness of William, and vice versa, that he received Charles Paget's lands, after Paget, a Catholic, had turned against the regime to join other refugees abroad for Mary's cause. Gilbert Gifford was one of these men, the son of John Gifford of Staffordshire. He met in Paris with Morgan and Paget in 1585, and it was decided that he was to travel to England with letters from Morgan to Mary. It was thought that Gifford would be able to create a new Catholic network in the area of Tutbury, where he had many acquaintances and relatives. However, Gifford was under surveillance by Walsingham's agents, even before he stepped on English soil. He was apprehended, arrested, and brought to Walsingham – a terrifying notion. For his life, Gifford agreed to betray the Catholic conspirators, and Mary. All the ingredients for a plot within a plot were now available to Elizabeth's men, and they wasted no time in pursuing their greatest task yet.[9]

Gifford made himself agreeable to the other conspirators, while William arranged for all letters going back and forth between Mary and her supporters to be intercepted. The plan was for all secret correspondence to be written in code. If those plotting to free the Scottish queen thought it was their idea, they were mistaken. It was Walsingham himself who planted the seed. Walsingham then employed one of his agents, Thomas Phelippes, who was an expert in ciphering secret code. Paulet was brought into the scheme, and it was decided that the letters would be brought to and from Mary in a beer cask. Gifford then informed the French ambassador that there was a way of communicating with Mary and so after some time of sending letters back and forth, they concluded that nobody knew of their secret, and thus began to plan. This is where Babington came into the picture. Every plot needed a figurehead, a noble, a man whom the blame could be placed upon. Unfortunately for this young man, he became entangled in the intrigue and excitement of something he knew scarce little about. When approached by one of the conspirators, a missionary named John Ballard, Babington was initially cautious. He indeed wanted to help Mary and aid the assassination of Elizabeth, of that he was certainly guilty, but to involve himself in yet another plot – of which many had failed, was a risk. By mid-1586 however, he had made up his mind to support the plot, and wrote to Mary exclaiming his wish to free her, and murder Elizabeth. Of course, this was exactly what William and Walsingham wanted, and Babington's fate was sealed. Babington's idea was for Mary to be freed before Elizabeth was assassinated, but the Scottish queen preferred to remain imprisoned until the task had been completed. This, in itself, can be seen as Mary's complicity in the plot, and her very suggestions that she remained in captivity until Elizabeth was dead, was enough alone to condemn her. Whether one believes that Walsingham had a forgery written or extra lines added to Mary's letters to secure her downfall has been a topic of great debate. But as Fraser stated: 'If this is not an endorsement of the murder plot…the English language has lost its meaning'.[10]

Walsingham now had total control over all information coming in and out of Chartley Hall. It is important to note that though Mary's complicity in the plot was due to Walsingham's agents' encouragement of the key conspirators, we must not dismiss her ignorance of Walsingham's plan as innocence.[11] On the contrary, Mary knew that unlike previous plots, signing her name directly, whether in a coded letter or not, which entailed details of any notion of freeing her from her incarceration or killing Elizabeth, was enough to justify her own execution. What we see by the end of 1586, is a woman at the end of her wits, with a hunger for freedom and autonomy. And so whether any postscript was added or nay, Mary's direct involvement and approval of the Babington Plot cannot be denied. Mary's and Babington's damning letters were copied and transcribed by Phelippes, who at the end of his copy of Mary's letter, added a gallows sign and many believe the postscript which asked Babington for the names of all those involved. This was why Walsingham allowed the letter to continue onto its destination to Babington, in the hope to entrap everyone involved. In the end, it was this copy that was used as evidence against Mary and the Babington conspirators. However, Walsingham's addition to Mary's letter rattled Babington, and he fled in fear of a much greater conspiracy than his own.[12]

By early August, Walsingham finally gave the order for all conspirators to be arrested. It took a few days, as Babington had fled into hiding. Those arrested were interrogated under torture until they confessed their treachery. Babington himself was taken to Ely House, which was Sir Christopher Hatton's London residence. He, amongst the others, was questioned intensely numerous times throughout the interrogation process. Where Walsingham was the genius who engineered the entire plot within a plot, it was William who questioned the conspirators. It seems that Walsingham was present for at least one of Babington's interrogations, but within the coming weeks, there were a number of trials and executions.[13] Babington was not difficult during this process, and revealed the whole plan and the roles of all those involved. It is not clear if Babington was tortured. Indeed, there seems to have been no need for such action and he was willing to confess his full endorsement of the enterprise. On 12 September, William wrote to Robert Dudley: 'Your lordship and I were great motes in the traitors' eyes, for your Lordship there and I here should first, about one time, have been killed. Of your Lordship they thought rather of poisoning than slaying.'[14]

William and Walsingham now had enough evidence to approach the topic of what to do with Mary. She was swiftly transferred from Chartley to another location close by. Mary was stripped of most of her personal possessions and everything including her own letters and personal papers were examined carefully. All of her personal staff were interviewed. The evidence against the queen was mounting and there was no other alternative than to put her on trial. This would most likely end her life, and as well as the realisation that they had succeeded, there was also the anxiety for both William and Walsingham, as to how to approach the queen. Elizabeth had always been anxious regarding Mary's treachery, and though she did not entirely doubt Mary's role in the many plots that had taken place over the past years, she was reluctant to put her cousin and an anointed queen on trial in a foreign country, where she was neither a subject nor inferior in status to Elizabeth. Plus, what would be the outcome of such an outcome for England? War? Regicide?

Elizabeth's reaction to the news of the plot was understandably dramatic. She was shocked that such a grand conspiracy had taken place, but was also extremely anxious for her own safety. She even encouraged that the executions of the men involved to be as Wilson puts it, 'carried out with the maximum cruelty'.[15] For there to be justification for Mary's death, there had to be a trial. This made Elizabeth anxious, but she would have known this was right. To carry out any assassination of the Scottish queen in secret would only make her a martyr. But William, Walsingham and the queen would soon find that whatever route they chose, Mary would serve as a martyr to Catholics anyway. Elizabeth was eventually persuaded to agree to a trial, but she would not agree to Mary being held in the Tower.

Instead, she was brought to Fotheringhay Castle in Northamptonshire. This would be the last time the Queen of Scots would be moved. Forty-two commissioners were appointed to see over her trial. William was unwell during this time, likely due to his gout, but he would have been eager to hear the deliberations. Mary, of course, was surprised when the copy of her letter was read out. However, she was not allowed to read or examine any paperwork throughout. She wholly denied her involvement, but her protestations did little to help her cause. By the end of September, the commissioners appointed had deliberated, and then announced that they found Mary Stuart to be guilty, and recommended that she should die for her crimes. Elizabeth was hesitant, racked by anxiety and guilt. But she was again persuaded to recognise the treachery that had taken place, and the very real threat to her life that Mary posed if she were allowed to live. By 3 December, the queen issued the proclamation that Mary Stuart was to be executed. But her decision remained clouded by doubt.[16]

William had much to be grateful for in a trusted friend and colleague like Walsingham, for he had much to contend with during the periods of the Throckmorton, Parry and Babington Plots. The queen's final courtship, that with the Duke of Anjou, was well and truly over by 1582. It was now a known fact that Elizabeth would never marry, nor produce an heir to succeed her. She was to be the last Tudor. However, this did not mean that the succession question went away, and with multiple conspiracies at large within and outside of the kingdom, there was much for Lord Burghley to worry about. Furthermore, by 1583, the situation in the Netherlands was more than troublesome. The Duke of Anjou had failed to stop the Duke of

Parma from advancing into the south. When Anjou died childless in 1584, any French intervention in the Netherlands ceased. William of Orange was also assassinated a month later. The deaths of Anjou and Orange would only have stirred the Spanish Philip. Elizabeth as always remained unsure of how to act, and she was reluctant to intervene. By the end of the year, it was clear that the French heir would be Henry of Navarre. But Philip and the Duke of Guise, Mary Stuart's maternal uncle, planned to exclude him from this. This was a serious threat to England's national security, and William decided that there was only one option, to intervene. The Treaty of Nonsuch was signed on 10 August 1585, but the delays in an English decision to intervene raised a few eyebrows, and of course, William was blamed for the queen's indecisiveness. William was also suffering from his usual bout of gout. [17]

By the time Elizabeth had issued any proclamation of Mary's guilt and sentence, she and even some of her council, were troubled by some doubt in the decision. It was clear from the verdict of Mary's trial, and the overwhelming evidence, that she was guilty. Elizabeth's guilt of killing her cousin, and a woman who she both feared and admired had less to do with her own hesitations. Elizabeth was seriously worried of the consequences of executing a Catholic queen and figurehead. However, as ever, William's words proved persuasive. It was his view that as the law must be abided by all, and that the law had found Mary guilty of crimes fitting the death sentence, then it was God's and the law's will that she should die. If it were not for William's dedication to creating a network of spies, agents and informants under Walsingham, Mary may have eventually succeeded in her hopes to seize Elizabeth's throne. To allow her to live would only stir further rebellion, conspiracy and internal turmoil for England. William may have underestimated the consequences of killing an anointed queen. Particularly in terms of the Spanish threat. The question of whether Mary was more dangerous alive or dead however, would soon be answered. On 1 February 1587, Elizabeth finally relented and called for Mary's death warrant. She hesitated again, but signed it. This was what William had hoped for so long, and now, he finally felt that England, and Elizabeth's reign, could be safe. Before Elizabeth had time for regret, the warrant was whisked to William and then to Fotheringhay where Mary awaited her fate. The queen did attempt to call it back but by the time her messenger reached William, the warrant was gone. The queen then wished to hear no more until 'the deed was done'.[18]

When Mary was presented with her death warrant, signed by Elizabeth, she was reputedly calm and exclaimed: 'The message is welcome; yet I did not think that the Queen, my sister, would have consented to my death...' She was not permitted a confessor to prepare her for death. Her faith was then argued upon by those present, and she was urged to renounce her Catholic faith, which she refused.[19] On 8 February 1587, one week after her death warrant was signed, Mary, Queen of Scots, awoke and adorned her finest black dress. Underneath was a fine, crimson velvet petticoat, the colour of Martyrdom. If Mary thought to dramatise her execution, it was she who was in for a surprise. The executioner butchered the job, and it took three blows of the axe to remove her head. The final blow ended decades of rivalry between two queens, and an endless thorn in William's side. Elizabeth was racked with guilt, and expressed her horror when told of Mary's death. She railed against William. In one moment, she seemed to forget all that had happened and would ask his advice, then she would remember, and banish him from her presence. Over the coming weeks, William was in and out of favour. However, he had done his duty, and at the very least, Mary was given a trial. If Elizabeth was horrified, the rest of Europe was completely outraged. Though William and the rest of the government had prepared for such backlash, they had not expected the whole of Europe to seek vengeance on England with such severity. By the end of 1587, war with Spain was looming, and an armada was on the horizon.[20]

The queen had initially ordered that secretary Davison be brought to the Tower as punishment for Mary's death. William was suffering from his usual ailment and had also recently fallen from his horse and therefore, was away recovering. William wrote to the queen himself beseeching her for forgiveness and requested that he explain his actions. He also offered to resign from his service to her. However, at the same time, he also criticised her for ordering Davison to be sent to the Tower, and reminded her that even in the days of her father, brother and sister, a loyal councillor was never sent to the Tower, besides those who were accused of high treason. The queen would not receive the letter. Again, he wrote four days later, and again, she did not open it. After some time, she relented, and told Thomas Cecil that she would listen to what his father had to say. She read his third letter. Elizabeth had forgiven William for Mary's execution by July, and Davison's life was spared.[21]

Following Mary's execution, men like William Allen, a Catholic exile on the continent, and his Jesuit counterpart Robert Persons, were petitioning Philip of Spain to act, by launching an invasion of England. Rumours had already begun to spread across Europe of an impending Spanish invasion, which would purge the kingdom of its heresy. Philip needed little encouragement however, and by the time he was petitioned, his infamous Spanish Armada was already under construction. Pamphlets began to circulate of England's impending doom. By the Spring of 1588, it seemed that the armada was almost ready. England was bombarded with news, rumours, and pamphlets all entailing details of the mighty armada. By July, it had already departed from the Spanish coast.[22] To say that Elizabeth and William were deeply worried is an understatement. William himself had read one of the pamphlets in June, written by Allen. The English government attempted to censor Catholic propaganda at this time, and it was deemed a serious danger not only to the kingdom's national security, but could ultimately sway England's Catholic minority to rally alongside the rest of Catholic Europe.[23]

The Spanish, and all those who endorsed the armada, were truly convinced that after thirty years, England could finally be conquered, and its heretic queen dethroned. By all accounts, their expectation of victory was not unfounded, for they believed that as an island nation, England was no match for the military might of Spain. The English Navy had neither the numbers in men nor vessels, and now with the Portuguese supporting Philip with their large fleet, England seemed like easy pickings. England had few friends, and none willing to intervene. The Spanish were then the kings of the sea, and with the papacy behind them, nobody expected the British Isles to stand a chance. The Prince of Parma was also in on the invasion front, and provided his own fleet and many men. The English were not slow to act however, and Elizabeth ordered that all necessary preparations for war be undertaken. The command of the English fleet was given to Charles Howard, Lord Effingham, who was the Lord Admiral of England. The position of Vice-Admiral was given to Francis Drake. Camden stated that along the southern coast, at least 20,000 men were assembled and positioned for defence. Robert Dudley provided 22,000 and around a thousand horses. A further 34,000 men and 2,000 horses were under Lord Hunsdon's command. England's best soldiers, both noble and common, were rounded up and prepared to defend from land.[24]

To think England lay idly in wait for the armada to form would be a mistake. The fact that so many men and horses, even within a few weeks of Mary's execution, were so prepared that their own fleet was under construction is admirable. Drake had already received orders to destroy the Spanish Armada in port, but William wrote to him hastily, ordering him not to do so. Drake's later destructive raid in Cadiz with several royal ships may have put the armada off for a time, but in the end it jeopardised an appeasement of Elizabeth's part, and she was ultimately blamed. Now there was no room for negotiation. It seems that the order may have come from the Lord Admiral. Either way, Drake's attempt to reach the enemy before they reached England's shores had consequences, and bad weather pushed them back to Plymouth. It would be that same wind that would bring the Spanish to England. He may have been tasked with defeating the Spanish, but there was a particular way to engage with one's enemy, and William understood this. The armada was initially delayed by bad weather, and the English fleet was also stuck in Plymouth Harbour. By 19 July, the armada was spotted off the coast of Cornwall and by the next day, it could be seen in the English Channel.[25]

The armada, which had sailed from Lisbon initially with around 130 ships, must have seemed daunting to the English. More ships and more men were meant to join it. The English wanted to avoid any battle taking place in their own channel, but this was not to be. However, the local knowledge of English waters, and their ability to seek reinforcements and further supplies, gave them a very good chance of fighting off the mightiest fleet ever seen. As the gunfire commenced, the hours became days, and reports flew in and out of the situation out at sea. The Spanish Armada may have been larger than any English fleet, but the Spanish themselves, doomed by the bad weather, found it difficult to overcome 'the veritable breath of God'. By the end of July, it was clear that an English victory was imminent. However, the idea that a small English fleet could have defeated Europe's greatest power without bad weather and a lot of luck has been refuted by most historians, and it is likely that without the wind and of course, the typically unmentioned fact that some of the armada's strongest ships did not make it to the English Channel at all, having returned for repairs, England may very well have been defeated. There was also the fact that though the Spanish and Portuguese ships looked bigger than the English ships, they were not. Nor were they equipped for such rough weather.[26]

As it became clear that the English seized the day, by whatever means or circumstances, the queen, the great statesman and the nation rejoiced. On 9 August, when much of the fighting had ended and most of the Spanish ships had been pushed away from the English coast, Elizabeth and William arrived at Tilbury to meet the English troops. The fact that the queen herself, though the sovereign, and a woman, would risk appearing before her troops at such a time, whether the battle was won or not, was extraordinary. This image of the virgin queen at the front line, encouraging her men and vowing to fight with them until the end was of course, one of the greatest Tudor propaganda stunts of the century. With her statesman at her side, her father's blood in her veins and her subject's devotion, it must have seemed like England's greatest triumph. In many ways, it was. We know Elizabeth did appear at Tilbury, but there is much myth surrounding what she actually said. Many accounts would purposely portray her in a mythological state – a vision of purity and power, riding among her men on a white horse, declaring: 'I know I have the body but of a weak and feeble woman, but I have the heart and stomach of a king.'[27] There are several problems regarding the evidence of this speech. The most important being that it was only published in 1654, based on a letter from 1624, decades after Elizabeth's death. Whether Elizabeth was ignorant of the victory until she reached Tilbury, and whether or not she spoke such powerful words is irrelevant, because England had triumphed.[28]

The English defeat of the Spanish Armada remains clouded by mythology and Tudor propaganda. Elizabeth's victory cannot be denied, and thereafter, she was known as 'Gloriana'. However, this victory was as much William Cecil's at it was Elizabeth's. In spite of everything, every tragedy, every loss, every plot and plight, William Cecil had risen to the highest office in the land, defeated his queen's enemies from all corners of the kingdom and afar. Through patience, policy, caution and as Smith rightly put it, 'sheer ruthlessness', England's greatest statesman had persevered. The moment Elizabeth had finished her greatest speech at Tilbury, whatever her true words were, the cheers of the English troops were enough to prove to him that the past thirty years of hard work were worth it in the end. His vision of England as a great Protestant, European power was finally realised.

So why was William so instrumental in the defeat of the Spanish Armada, if we can safely say that the day was won by 'God's Breath'? Between 20 July and 10 August, William was the most present councillor at every meeting. The council had met every day in between these dates. It was absolutely crucial that they received news and reports of the battle going on out at sea. Every move they took mattered. Indeed, as the battle raged on, there was little that the men of the council could actually do, but given that they received daily reports on the situation, it must be considered that they were readying themselves for defeat, as much as they were praying for victory. It was essential to plan ahead for every outcome, whether it be victory or defeat. William himself was influential in terms of the Tudor propaganda that came after the destruction of the armada, and therefore, he is to an extent, responsible for how we view England's victory, Elizabeth as Gloriana, and that unexplainable sense of British Naval pride. He commanded how the Navy should be divided into two fleets, and negotiated the funds for the necessities – ultimately by loans and taxation. The many letters and pamphlets that were sent out after Spain's defeat were also due to William's influence. The queen may have seemed the vision of strength at Tilbury, but as the weeks passed after the armada, she would rely on William more than ever. For with every high, there must come a low, and Elizabeth was about to reach her lowest ebb in decades. The only man that could pull her from such darkness, was William Cecil.[29]

Everyone had their place and role when it came to the defeat of the armada. Elizabeth was every bit the leader, a hot-blooded Tudor. If any of her subjects had questioned her ability or legitimacy up until her speech at Tilbury, they certainly did not thereafter. Drake, despite his deviance which may have quashed any possibility of negotiation, was still a celebrated war hero, and Elizabeth celebrated and rewarded his loyalty. William had been hard at work during every moment of the conflict itself, and had been up until the moment the armada arrived, working with a man named Christopher Saxton to map all the English and Welsh counties. This may seem like a trivial task hardly worth mentioning, but it allowed for William to keep tabs on the locations of every Catholic in the land. Not to mention much of the mobilisation of thousands of citizens long before the Spanish arrival, was due to William's preparations.[30] However, many forget the importance of Robert Dudley, who stood by his queen during this time of turmoil, and who commanded a considerable number of men who contributed to England's victory.

England erupted into celebrations and Elizabeth even conducted a progress through London on 24 November, with Dudley by her side. There was a large ceremony at St Pauls, which William most definitely attended, along with all the other nobles and peers of the realm. Dudley had been in the Netherlands recently, attempting to control the backlash for Mary Stuart's execution. He had served his mistress well in so many ways. It was he who was also responsible for erecting the fort at Tilbury, therefore being the reason for the queen's visit and her great speech. However, as celebrations went on, Dudley left court with her permission, and went on to Rycote to visit the Norris household. From there he sent her a letter, which would be his last.[31]

Robert Dudley died on 4 September 1588 on his way to Buxton in Derbyshire. He was apparently going to take the baths. His health had been declining for some time, and during the armada crisis, it went further downhill while he was abroad. Historians still debate on the root cause of his death, some considering malaria, whilst others cancer. Whatever the cause, one thing was clear, one of Elizabeth's great loves was gone. The queen was inconsolable. William had never been Robert Dudley's greatest friend. The pair had often quarrelled for the queen's ear, with Dudley often coming out on top. The relationships between the queen and her suitor and her statesman were very different. However, this is not to imply that William did not respect Dudley greatly, as he did all noblemen of the realm. Elizabeth had great faith in Dudley, and had given him titles and many offices throughout his life. And had even named him as Lord Protector should she have died from smallpox in 1562. Luckily for William, this never came to pass. There is no record of William's reaction to Dudley's death, but he certainly benefitted from it for the next decade, as the ageing queen became more and more dependent on her old advisor, who himself was an old man by the end of the 1580s.[32]

After some time of mourning, when William tried to show patience, the queen came back to her senses. She was never the same, but at least she returned to her duties. By January 1589, Elizabeth wished to thank her greatest advisor by granting him the earldom of Northamptonshire. Despite William's respect for the English nobility, it seemed that a barony was sufficient enough. He claimed that he was too poor to be an earl, yet his many properties, lands and high offices contradict this statement. Loades states that this was due to William's sensitivity towards status. But what does that actually mean? William had grown up and come up in a time where powerful men, men behind the throne such as Cardinal Wolsey, Thomas Cromwell, Edward Seymour and John Dudley, had all risen high in status due to their closeness to the monarch and their service to the crown. All of these men were quick to lap up titles, fortune, lands and even greater powers, and they all ended up disgraced, or executed for treason. William therefore not only revered great men of noble birth, but he was also extremely cautious and careful to remember where he came from, what he worked for, and knew the consequences of rising too high. The queen proposed several more promotions over the next few years, but William time and again, turned them down. It is also likely that by this time, the great statesman felt that he was too old to bear the brunt of responsibility for any further offices. It is also notable that he was training his younger son Robert for the eventual inevitability of his own death. William was also likely put off any further promotions as the death of his wife Mildred that April plunged him into depression.[33]

Though the defeat of the Spanish Armada has been passed down through history as Elizabeth's victory, and while the glory certainly belongs to her – as we do revere her as 'Gloriana', it can safely be said that the victory also belongs to William Cecil. It was through William's connections with men such as Walsingham, his spies, his web of informants, and his insatiable appetite for knowledge, that brought down England's enemies. Mary Stuart was a deadly threat to his vision for decades, as were the succession crisis and the powers of Europe. Yet, he was able to mastermind a way to free England from every threat, secure Elizabeth's safety and the regime in her name, while also carving out his own legacy. The very sense of national pride and 'Englishness' so present in every British person today, stems from William's vision of England as an independent, strong European power. Indeed, centuries later in the 1940s, when Britain was under threat of invasion once again from another great European power, Germany, that British defiance in the face of peril could certainly be said to have originated with the legacy of the first Elizabethan state. Therefore, it is through William Cecil, that every British person today, owes their pride.

Chapter 10

The Final Decade

The final years of William Cecil's life are probably the most interesting in terms of understanding the man that he became, and how he is remembered. He remained as busy as ever, but had his well-trained son, Robert, at his side when needed. In April 1590, Francis Walsingham died. Much like his friend William, Walsingham was always prepared for the inevitable. He had made his will a year earlier, and though he started to show signs of ill health, he would never have resigned his offices, nor even thought of retiring, until it became clear that he had weeks to live. He must have known for some time that he was on the way out, even before the armada had reached the English coast, for he had been bedridden for the last several winters. William and Walsingham were similar in their outlook on life. They worked themselves to the bone, until they became ill and were forced to take respite. This became habitual for both men and it is therefore unsurprising that it took its toll. Many have claimed that Walsingham died in poverty. However, as Wilson points out, he had cleared some of his debts along with Philip Sidney's. But, his wife and family were not left with much, and he remained indebted to the crown for more that £40,000. However, it is impossible to think that this was an uncommon factor for many courtiers during the period, and many courtiers ended up bankrupt from at least one visit from the queen during progress. Walsingham's debt was therefore fairly modest by the standards, considering the financial complexities of Tudor courtier life. His funeral was simple and his burial modest.[1]

William's reaction to his friend's death can be summed up in a letter he wrote to Walsingham's friends in Florence: '...the death of Mr Secretary Walsingham who left this world the 6th of April...the Queen's Majesty and her realm and I and others, his particular friends, have had a great loss, both for the public use of his good and painful long services and for the private comfort I had by his mutual friendship.'[2] William had clearly not only lost a much needed confidante and colleague, a man of great talents, but also a very close friend. In fact, many of William's friends and contemporaries were long dead, ill, or died soon after Walsingham. Philip Sidney had died in 1586, and Christopher Hatton died in 1591. However, the old statesman was not finished just yet. Francis Walsingham had taken the office of principal secretary in 1573 and it was his until his death. William had once enjoyed the office himself and he owed much of the success of his career as secretary. William and Robert Cecil, along with other members of the Privy Council, likely took on the many duties of Walsingham for the next year or so, but by May 1591, it was clear to William and the queen, that Robert had come into his own, and was more than capable of the job. He took over the many duties of principal secretary. This was convenient for William as he was feeling his age, was often ill and wanted some form of semi-retirement as Loades puts it. He also wanted such a position for his son, as he knew he was capable and wanted to pass on his political legacy to his own kin. Thomas Cecil may have turned out to be a good man in the end, but he would inherit the Barony, based on primogeniture. Therefore, William had to leave something for his second son, and that was his political career. Though it was William's wish for his son to succeed him in this way, he and Elizabeth were acutely aware that many viewed the Cecils as the true rulers of England, and when Robert was knighted in 1591, it irritated many a courtier, and William knew it.[3]

With Robert acting as Walsingham's replacement, and a young man named John Puckering to replace Hatton, it seemed that though the queen and William were ageing, new blood was beginning to flow into the council. Whether this was seen as a positive change or negative can be speculated upon, however, with new men came new ideas, and new ideas could be dangerous when the sovereign so outwardly rejected change. The queen may have been hesitant when William approached the idea that his son would officially take over many of his duties and one day succeed him in his role entirely. William was not a man to simply give up, but he was certainly tiring from the volume of work. He had not yet reached his seventieth year, but he knew that he could not live forever. The queen may have been hesitant due to Robert's young age, but he proved to be more than capable, and may have surprised her. He would not be officially appointed as secretary for some time, but now more than ever was the time to prove himself, for he was not the only young man on the rise. Indeed, though he had sat in the Commons from as early as 1584, his ambitions mirrored that of another, perhaps more dashing and daring young man whom he was familiar with – Robert Devereux, 2nd Earl of Essex. He was the son of Lettice Knollys and her first husband, Walter Devereux. He was therefore the stepson of the queen's late favourite Robert Dudley. If the rivalry between William Cecil and Dudley was anything to remark upon, the tension between the young Robert Cecil and Devereux was far more tenuous. The two men couldn't have been more different. Robert was dutiful, quiet, studious and not the most handsome man by any means. Devereux was three years younger, extremely handsome, athletic and bizarrely pompous, and already embarking on his own political career.[4]

Devereux began to find a place in the queen's affections. She seemed to be happy with the way things were going, with William remaining in his place and officially residing over the principal tasks of secretary with Robert's help. However, if there was any notion of competition between the two Roberts at the beginning of 1591, by 1593, tensions were boiling over. William had finally defeated Elizabeth's greatest foe, Mary Stuart, and the Spanish Armada had safely been blown away from English shores, crashing off the west coast of Ireland and beyond. But that did not mean that plots on the queen's life and position had joined the watery grave of the Spaniards. Indeed, as Elizabeth grew older, she became much like her father. Desperately paranoid about assassination and conspiracy, Robert Cecil certainly had his work cut out for him. The first hint of what is now known as the Lopez plot arose towards the end of 1593. Rodrigo Lopez was a Portuguese Jew. He had emigrated to England within the first year of Elizabeth's reign due to persecution. He became a renowned and respected physician and the queen eventually came to hear of his talents. The fact that he was foreign, Portuguese or even a Jew mattered little to those who sought respectable and professional services. Devereux had just been officially appointed to the Privy Council, and eager to make a name for himself and prove his loyalty to the queen, he suddenly denounced Lopez as a traitor and stated that the latter has been conspiring with the Spanish to poison the queen. There is absolutely no evidence to suggest that Lopez was plotting to murder the queen. Indeed, the notion that he would serve Elizabeth so loyally for decades, during many risings, plots and even war, to end up poisoning her in her old age is entirely ludicrous. Both the queen and Robert Cecil initially defended Lopez, but Devereux and his lackey Anthony Bacon whispered poison in the queen's ear. In the end, the queen's paranoia likely had the final say, and Lopez, who professed his innocence, was executed in June 1594. More than anything, William, Robert Cecil and Robert Devereux all found the plot to be positive in terms of promoting an anti-Spanish propaganda across England. William even wrote and published *A true report of sundry horrible conspiracies* on the matter.[5]

William Cecil's final decade was perhaps his busiest. This was likely due to the growing power of much younger men entering the Privy Council. By 1593, William was struggling to keep his grip on power. This was not in the sense that the queen was willing to let him go or resign entirely from his duties. However as he aged, his mind may have remained sharp, but his body was ailing him. The military, its expansion and the expansion of what were the beginnings of the British Empire, not to mention the situation in the low countries, dominated English politics. William had worked his whole life to secure England's national security and securing it as a real power in Europe. As more young men poured into Elizabeth's government, men that were replacing William's generation, the queen inevitably had to go with it. But tensions began to rise, and not only those between Robert Cecil and Robert Devereux. Devereux had married Walsingham's beloved daughter, Frances, after her first husband Philip Sidney died in 1586. By 1591, she had given birth to their son Robert, named for his father. After begging the queen for his first commission and with the help of William and Hatton who had not yet passed, Elizabeth gave in. With the tensions in the low countries mounting, she tasked him with leading an army in Normandy to support the French against the Spanish. But the queen was nervous of Devereux's inexperience, youth and brash nature. Ultimately, she allowed him to go, but he was sent with a number of advisors who would report back to William of the young Earl's doings and sayings. Devereux went against the queen's commands in travelling and besieging enemy territory, but in the end, he met with the French king. Though a successful encounter of great pomp, Elizabeth was furious with her favourite, who it seemed was more daring and dangerous than his step-father or mother had ever been. By September, Devereux was severely ill, but he recovered. By October, he was ignoring Elizabeth's direct orders and even knighting men. By the time he returned, he found himself at the mercy of Elizabeth's wrath and she sent him back to France, only for him to return in the beginning of 1592.[6]

Though Devereux's influence on the queen was growing, as her closest advisor was ageing, the 'Essex Faction' underestimated the level of influence and power that remained in the hands of the Cecils. However, it would be too easy to think that the Cecils themselves thought that they were untouchable. Indeed, as William got older and became less able for the mounting work expected of him, he needed Robert to keep a grip on that power. William's last years may have been his most busy, but they were also plagued by ill health and thus, periods of respite. The uncomfortable nature of his ailments never left him entirely, and it must be considered that his final years were shadowed by considerable physical pain. Robert took on many of his father's duties without any hesitation, and dove right into the preservation of the Cecil administration and thus, the Elizabethan regime.[7]

The question of whether it was assumed by all, including Elizabeth, that Robert Cecil would one day replace his father and take up all of his political duties, is rather poignant. Firstly, we must consider how Elizabeth felt about Robert's growing influence, power and ability. Why was it that she was cautious to make him principal secretary officially, despite his father's diligent training and the young man's ability for the role, when she was persuaded by the young Earl of Essex to allow him to venture out into the world and represent her and the English military, when this was an evidently disastrous notion? The answer to that may be impossible to come by. We can speculate that it was due to Elizabeth's apparent lust for Devereux – his charm and handsomeness only deepening his hold on her. But we can also view it as Elizabeth's reluctance for change and anxiety towards losing William Cecil. To knight Robert Cecil was one thing, and to allow him to take up much of his father's work unofficially was another, but to give him an official position of secretary would have pushed William further away from governmental administration, and Elizabeth was not ready to let her *Spirit* retire. Secondly, William himself was eager for Elizabeth to accept Robert as his replacement, perhaps not simply out of principal or for the legacy of the Cecil name, but rather because he feared Elizabeth taking on evil counsel once he was gone.[8] The key to avoiding the queen's corruption was to replace William Cecil with another Cecil, and in William's view, what better man than his youngest son and protégé?

In 1596, under Devereux's command, the English and Dutch captured the Spanish port of Cadiz. This was helped by the Duke of Parma's death and also the diplomacy between England and France. Though a great victory for Devereux, who was celebrated upon arriving home in July, Robert Cecil also had reason to celebrate, as he had been officially appointed the position of Principal Secretary of State, likely much to his ailing father's joy. For all of Devereux's charm, charisma and glory abroad, it was Robert Cecil who was honoured to carry the queen's signet, and as Loades states 'free to act without any commission in any matter'. One can only imagine the bitter taste in Devereux's mouth as he arrived back at court, having been cheered by the crowds of London, only to find his political enemy at the heart of English politics, and at the right-hand side or Gloriana herself. The new secretary, unlike his counterpart, was not a man to begrudge his political foes. In fact, both Roberts were happy to put their differences aside until concerns regarding the earl's conduct whilst in Cadiz arose. It was also apparent that as soon as he left, Cadiz was reclaimed. Any plunder from Cadiz found its way into Devereux's personal purse, and so, the massive expense that went into claiming the port was not for the greater good of England, but for his own glory and wealth. The cost of taking Cadiz was massive, and in the end, it was Robert Cecil who had to balance the accounts and exchequer.[9]

What Elizabeth wanted from this venture was the great deal of cargo worth around twelve million ducats. However, a fire was set so that the English could not claim the plunder they wanted and so though he had secured the town and port, he would be blamed for the loss of plunder. The queen was furious with Devereux and the fact that the people had cheered him on, only worsened her anger. His need for self-glorification outweighed his sense of duty to his country, if he even had any, and his narcissism had cost England a fortune. If it were not for the ability of Robert Cecil in finding ways to replenish the treasury, the earl may have found himself in an even more dire situation. However, within days, Devereux had convinced the queen to forgive him. He altered the narrative of the events that took place. Though it does seem he attempted to capture Spanish ships on the way home and therefore, his courage and advantageousness cannot be dismissed. William even backed the young earl when the queen wished to take his cut of the plunder in order to pay for the massive cost. This may seem an unusual act, considering Devereux's indifference towards William's son and political successor, but he was fond of him.[10]

Spanish prisoners were taken back to England as a means of ransom. This was common for the period and indeed, Devereux expected to get his cut from the profits. However, as the venture was mostly a failure due to Devereux's misjudgements, Elizabeth felt that it should have been her who reaped the profits from ransom. William was fond of Devereux, but he was not disillusioned towards the new favourite's true colours. Still, he spoke up for him and pointed out that as a rule of war, the Earl of Essex was entitled to such profits.[11] Indeed, in the end, the ransom was paid, and so was Devereux. On 22 September 1596, William wrote to Devereux regarding this matter. Here, it is clear that William was not only unwell, but also had put himself in a difficult situation by defending the earl:

> My Lord, – My hand is weak, my mind troubled, and therefore my letter must be shorter that the subject offered me…I came from the court with the burden of Her Majesty's displeasure, expressed as my L. Buckhurst and Mr. Fortescue did head with words of indignity, reproach, and rejecting of me as a miscreant and a coward, for that I would not assent to her opinion that your Lordship ought (not) to have the profit of the prisoners… [He continued:] …Her Majesty chargeth and condemneth me for favouring of you against her…[12]

Devereux's reply to William seems gracious enough, and indeed, it appears that his own fondness for William was genuine. The pair had an equally as good a relationship as William and his son, and Devereux had spent much of his childhood and adolescence in the Cecil household. It was two days later that the earl replied:

> My very good Lord…The honor your L. doth me to write upon the first notice given you, that I had sense of some unkindness form you, is greater than I could challenge…Your L. applieth to me the phrase of displeasure, and to yourself of being kept down, when both the matter and the manner of my speech was full of reverence to your L., and humble in itself. I know the weakness of mine own state; and I am striving every day to make the world know the quietness of my hurt, and the temper of my affections, so as if I should receive hurt from your Lordship, I would rather sit down with loss, than seek to right myself by contention.
>
> [He continued:]
>
> …I pray your Lordship believe that I have no ambition but her Majesty's gracious favour and the reputation of well serving her. And if your Lordship shall hear or apprehend anything that may make you think I deserve them not, if you make me know it, I will either be cleared by my just apology, or reformed, when once my fault is proved to me, and by your lordship sooner than by any man. For I have ever desired, and so do, that your Lordship were well edified of me.[13]

Towards the end of 1596, William, though tired, was appointed to a committee to discuss and negotiate the situation in the low countries and England's role in the war. The situation was becoming more strained and with Robert taking over much of William's work, he was able to eventually leave court as the strain of his work was becoming too much. He wrote to Robert on 10 October: 'I myself am so desirous to know her Majesty's pleasure whether I shall in the term time attend on her both at Court and in her service at Westminster, which will be very hard for me in regard to my weakness, which I am sure will increase towards winter. But yet I shall willingly strain myself to my uttermost to obey her commandments herein.' Regardless of William's attempts to get away from court and relax, the work of the committee followed him and there is at least one account of a meeting being held in his own home away from court, likely not outside of London, of which he probably presided over.[14]

As the Cecils and Devereux settled into some form of collaboration, which saw any tensions between the two Roberts settle for a time, there was much more to contend with than simply the Spanish and French situation. Indeed, it seems that though Mary Stuart was long buried, the ripples of her death and the remnants of the defeated Spanish Armada only served more conspiracy, strife and a struggle for the survival of the Elizabethan state. The Nine Years' War, also often referred to as Tyrone's Rebellion had begun in 1593, and would last until 1603, the year of Elizabeth's death. Though tensions between Ireland and England had been brewing for much longer, and indeed, this was not the first example of an Irish rebellion against the Tudor administration of Ireland, it was certainly the last Gaelic response to the continuation of the Tudor conquest of Ireland. Led mainly by Hugh O'Neill of Tyrone, with the support of a number of other Irish lords, their alliance was a seen as serious threat to England's national security during a time when England should have been preoccupied with the situation in the lowlands and between France and Spain in general.

The rebellious alliance was also made up mostly of Catholics who feared that the tightening of the English grip on power in Ireland would bring about the further spread of Protestantism and the destruction of the Catholic faith and church. Elizabeth, at the pinnacle of the English Protestant Church, along with her ministers and council, represented all that the Irish lords resented. By 1596, the situation in Ireland had become perilous, and the rebellious alliance that had been formed was continuing to gain members. For all of William's past diligence, this had seriously gotten out of control. By the time Robert Cecil felt that an intervention was needed, William's illness was only worsening, and the council began to panic. To restore order in Ireland, there would have to be a large military effort, under the command of a great leader. But who could lead such a campaign – a campaign that had no room for trial and error, where defeat was not possible?

Of course, many had their own ideas of who would be the best man to lead such an important expedition. Devereux, who was again in the queen's favour, suggested that George Carew was the right man for the job. However, many, including the queen, disagreed. The open opposition to the earl's idea was not uncommon during such meetings. Indeed, William had often fought to convince the queen of his own suggestions. Devereux reacted to the queen's dismissal of his suggestion in the most appalling manner. He turned his back on the queen to leave, which caused her to lose her temper and box his ears. He then reached for his sword. To draw a weapon in the presence of the queen was not only illegal, but to draw a weapon on the queen was treasonous. The men of the meeting grappled to seize Devereux and he was removed from the room. He stormed off, and though Elizabeth would later forgive him, his actions left a bad taste in the mouths of all those present and he would never fully recover from his disgrace in the eyes of the council, especially that of Robert Cecil and the ailing Lord Burghley.[15]

A year previously, O'Neill's demands on Elizabeth for a presidency or some form of authority over Ulster were denied. She refused to bow to any conspiracy or rebellion. The authorities ruling from Dublin Castle for a time remained ignorant of the true threat that the rebellion in Ulster posed. Whereas in England, William and Elizabeth became more and more anxious to avoid any idea of all-out war with Ulster if possible. It was O'Neill's request of Philip II of Spain that worried them the most. If Ireland and Spain were to form an alliance whereby Spain would invade England by using Ireland as a gateway, the situation could have been dire for England's west coast. Philip did supply an armada for O'Neill's purpose by 24 October and though it was unsuccessful, William, who was still ill and living away from court, became increasingly nervous of the implications of a Spanish-Gaelic alliance. On 31 October, he wrote to Robert:

> I neither can myself write, nor yet forbeare to expresse the grief to thinke of the dangerous estate of hir ma[jes]ties Armie in Ireland. Wheare all the treasure sent in August is expected, and the Armie consistinge of the number of abowt seaven thowsand widening [withdrawing?] paie of her ma[jes]tie, besides a great number of others having extraordinarie payments by waie of pentions such like…for which the treasurer hath never a pennie in Ireland & nowe this charge doth presentlye followe the charge of 2,000 newe men already levied and appointed to be sent thither for whome at their arrival there, there is also now monie to entertaine them…[16]

Clearly, what worried William the most was the cost in men and money, which should have been sent to and spent on the Anglo-Spanish war and the situation on the continent. The continued friction between the English, Spanish and French may have been convenient for O'Neill, but it spelled disaster for the English authorities. Especially that it was clear to all now that O'Neill had no intentions of simply remaining as a lord, but perhaps had his eye on a crown. William's language towards the end of the letter not only reveals that he was worried about the situation in Ireland greatly, but also that he was a man who believed that he was on the way out. He continued:

> What great danger this maie be I doe trembell to utter, considering theie will force the Countrie with all manner of oppressions, rather than furnishe. And thereby the multitude of the Q[ueen's] Loiall subjects in the English pale tempted to Rebell. Thes unpleasant lines I am most sorie to be presented to hir ma[jes]tie, but I cannot endure to bethink my self of the peril. ffrom my howse in the Strand this last of October, 1596...[17]

William's relationship with Ireland is an interesting one. The English government had so far resisted any crisis between Ireland and England. There had been previous moments of strife, but not as organised and powerfully represented as O'Neill's rebellion. Also, Ireland and England may have been sister islands, and indeed shared a long history of colonisation, warfare and social change, but Tudor Ireland was culturally and socially very different than England. William, out of every previous chief advisor to the Tudor monarchs, was the most intent on working alongside the Irish and those settled within the pale to govern Ireland. This is a topic not often enough discussed by historians, especially Irish nationalist historians. This is not surprising however, considering William's position towards France, Scotland and Spain during his career. Indeed, he hardly had the time to make the impact he likely wished on Ireland as a neighbouring island. William, unlike Devereux, never travelled to Ireland. But his interest in its ruling families' genealogy, history, and even geography is evident. He spent many years compiling maps of Ireland. However, his interest in the geography of the island likely played a part in his efforts to overcome rebellions and possible alliances with Spain as he had with England and Wales. Indeed, if he knew the ruling families, their history and where they were located, then it would be much easier to intercept any rebellion or conflict. He was even made the chancellor of Ireland's first university. His work as a genealogist and historian of Irish history may seem unusual, but it was due to both his interest in the topic and the benefit of knowing the country and its rebellious inhabitants from which it originated.[18]

By 1598, Ireland was fully involved in the Anglo-Spanish conflict. William had remained ill for much of this time, although continued to work where and when he could. Robert Cecil had been to France and had returned with the report that Henry IV and Philip of Spain had long been in private negotiations. If France and Spain were to ally themselves and bring Ireland into the fold, England would again be alone against the might of Catholic Europe. Devereux wanted to take immediate action, but most felt this was irrational and the council wished to avoid any further destruction or war. William, above all else at this stage of his life, wanted peace. England could not afford to continue in a war with Spain, France or Ireland. The queen still favoured the Earl of Essex but had become weary of his bad attitude, hunger for power and lust for warfare and bloodshed.[19] The memory of the earl drawing his sword on the queen remained at court and the council's patience with Devereux was wearing thin.

William Cecil's last days are some of the fewest recorded in terms of his own writings within the Cecil Papers. His correspondence with many of his friends and confidantes becomes sparse, besides that of his communications with either his son or the queen, and some to the Earl of Essex. He did attend meetings but for the most part, he remained away from court at his own private households. He did miss one meeting in January 1597 if the records are correct, and indeed, he was away for much of February and March. Most letters regarding state affairs were directly sent to Robert, but that does not mean that William gave up all official duties to his son entirely. He most certainly trusted him with the affairs of state, but his loyalty and razor-sharp mind never faded throughout his physical decline.

When Christopher Hatton died, along with his old friend Lord Cobham, who happened to be Robert Cecil's father-in-law, William's physical ailments were not all that plagued him. He had lost two of his daughters, his beloved wife, his mother and many of his close friends and confidantes by his final year. He was by this time seventy-seven years old – an ancient age for the Elizabethan period where the average lifespan was between forty and forty-two years old. By the end of the year, his attendance at court and council meetings fluctuated. In August, he missed most of the month of work, but by September he seemed to come back to himself. Then in October, he missed many meetings and then for the final two months of the year he was again in attendance. The queen herself was by this time an old woman, and her relationship with her *Spirit* remained as strong as ever. They had had their disagreements and there was many a time when William was out of her favour, but he kept his word from the moment he entered into her service and gave her sound and practical advice for more than forty years. No other advisor had ever served a Tudor monarch for so long, and indeed, no Tudor had reigned as long as Elizabeth. A feat which in itself owed much to William's success as a statesman, a loyal subject and an eager counsellor and mentor. During the moments where William was able to attend Privy Council meetings and attended court, the queen was present, and it must have occurred to her that her most loyal servant was not long for the world.[20]

William stopped writing in his diary by January 1597. Why exactly he stopped at this point is unknown but it is likely that he believed it would be his final year. He remained dutiful but detached somewhat. He had accomplished many triumphs during his long life, but he was unable to resolve the issue of the Irish Rebellion. This would be left to Robert. It was perhaps equally as tragic for William that he was unable to bring Robert and the Earl of Essex together. It appears that Elizabeth too felt that the end was nigh for her old friend, and instructed Charles Howard, the Lord Admiral, to write to William on her behalf, thanking him for his years of service and loyalty:

> Her Majesty commanded me to write this to your Lordship, that you do not give her so many thanks for that she did to your son, as she giveth herself for the doing that which may any way comfort you. And also to give your Lordship thanks from her for your kind and most dutiful letter – and saying although you have brought up your son as near as may be like unto yourself for her service, yet are you to her in all things and shall be Alpha and Omega. Her Majesty also prayeth your Lordship that you will forebear the travail of your hand, though she is sure you will not of your head for her service.
>
> Her Majesty… prayeth your Lordship to use all the rest possible you may, that you may be able to serve her at the time that cometh...

It is likely that Elizabeth still had some hope that he could recover however. Clearly, the Lord Admiral was moved and felt that he was unable to portray the emotion conveyed by Elizabeth as she dictated this letter and he ended by adding:

> My honourable lord, let me crave pardon that for want of memory cannot so fully write her Majesty's gracious words… It sufficient that your Lordship knoweth her excellency and my weakness to express it: but I protest my heart was so filled with her kind speeches as I watered my eyes…[21]

For much of 1598, William's health fluctuated. He continued to attend council meetings where possible for much of July but by the end of the summer, he remained in his house on the Strand. It wasn't Theobalds, as he likely wished, but he was able to shut himself away comfortably and yet remained as close to the queen and council as possible. The man who had once been so strong, with a love of life and hunger for knowledge, grew weaker by the day. He took to his bed and there he stayed. Gout had plagued him for decades, but towards the end, William began to also complain of a pain in his chest.[22] Up until his last couple of days, he continued to dictate letters and accounts, never fully ending his servitude to the queen. Besides aches and pains, the old statesman seems to have been wracked by some mental strain in his final weeks and days. As Read mentions: '...he [William] seems to have been much troubled by discontentment and grief of mind, which caused him oftentimes with tears to wish for death'.[23]

William's greatest desire was to leave England, Elizabeth and the reign that he had worked so hard to build and protect, safe. The fact that he knew he was dying and was unable to do so knowing that Elizabeth would remain safe is probably the most tragic factor of his departure. However, when the queen knew he would not rise again from his bed, she was said to have visited him in his final days to comfort him, even feeding him with her own hands. William's reaction to his mistress's gesture is magnificently preserved in what would be his final encounter with the woman he had served for decades, and poignantly, likely one of the last if not the last letter to his son Robert, addressed: 'To my Vearie Lovinge Sonne Sir Robert Cecil...'. It reads:

> Thiugh I knowe yow connt it yowr duty, in nature so continually, to shew you carefull of my state of helth, Yet war also unnatural, if I showed not tak comfort therby, and to besek almighty God to bless yow with supply of such blessynges, as I can not in this infirmyte yeld yow.
>
> Only I pay yow diligently and effectually. Let hir Ma[jes]ty understand how hir singular kyndnes doth overcome my power to accept it. Who though she will not be a mother, yet she sheweth hirself by fedyng me with hir own princely hand, as a carefull Nurss and if I may be wayned to fede my self, I shallbe more redy to serve hir on earth. if not I hope to be in heaven, a servitor for hir and Gods church and so I thank yow for yowr partriches...

It is his last line of this letter that is a true testament to the man that William was, his duty, loyalty and his faith never faltering: 'Serve God by serving of the Quene for all other service is in dede bondage to the devil…Your languishing father, W. Burghley'.[24]

William Cecil may have been Elizabeth's most loyal subject and councillor, but she, his family and much of the English nation was just as loyal to him. On his last day on earth, his living children and grandchildren remained by his bedside, praying and awaiting the inevitable. William himself, recited the Lord's Prayer in his final hours, before drifting into a sleep from which he would never wake. William Cecil, Lord Burghley, the great statesman and perhaps the founder of the Elizabethan and Early Modern British State, died in the early hours of 4 August 1598. He had not yet reached his seventy-eighth birthday. He had lived an incredibly long and eventful life, and had served his country and his queen to his utmost ability. He left behind his two surviving sons and many grandchildren who were no doubt devastated by his death as he had likely been by the death of his grandfather, David Cecil. His close friend William Camden lamented his death and wrote that he was 'a most excellent man'.[25] The people of England likely never knew how great a debt they owed him. Yet he passed in his own bed, surrounded by a loving family and loyal friends – a privilege which had not been granted to many an advisor to a Tudor monarch.

Elizabeth's reaction to William's death is telling in terms of how she valued him not only as a councillor but as a friend. Her reaction was much like that of the death of Robert Dudley or the Duke of Anjou. The queen had not publicly been able to lament the deaths of these two latter men, and upon Walsingham's death, she mourned little. But the death of William Cecil devastated her. For months after William's death, Elizabeth was seen to openly shed tears for the loss of her old friend and adviser. Robert Cecil, though clearly grieved by his father's death, was already grieving the death of his beloved wife Elizabeth. The situation in Ireland continued to take up his time and as tensions mounted, he likely heard his father's final words of advice ringing in his ear. He had no time for sorrow, that could wait.[26] William's body lay in state for six days before being transported up the Great North Road. Funeral rights were performed at Westminster Abbey but also at Stamford, where he was buried at St Martin's Church. Both funerals were performed with great splendour and pomp, and no expense was spared.[27]

William Cecil had left an everlasting legacy, his genius, shrewd character and ability to survive and prosper through four of the five Tudor reigns continue to fascinate historians and readers alike. Yet the man behind the often cold and stern exterior was one who loved life, was deeply religious and a devoted husband, father and loyal friend. His relationship with Elizabeth and the extent of his true power continue to spark discussions and debate amongst scholars, yet his unwavering sense of duty and loyalty to the crown has never been and can never be doubted. Now the reins of power and influence transferred from one Cecil to another. His son Thomas may have inherited the title, but Robert Cecil inherited something far greater and longer-lasting than a barony. William Cecil carved out the foundations of the Cecil dynasty, but Robert Cecil was far more daring and ruthless than his father, and it was he who would cement and preserve the Cecil legacy.

Chapter 11

The Cecil Succession

When William Cecil died, he left behind a much safer, richer and prosperous England than he had been born into. Once the old statesman was gone, his legacy took on two different forms, went in two different directions. On one hand, there was his son Thomas from his first marriage to Mary Cheke. Thomas was William's designated heir to his estate, titles and fortune based on the age-old practice of primogeniture where the eldest son inherited his father's title(s) and everything else that came along. All of William's children had grown up in privileged circumstances. Though Thomas was well educated at home, he was not the brightest Cecil, and as he grew up, he became somewhat of a disappointment to his father, given the fact that he was to inherit most of William's wealth and houses. Before Robert was born in 1563, during Elizabeth's early reign, Thomas was William's only heir and he may have worried that he would be his only son. However, it may have been William's fault that his first son became somewhat of a lout and was only successful much later in life after marrying Dorothy. William himself admitted that perhaps he could have been a better father stating: 'I never showed any fatherly fancy to him but in teaching and correcting.' It likely didn't help that William grieved deeply for the loss of Thomas's mother and therefore it could be suggested that while caught up in his grief, he neglected his only child and the only part of Mary he had left. Indeed, as Loades states, by the time William later married Mildred, there was already a distance between father and son. Mildred undoubtedly would not have helped the situation, given that she was not the warmest individual.[1]

It seems rather unfair that Thomas has been branded as the least successful of the Cecil children. Though he was more modest than his father and brother, he was nonetheless a successful politician and courtier and was given the title of Earl of Exeter during the reign of James I. Thomas married twice, and children came from both marriages, despite him marrying his second wife when he was seventy years old. Indeed, as a Cecil, Thomas mattered greatly to Elizabeth's successor as much as his brother Robert. Robert may have been the shrewd politician and genius like his father, and was also made the Earl of Shrewsbury during the new king's reign, but Thomas carried on the Burghley name, title and legacy. His own son would inherit the political role that meant so much to William and therefore, the contrast between both brothers should be regarded as a positive, for both preserved their father's dynastic legacy in different ways. Smith's interpretation that Thomas was 'stupid' in comparison to Robert who was 'capable and assiduous' lacks substance and depth and any interest in understanding the successes of Thomas Cecil's career as a military man, rather than an astute, political weapon which William had molded Robert to be.[2] Indeed, Loades also concurs that though Thomas lacked his father's genius, nor had the 'aptitude for study' like Robert, he would have done much better if educated in a more militarily focused household, of which William had many connections.[3]

Thomas Cecil's marriage was probably the making of him, although the current interpretation of him as a wayward youth and good-for-nothing is likely misinterpreted and William's reaction to his son's affairs and conduct in France as a young man were likely over-dramatic. Either way, Thomas and his first wife Dorothy had thirteen children, ten of who survived to adulthood. Given that infant mortality was extremely high during the period, it is likely that Dorothy carried even more children that we do not know of that resulted in miscarriage or stillbirth which were also common. Dorothy was a relation of Sir Henry Percy and therefore, her connections to the nobility and high society not only suited William when he matched his eldest son and heir, but it likely suited Thomas himself as she was considered quite the looker, and according to Sir Henry Percy himself, was 'very wise, sober of behaviour and womanly'. Their marriage lasted until Dorothy died in c.1609. In 1610, Thomas married his much younger second wife who eventually produced one child – a girl named Georgiana who died in infancy.

Thomas's political career was extremely successful. By the time his younger brother Robert was born in 1563, he was already an MP for Stamford and later represented it again twice. He was elected in 1584 for Lincoln and 1592 for Northamptonshire respectively. Though talented, his offices were likely given due to the influence of his father. How much William Cecil influenced both of his son's careers is uncertain, but it must be stated that their successes were due to their own abilities more than that of their father's influence, as after his death, both Cecil men continued to have successful careers and happy lives. Indeed, in hindsight, William may have been shocked but delighted in the successes of his two heirs.[4]

Thomas may well have been a talented politician, but he was a solid soldier and officer before all else. He proved useful several times during rebellions such as that in 1569, and tensions abroad such as the war in the Netherlands. Elizabeth I herself favoured Thomas and knighted him in 1575, and it would be he who protected her against the possibility of invasion during the Spanish Armada by acting as colonel and forming a special army to defend the queen's 'person'. Later, he would assist his own brother, despite their differences, during the Essex Rebellion, and he was instrumental in crushing it. Under his brother's regime, just one year after William's death, he became Lord President of York, and later a member of King James's Privy Council. To conclude on Thomas Cecil's successes, he was a family man, a good politician, an officer and later, surprisingly studious. Overall, he may not have inherited his father's genius as did Robert, but he did mirror him in many ways and proved to be successful. He even inherited his father's lifelong ailment – gout! Indeed, it may even be stated that he would have made his father proud. Many Cecil biographers would claim that Thomas was a man of 'ordinary ability' or 'undistinguished'. However, as Richard Milward has pointed out, Thomas became a success despite his rather lonely childhood and distant father. He had a large, happy family and was well liked by Elizabeth I and James I. He was less severe as an individual as his father or brother and was known to be generous. By the time he had died, he was one of the richest men in England and as he had so many children, including sons, he was able to preserve his father's bloodline and dynastic legacy in a way which Robert Cecil could not – by passing on the title of Lord Burghley.[5]

Robert Cecil, his career, personal life and dedication to protecting Elizabeth I's legacy and creating a new Stuart legacy has fascinated historians, authors and readers for decades if not centuries. He is known to have been far more ruthless, zealous and rigid than his father. Yet, it might surprise many that there was more to this man than his religion and politics – just like there was much more to his father than how we view him as the old statesman. Robert Cecil was born during the early years of Elizabeth's reign – a much safer one than that of his elder half-brother Thomas. By the time Robert was being tutored at home by Michael Hicks, his father was working hard to preserve the integrity of the Elizabethan reign and the Protestant faith. The fact that he was born into such an era and undoubted privilege as the younger son of the most powerful man in England, actually served him quite well. Robert, despite his health issues that no doubt worried his parents greatly, was notably scholarly, studious and dutiful, much to his father's delight. He excelled in languages, philosophy, cosmography and theology – especially Protestant theology. By the time his father became Lord Burghley, Robert was showing signs of true genius.

He likely attended Saint John's at Cambridge and followed one of his tutors there when he reached an appropriate age. Despite his physical disability, he would not be held back and as well as becoming a successful student, he made many life-long friends that would serve him well in the future. In every way, he attempted to emulate if not outdo his father from an early age.[6]

By the late 1590s when William's health was declining and the Spanish threat was once again emerging – not that it had ever really gone away, Robert had established himself as a useful and tactful member of Elizabeth's council. In 1596, he officially became her secretary of state, yet his abilities were far greater, and his father could see this. William's success with regards to the fall and execution of Mary Stuart and the defeat of the Spanish Armada cannot be doubted, but this did not mean that Spain was no longer a threat, or that another armada could be formed. Indeed, when the second armada was defeated, and English forces remained on the defensive, it was down to Robert's ability to intercept foreign intelligence. The web of informants that he spun would make Francis Walsingham's look meager, and by 1597, he had agents in several corners of Europe, infiltrating Spanish intelligence and it was one of these informants that had discovered the plot for the second armada in 1596. In many ways, Robert's training under his father had prepared him for multiple plots and dangers that William could never have even predicted at such an age. Where William was careful to employ trustworthy men such as Walsingham, Robert himself became a blend of both shrewd politician and ruthless theorist. Indeed, as Alford mentions: 'So expertly trained by his father in every aspect of government business, Sir Robert was a practical man as well as a theorist: he decided what information he needed to know and the best ways he could devise to discover it.'[7]

Robert Cecil's relationship with the Elizabethan government – subjects, Elizabeth's favourites and the queen herself – differed somewhat to that of his father's, and the explanation is rather simple. William Cecil had risen wholly on his own accord, ability and perhaps some luck. His father and grandfather were indeed already connected to Margaret Beaufort, Henry VII and Henry VIII before William's career even began to take shape. However, Robert had grown up knowing no other world than that of which his father was a leader. He was educated and groomed to fit his father's wishes so that he would one day succeed him politically. Though there are some historians who suggest William's hand in Robert's success or opportunities was not to the extent one may think, the fact remains, he was his father, and had no hope of ever leaving his political legacy to Thomas, however well he may have turned out in the end. Furthermore, William was not as outwardly defensive, fierce and staunchly anti-Catholic and zealously Protestant as the son he had indoctrinated to be. Even prior to the armada, William came under scrutiny in the summer of 1585, as part of a campaign to displace his influence. He was defamed and accused of not being as committed to the preservation of Protestantism as he should have been. We know now in hindsight that there was no other man in the kingdom of England who wished to preserve the Elizabethan state and the Protestant cause more than Lord Burghley, but he was not understood this way by a large portion of the public, and therefore this slander suited his opposition. This was when it became clear that many felt England was ruled by the Cecils and was referred to by William's opponents as *'Regnum Cecilianum'*. By the time Robert's education was complete, and he had joined his father in a bid to learn all he could to succeed him, the fact that he rose to prominence, favour and success so easily, so rapidly, increased this slander and ideology towards a ruling Cecil dynasty. There may have been a degree of respect for William Cecil by the time he died, even by those who opposed his influence, but that level of respect would never be owed to his youngest son, and Robert would have to navigate the waters of politics, favouritism and treachery to preserve his family name in history.[8]

As Read stated, William Cecil 'did his best for his offspring, but much of what he did turned out to be wrong'. Indeed, Thomas Cecil may have turned out well in the end, but that was likely much to do with his wife's influence, and even so, he was not as politically astute as his younger half-brother. Ann and Elizabeth had both married, yet both died young and Ann left children of her own behind. Ann's dreadful marriage caused a scandal, and Elizabeth barely lived long enough to cause any. Robert it seems, was the exception of a rather dysfunctional family. Robert was sent to Paris in 1584, to spend time with Sir Edward Stafford, as his brother had. Where Thomas had sowed his oats and apparently disgraced himself and his father's name, Robert bloomed. He expanded his knowledge of the world, satisfied his inherited hunger for knowledge and influence, and had made a number of notable contacts by the time he returned to England. He was elected to Parliament before his twentieth birthday and in 1588, William gave him a commission in the low countries to discuss a peace treaty. Indeed, it seems that by the time his father was dying, having been thoroughly educated for the job, on good terms with the queen, a diplomat of high standing, and having sat in parliament on at least five occasions, there can be no doubt that Robert Cecil was ready to take on the reins of power and steadily steer England into a new era. Despite the growing hostility to Cecil power and influence, Robert would bring Elizabeth through some of her darkest, and ultimately, her final years.[9]

So, we know Robert had a close relationship with his father, we know he was successful and gifted despite his physical afflictions, and we know that he shared his father's vision for England. But what made him different from his father, and brother? And how did the Cecil brother's aim to live up to their father's great name?

By 1582, though William had many years left in him, he was probably urged to write up instructions for Robert for when he was gone, and he had actually done the same for Thomas at some point. William's last will and testament was extremely detailed and covered everything he could possibly think of. He went over it and re-wrote it many times. Firstly, his burial was most important to him, but it was not to exceed the sum of a thousand pounds. Secondly, by right, Thomas Cecil inherited the title of Lord Burghley, and therefore Burghley House and its accompanying Lincolnshire estate and the larger family home in London. Robert, his *de facto* political heir, inherited the properties at Theobalds and Rutland and all of the Hertfordshire estates. He did not instantly become the Lord Treasurer, but he was given the office of the Master of the Court of Wards. This offered a grand revenue, of which Robert was not humble enough to decline. However, neither was he as eager to profit from such an office as his father had. He had his own home in London and did not need the properties he inherited, but inherit them he did. William's daughter Ann's children Susan and Bridget were also provided for in terms of furnishings and generous dowries. He also provided for his sister Anne in terms of lands and annuity. All in all, William's scrupulous nature comes through in this document. His final wishes were granted to every inch of his specifications and indeed, he did his best to provide for his sons and remaining family as equally and generously as possible. What his will eluded were his concerns with his political legacy in Robert as well as his genealogical, dynastic legacy in Thomas. In his final provisions and requests, William Cecil was laying the foundations for his children's futures, and that of their children and children's children. Despite Thomas being his official heir, it is evident that in the end he held no preference, despite being closer to Robert, especially in his final years.[10]

Robert Cecil had much more to contend with than the opinions and opposition of other courtiers and nobles, who wanted the power and influence once harnessed by the late Lord Burghley. The queen herself had become melancholic, unpredictable, and as Croft has pointed out, much more autocratic.[11] Another main issue was England's difficult financial situation. Lord Burghley may have been loyal and scrupulous, but he was not above meddling with his own taxes. Indeed, before his death, a crisis over embezzlement, monopolies and financial corruption had risen. William had been covering up this corruption for years, and as his life began to fade away, and his lasting legacy became more important than ever, it was revealed that a large amount of courtiers, nobles and other elite families had been using crown money for their own luxurious lifestyles and advancement. Even William 'fiddled with his taxes'. The queen's monopoly grants, which were meant to protect and fund lucrative industries, only led to further corruption, inflation and misuse of the crown's money. The queen asked for several grants to be investigated but the chain of corruption was so long that in the end nothing was done. William had been complacent for so long. But as tensions boiled over, he agreed with the queen that something had to be changed. In the end, changes were made, but they were so subtle that most monopoly grants remained the same as they had before.[12]

Robert put all of his energy into his newfound position. He had tragically lost his wife Elizabeth, also the queen's goddaughter, in 1597 who he had married in 1589. The couple were happily married and had two children, a son named William for his grandfather, and a daughter named Frances. Though he was a warm and loving father, his children were the least of his worries by the end of 1598, his priorities were elsewhere, and his grief did not last long. Robert was keen to see an end to the conflict in Ireland, but found it difficult to keep up with his mistress's changing moods, favouritism for the Earl of Essex, and the factions beginning to divide the court in a way that had never been seen before. Robert was in many ways like his father, but he was not as honest as him and indeed, saw no issue with rising to favour with the queen above all others if it meant advancing his own career and accomplishing his own vision for England. In this, we can see that he was more selfish than his father when it came to politics, and thus, with his grand education and grooming, he was perhaps capable of being the most dangerous politician in England. His father, mother, grandmother, sisters and wife had all died. And it was up to him to carve out a new path for the Cecil family. His brother could enjoy the grandeur of the barony and the houses and style that came with it. William had created perhaps the most perfect Tudor minister in Robert. Essex may have been Elizabeth's favourite, but Robert could offer her something far greater than looks and charm. By mid-1599, Robert had settled well into his new position, and was working to come to a peace treaty with Spain. This was something that Devereux could not offer the queen, who had already left for Ireland.[13]

Philip III, the new king of Spain, was willing to negotiate peace with England on the condition that the English traders leave the Netherlands.

Where William and Philip II were unwilling to see eye to eye and negotiate, Robert and Philip III were not their fathers, and at this stage, peace suited them both. But neither were willing to concede to the other's conditions, and Robert was well aware that the money taken in from trade in Antwerp was necessary to expand the English treasury following the revelation of the monopolies scandal. While negotiations had stalled, it then became clear that Robert had more to worry about than England's financial situation, for it was reported that a Spanish fleet had landed an army on the Isle of Wight. Though it turned out to be a fleet of fishermen rather than a revival of an armada, the panic that ensued from the report made Robert realise how vulnerable England remained. Elizabeth was ageing beyond recognition, new men were rising at court, new kings were treading the waters, and the great Cecil name was in danger of being overshadowed by the rise of the Earl of Essex. Robert's intelligence web that he had inherited from his father and Francis Walsingham had failed him this time, but he would make sure that this never occurred again. And while Devereux likely thought that he could do no wrong in the queen's eyes, and would bring victory to her final years, his delusions and fancies would soon be revealed, and Robert Cecil would become her Alpha and Omega.[14]

But what was Robert Cecil's relationship with the queen? How close were they? And what impact would this have on the fate of Devereux and England? By 1590, Robert Cecil was on the rise, and though there was no sign at this point of his father slowing down to the extent he later would, he was well-trained for a life in politics. He may have only been twenty-seven, but he had already taken his seat in parliament. It is important to note that these years behind the scenes were crucial to polishing off Robert for a life in service to the crown. It has been suggested by Loades and indeed, others, that it was the death of Francis Walsingham that really allowed Robert to fade from obscurity and make his mark on the world. However, it was likely mere coincidence that Robert's star began to rise at the same time that one had fallen.

Though there is no doubt that Walsingham's death influenced this shift in office, it must also be noted that Robert treaded the waters carefully, and did not take up the position of secretary officially for some time. Indeed, it could be said that he remained in the background, now doing more work than ever, but without the prestige or honours. It must also be remembered that Robert was groomed for his position, and that his expensive education was indeed intended to prepare him for a life of public service, and service to the queen. The next year, Elizabeth would take notice of the young man, and wish to know him better. She did just that when she visited Theobalds for ten days. By 1596, he had been knighted and secured the office of principal secretary officially, just in the nick of time before his father's death some two years later.[15]

Elizabeth clearly favoured Robert to an extent, and though he was more frigid than his father, he likely reminded the queen of a younger Lord Burghley, especially when his father had passed, along with many other contemporaries of the queen's. Robert's deformity – his hunched back and unusually short stature, even for the time, made him a target for cruel remarks and mockery. Elizabeth's favouritism for him and reliance on his abilities did little to help. Francis Bacon portrayed Robert as a savage, deformed slave and 'a born Devil'. The queen herself even nicknamed him 'Elf' and the more commonly known 'Pygmy'. To be nicknamed by Elizabeth was considered an honour. Many of her courtiers and favourites had their own pet names. Though he outwardly accepted the queen's cruel names, he may have been inwardly hurt by them. Indeed, as Guy has mentioned, Robert told his father that the reason he did not 'dislike' the name was because 'she gives it'. By this he was indicating that as Elizabeth was queen, he ought not to dislike it.[16]

Elizabeth had long established favourites throughout her reign, it was no secret. Lord Robert Dudley, Earl of Leicester and William Cecil were only two of many. Both had known the queen before her accession, and she valued their friendship and advice in different ways. There may have been some sense of rivalry between the pair, but they were able to come together when necessary and towards the end of Dudley's life, they had long reconciled their differences. The debate on whether court factions existed during Elizabeth's reign has continued for decades, with Read and Neale arguing for factionalism throughout the Elizabethan reign. Simon Adams argued that at the root of such analysis, there is the problem of authorial bias from the sources used due to the popularity of writings about kingship and corruption during the late sixteenth century and seventeenth century. Natalie Mears has demonstrated that though factionalism dominated Elizabeth's brother's reign due to the conflict between the two domineering protectors, that her early reign was not subject to such definitive splits in terms of religion and policy, but the latter years of her reign may indeed have been subject to factionalism.[17]

So what does this mean? And what does it say about Robert's relationship with Elizabeth and how it differed from his father's? During William's tenure at Elizabeth's side, the political, religious and social situations differed greatly than that of the 1590s. In particular, during the 1560s, Dudley was preoccupied with Elizabeth in an intimate nature that also differed greatly from that of his stepson's with the elderly queen. Elizabeth and Dudley had known one another for many years, and as many would believe, their relationship went deeper than that of a platonic friendship. One could even go as far as stating that during the 1560s, Elizabeth and Dudley were romantically committed. This is not to say that their relationship was sexual in nature, but it can most certainly be stated that it differed greatly than her relationship with William Cecil, whom the queen also admired and trusted for different reasons. The two men clashed, but this never resulted in dividing the court and it never really became a topic of public scrutiny. William wanted to push England into a new age and was preoccupied with the succession and the queen's marriage. Dudley, already a man of reverence with a good military standing, wanted to simply be a part of that world and share it with Elizabeth. These two very different relationships with two very different men did not lead to two warring factions, simply because it was not necessary.

However, by the time the 1590s were coming to a close, Elizabeth was an old woman, with an ever-changing mood. Robert Devereux had been her favourite for a number of years and though he had pushed her on a number of occasions, she always forgave his arrogance. Robert Cecil, on the other hand, was preoccupied with much of the same issues his father had – the succession, the situation in Europe and the future of the Protestant state. The reason why the issue of factionalism arose in the latter years of Elizabeth's reign therefore was due to the very thing that concerned her the most – her age. As she aged, so did others, and many of the men that had come up with her at the time of her accession were dead and buried. Elizabeth had always been a vane woman, and as she aged, the idea of a dalliance with the young, handsome and charming Earl of Essex took over any notion of sensibility she had left. Of course, the situation was much more complicated than this, but most notably, Elizabeth's fragility allowed Devereux to establish a serious amount of power and influence at court and within the council. Indeed, as this led to his leadership in the military support of the Dutch and French Protestants during the conflict on the continent, the Earl of Essex became more than just a favourite, but a figurehead in his own right. Something that Robert Dudley and William Cecil had never done, and something that Robert Cecil had not considered doing. Therefore, the idea that Elizabeth's favouritism of both Robert Cecil and Robert Devereux in the latter years of her reign did not result in court factionalism must be re-considered.[18]

The relationship between Robert Cecil and Robert Devereux also changed after William's death. Both men, though in their own ways aggrieved by the loss of the great statesman, were also liberated. Robert was now free to take the reins of Elizabethan polity, and though he moved through the ranks slowly, and many questioned his new found position, his accession to his father's station was definitive as Elizabeth needed him. With William now gone, Devereux also had greater influence on Elizabeth. This is not to say that the rivalry between both men meant that they could not work together. Indeed, both pressed the queen to elevate Francis Bacon to Solicitor-General. Why Robert Cecil would push for the advancement of a man who previously publicly ridiculed him is uncertain, but it is likely that he was more concerned with the benefits of this politically rather than any personal biases. The queen opposed the idea either way, but this small matter shows that both men had a vision for England, and sometimes shared the same concerns and ideas. But who was to blame for this shift in influence and factionalism? The truth is, if we are to go down the road of blaming individuals for the catastrophic final years of Robert Devereux's life, we must look to Lord Burghley and Elizabeth as the culprits. Despite all the warning signs, William favoured Devereux and allowed his rise to prominence and favouritism without much concern for the political implications it could bring about. Elizabeth is also to blame as she knew that with William gone, a factional split in the court amongst favourites, eyeing up the vacant position of power, was very possible, if not probable. Two factions forming behind two men of great power and influence could pose a threat to Elizabeth's own position – something she would learn the hard way.[19]

Chapter 12

Crisis and Rebellion

Robert had reason to worry about the Earl of Essex, his supporters and the queen's blindness to his lust for power. On 25 March 1599, Robert Devereux was appointed Lieutenant and Governor-General of Ireland. By the time he arrived in Dublin he was unwell, but he was now at the very pinnacle of his power. With the war to contend with, he commanded a colossal army of around 19,000, including both men and horse, to attack Tyrone in the north. But there was already rebellion within the Province of Leinster anyway and reinforcements were needed. The plan of attack was agreed upon by the queen and council, and he had much success while en route despite meeting much resistance. However, he was dismayed by the lack of Elizabeth's support and in a letter he lamented this and those at court. Though Robert Cecil had the queen's ear while Devereux was away, if the earl thought that the lack of Elizabeth's gratitude had anything less to do with his own lack of competency, he was deluded. He knighted many men, though he had been commanded not to, and he had not dealt with the Earl of Tyrone as Elizabeth had wished, despite being in Ireland for over three months. Devereux wanted to return to court but Elizabeth would not allow it and wanted him to continue on in what had become an expensive venture.[1]

What Elizabeth and Robert had intended to be a great victory to bring an end to the Irish rebellion was truly nothing short of a disaster. All the earl had done was cause chaos and destruction where it was not necessary, and spend a fortune on supplies and men that served little purpose. Robert was slow to realise the true severity of Devereux's situation in Ireland. But when the earl returned to Dublin, and wrote to the queen of his despair for the situation that he himself had created, Elizabeth was quick to act. She knew the earl's next move would pose some serious consequences. She ordered him to remain in Ireland and to see out his duty as had been outlined – attack Tyrone and the rebels in the North, and bring an end to the conflict that had thus far costed an absolute fortune.

Unfortunately, by the time the letter was put in Devereux's hands, his army had broken up significantly, with many of his men leaving Ireland and returning to England. It was a spectacular failure, and it was Devereux's fault. It was clear that he wanted to return to court to keep the queen's favour, but it was out of the question. Eventually, Tyrone offered to negotiate with the earl for peace. This was negotiated in person on 7 September. The earl certainly had the best intentions and wanted to find a way to protect Elizabeth and her power in Ireland. Of that there is no doubt. However, the lack of an official witness to this agreement gave Elizabeth cause for anxiety. Devereux's trust in Tyrone was apparent but the queen knew the word of a rebel had to be taken with a pinch of salt. This anxiety was further elevated due to the reports of Philip III's plans to send a new armada to defeat England, and possibly use the east coast of Ireland as a back door into England for a full-scale invasion.[2]

The Earl of Essex's irrational behaviour has often perplexed historians, just as it must have astonished Elizabeth and Robert Cecil back in England. His paranoia and bad counsel clearly culminated in a military disaster that should have been a success. It is evident that he even considered returning home with his army in a rush prior to meeting with Tyrone, in order to regain the queen's favour and confront his enemies at court – men who were genuinely interested in the protection and preservation of the state. Robert Cecil may have been somewhat more self-serving than his father when it came to his position and politics, but if anyone can be accused of having been self-serving, it was Robert Devereux. He may have been loyal to the queen, and genuinely wanted to succeed on her behalf, but his loyalty had a cost. Absolute favouritism. Robert Cecil's duty held no such condition. The fact that the number of men and high cost of the venture was to crush Tyrone's rebellion once and for all – yet had not due to the earl's incompetence, was too much for Elizabeth to bear, despite her favouritism for him. However, it was also his disobedience that shocked her. He had also negotiated terms with Tyrone of his own imaginings without consulting the queen or council. All in all, his actions had thus far proved rather more treasonous than victorious.[3]

The existing evidence suggests that Cecil and his cronies in England were not in fact working against the Essex campaign (for, why would they?), but were as eager as the queen for his success as there were more pressing matters to deal with other than Ireland. Indeed, it seems that though Devereux has dismissed the queen's orders to directly take on Tyrone, not to knight men or bestow favour, and that negotiating with the enemy without royal approval was dangerous, the act of negotiation was somewhat successful. Cecil later wrote that it was actually the queen herself who ordered that the areas which the earl had travelled through be secured prior to meeting Tyrone head on and that the peace with Tyrone was 'so seasonably made...

as great good has grown...by it'.[4] Whatever the queen's true thoughts on Devereux's disastrous campaign, he soon returned to England, despite the queen's orders that he remain in Ireland until the true nature of Tyrone's peace terms were understood. Elizabeth was at this moment staying at Nonsuch palace, the pleasure palace that her father had built during his mid-reign. However, there was nothing pleasurable about Devereux's next encounter with the queen. By 24 September, he was again on English soil.

Four days later on the morning of 28 September, Elizabeth's ladies were busy readying the queen for the day. Elizabeth often took hours to get ready and by the time she met with Cecil, a true transformation had taken place. Nobody but the queen's ladies had ever seen the process of this transformation take place, and to all who beheld her image at court, she must have always seemed perfectly put together. On the morning of his arrival, without any ceremony or permission, Devereux barged his way into the queen's privy chamber, where nothing but a thin, frail and balding old woman sat as her ladies attended to her. The earl himself was far from dashing as he hadn't changed his travelling clothes since setting off from Ireland days earlier. The queen was taken aback by her favourite's outburst, but kept her composure and insisted that she would dine with him once she was ready. However, as Elizabeth continued to dress, and transformed into Gloriana, her anger boiled over.[5]

Meanwhile, Robert Cecil was also busying himself. He had recently been working on intercepting Philip III's apparent invasion fleet but was sorely let down by his own informants. There would be no second great defeat over a Spanish Armada for Robert to match that of his father's. However, on the morning of Devereux's intrusion, Cecil was called by the queen, who needed him at her side. When he arrived, the queen was again perfectly put together and composed. She was sure that the earl's outburst was not a part of any coup, and thus she could deal with him personally. Devereux was summoned before the queen and her council. He must have begun to realise what he had actually done that morning as his erratic behaviour had somewhat calmed. Yet he remained outwardly delusional as ever. He calmly explained that his actions were necessary in order to speak to the queen directly. The whole council disapproved of his behaviour and lamented him for his intrusion on the queen's person, stating that no such pressing matter should call for him to leave his position in Ireland without permission and to call on the queen's person likewise without appointment. The queen remained calm, as did Cecil, but the Earl of Essex was later apprehended and taken to York House under arrest. He was not permitted to speak to the queen or communicate with anyone outside of his holdings.[6]

The council denounced all of Devereux's actions while in Ireland. This was Robert's moment to take note of his foe's failures and from henceforth, he would take care to take record of all the earl's wrongdoings. Devereux was stripped of all his royal offices and appointments. He kept his earldom, but just about. He went from Elizabeth's favourite to her prisoner, and it was recommended that he retire from all public duties and retreat to live a quiet life away from court and out of the queen's sight and mind. This was likely more so Cecil's wish than the queen's and she soon loosened the terms of the earl's imprisonment to suit her own needs. However, the more that Robert Cecil investigated the earl's conduct and expenditure, the more Elizabeth realised that he had used her and had amounted a colossal dept that only she could realistically pay. Not only had he cost her a number of men and a lot of money in his attempt to subdue Ireland, but he had long benefitted from the queen's favouritism for him. In essence, he became too accustomed to having whatever he wanted. The basis of the earl's income was the lease of sweetwine, which allowed him to acquire a lifestyle fit for a king. Despite this grand income his depts were high and the queen had no choice but to revoke his lease in order to take financial control. Though she had loosened the terms of his incarceration, he was nonetheless a prisoner, and without his offices, income and the queen's favour, he was just a man. This likely pushed him over the edge, and it is possible that he felt that the queen's revoking of his income was a punishment. Who else could he blame but Robert Cecil?

However, if Devereux was outraged by the queen's punishments, his followers remained duly loyal to him and were out for a fight. Indeed, much of this discontent came from the suspicion and dislike of Robert Cecil more than it was for support of the Earl of Essex, but nonetheless, his cause gave purpose to the faction opposing Cecil's power.[7]

For all of Devereux's support, whether it was the result of factionalism or not, he was no military genius. The man that became the queen's favourite towards the end of her long life was indeed charming and charismatic. His sense of self-importance may have been a true sign of what we now refer to as narcissism, but time and again, his flaws surfaced. In the end, by the time he was technically under house arrest, he was desperate. It is surprising when considering his disastrous military career that he had a handful of followers at all. Yet, as soon as the queen loosened the earl's reins, and he was able to communicate with the outside world, he began to plan his comeback, or rather, his own downfall. Whether Robert Cecil was aware of the danger the earl posed at this time is unclear, but he, like many, did not trust him. Those who supported the earl were rallying around, trying to find any means of support. His own family, including his mother, Lettice Knollys, Elizabeth's lifelong enemy, was trying her best to protect her son. His wife who had recently given birth, begged for an audience with the queen, but she was ignored. The council were already in the middle of making a case against Devereux and though the queen momentarily gave him a little taste of freedom, it was something she would soon regret.[8]

Devereux's next actions were superseded by a period of physical and what would now be referred to as mental strain or illness. His period of captivity, failure in Ireland, and falling out of favour with the queen proved too much for him to bear. By January 1601, he was likely aware that Cecil was out to get him. Robert was pressing for a trial against the earl, and though Elizabeth considered it for a moment, she was likely struck with visions of the trial and execution of her cousin, which though proved successful in terms of eliminating her as a threat personally, brought on a whole new threat – the Spanish Armada. Elizabeth was aware of Devereux's support, and therefore deemed his political and financial ruin as punishment enough. However, as the earl's health recovered over the month of January, he mustered a plan that would become Robert Cecil's first great crisis, and Elizabeth's last. Devereux's supporters rallied behind him and a plan was made to force the queen to grant him access to her, and to depose what they deemed as her evil councillors – men like Cecil.[9]

However, the queen and council were far from ignorant of the earl's plans, and word spread – likely due to a combination of rumour and Robert Cecil's web of informants, that the earl was conspiring and planning some movement, of what nature at this point was unclear. They summoned the earl for questioning, but he ignored them. When men were sent out to fetch him, he refused to go with them and even took a number of hostages. It was now clear that Devereux was a serious threat to Elizabeth's safety and therefore a risk to national security. The following day, 8 February, the earl had assembled up to 200 men to lead an outright revolt against Elizabeth's council. Accounts of the actual number of men behind Devereux vary, with Leanda de Lisle stating it was somewhere around 300, but the exact number matters little. It was enough to cause more than a little chaos. Devereux's apparent wish was to protect the queen from their evils and to re-emerge as her champion. With his men rallying behind him, the Earl of Essex marched from his house on the Strand right in and through the inner city of London. He himself and a number of his men shouted in the streets, exclaiming that he was there as their saviour and wanted to protect the queen and remove the evil councillors she had surrounded herself with.[10]

If Devereux thought he could win the public over with his charm as he had the queen and his followers, he was deluded. The citizens of London shut themselves up in their homes or appeared shocked and outraged. Robert Devereux was many things, but he was not the queen. Nor could he have understood the unique relationship between Elizabeth and her people. Some people had never known a life without Elizabeth as queen and their loyalty to her is evident in their reaction. It must also be noted that the Cecils had steered Elizabeth's reign from the beginning. The regime was safe and familiar to the English people, and without men like William and Robert Cecil, there could be no Elizabeth in the way she is understood now, and was then. Robert Cecil was quick to act. Devereux and his men were incredibly outnumbered and could not have possibly overcome Elizabeth's troops. They were pushed back by the end of the day and the Essex Faction was broken up. The earl himself returned to his home in panic, but there would be no more mercy. The order was given to fire cannon and his rebellion was crushed with all of Cecil's might. By the evening, he surrendered, and Elizabeth was finally safe again. The earl and the remainder of his men were arrested. Elizabeth was in no mood for mercy.[11]

The Cecils pulled together on this occasion, with Thomas Cecil, Lord Burghley, proving to be more useful than his younger brother had ever anticipated. It was his soldiers that successfully put down the Essex Rebellion and without his military prowess and Robert's interception of the revolt itself and quick action, the chaos may have gone on for much longer. There is really no doubt that Devereux's rebellion would have fallen either way, but the devastation left in its wake was minor. The very next morning, a commission was held to examine the actions of Robert Devereux, and what was to be done with him. Interestingly, when Cecil did get to speak, he stated that the Earl of Essex had for some years, wanted to take the throne for himself. Meaning that he wished to depose Elizabeth and make himself king. However, there really is no evidence that Devereux wished to be king, or to suggest that he considered deposing or harming Elizabeth in any way. It is more likely that his expressed intentions were true and that he simply wanted to gain her favour again and remove Robert Cecil from the situation. This does not mean his actions were any less treasonous, but to observe his revolt as a quest for the throne is unfounded. Cecil's notion likely came from his own feelings towards the earl and vice versa. The trial was conducted on 19 February. Cecil himself was not present officially as he was not a peer of the realm at this stage, but he was certainly there in the background. Some other conspirators, such as the Earl of Southampton were pardoned but Devereux was now considered too dangerous, and he was found guilty of treason and condemned to die.[12]

As soon as the Essex Rebellion was crushed, the earl's seemingly staunch supporters disappeared. Immediately after his capture, over one hundred of his followers were arrested. The queen likely understood at this point that a trial would have been necessary and that her favourite had to die in order to preserve her safety and reign. If Elizabeth and Cecil thought the danger had evaporated, they were mistaken. Only days later, a man named Captain Thomas Lee was apprehended just outside Elizabeth's Privy Chamber with a dagger in his possession. It was discovered that the man was a supporter and distant family member of Devereux's. Cecil himself had called the Essex Rebellion a 'dangerous accident', but it was clear that the earl's poison had seeped much further than anyone could have expected.

The very next day, Lee was tried for treason. His connections to the Earls of Essex and Tyrone were discovered and he was soon executed. All of this did little to help Devereux's cause. It was, however, useful to Cecil. Much of the evidence for Devereux's trial and execution had been gathered over a period of weeks and months. Robert Cecil housed both the qualities of his father and of Francis Walsingham. Even before the rebellion had taken place, the Earl of Essex left breadcrumbs behind him, which only served to seal his fate later on. Robert Cecil's interrogations were many, which included those who were involved in the conspiracy and those connected to it on a social or familial basis. He left no stone unturned, and it was even revealed that the Globe Theatre and Shakespeare himself, albeit unknowingly, played their part in the rebellion. Before the rebellion began, Devereux found it absolutely necessary to create some form of propaganda to stir support for his cause. It was revealed that his followers had approached the players of the Globe and asked them to preform Shakespeare's *Richard II*, and crucially the scenes of his deposition and the killing of an anointed king by his own corrupt ministers. The intention behind this can be taken in more than one way but it matched well with Devereux's reasons for rebellion. The only reason Cecil did not know about the connection between the play and the rebellion sooner was that it was held the day before the Essex Rebellion. In the end, Robert Devereux became his own version of Richard II. He was executed on Wednesday 25 February 1601 by beheading in the courtyard of the Tower of London, aged thirty-five years.[13]

Many accounts state that Elizabeth was indecisive when it came to signing the earl's death warrant. It has been suggested that as she had previously been unable to sign Mary Stuart's death warrant, and was wracked with guilt when the order was finally given, she was aware of the backlash or even guilt that would come from signing Devereux's execution warrant. However, though she did sign it after some time, only to call it back the next day and then send it again, the queen knew that the earl had to die, despite her remaining feelings for him. Whether she really hesitated due to her feelings for him cannot be certain. The day before the execution took place, she showed great strength and leadership in signing the Earl of Essex's death warrant and sending it on.[14] The betrayal had been too much for her to bear.

The queen was clearly moved that her people had supported her and refused to take part in the rebellion. This is evident from the *Proclamation on the seizure of the Earls of Essex, Rutland and Southampton for rebellion*:

> Our good subjects of our city and elsewhere having showed themselves so constant and unmovable from their duties towards us, as not any one of them of any note (that we can yet hear of) did offer to assist the said Earl and his associates, we have been contented, in regard of the comfort that we take, to find by so notorious evidence the loyal disposition of our people (whereof we never doubted), not only to make known to all our said subjects of our city and elsewhere in how thankful part we do accept both their loyal persisting in their duty and stay from following the false persuasions of the traitors, but to promise on our part that, whensoever we shall have cause to show it, they shall find us more careful over them than for ourselves.[15]

However, the proclamation also reveals Elizabeth's defense for her councillors, and this is important as she wished her subjects to know that the men she surrounded herself with were not corrupt or evil as Devereux had suggested. This open support for men like Cecil was absolutely necessary in order to quash any further suggestion of corruption in what was in fact the new '*Regnum Cecilianum*' in many ways, because to undermine or corrupt Cecil's position was to also undermine Elizabeth's power as monarch, who placed him in his position.

The queen's defense of her ministers may have been the last point addressed in the proclamation, but it was by no way the least important. The queen continued:

> And hereby also, in regard of our gracious meaning towards our good people, to admonish them that, seeing this open act

was so sudden as it cannot yet be thoroughly looked into how far it stretched and how many hearts it hath corrupted, but that it is to be presumed by the common example of the manner of proceeding of all rebels in like actions that it was not without instruments and ministers dispersed in divers places to provoke the minds of our people to like of their attempts with calumniating our government and our principal servants and ministers thereof, that they should do well (and so we charge them) to give diligent heed in all places to the conservation of persons not well known of their good behavior and to the speeches of any that shall give out slanderous and undutiful words or rumours against us and our government...[16]

In terms of the apparent grief that Elizabeth felt for signing Devereux's death warrant, it appears that she did later suggest to the French ambassador that she regretted the earl's death, and that if she could have saved him, she would have. However, this seems eerily similar to her apparent guilt over Mary Stuart's execution, where she blamed and raged at William Cecil. Her indication to the ambassador that the decision was not entirely hers and if it were that the earl would have lived, was a subtle way of indicating that his death was decided by her government.[17] This was Elizabeth's way of placing the blame on others. However, it is clear that without her signature on both the death warrants of Mary Stuart and Robert Devereux, their executions could never have taken place. In the end, it was Elizabeth who made the decisions, and as her proclamation stated, the Cecils were merely her 'servants'.

With Robert Devereux now out of the way and his memory disgraced, there was nowhere else for Cecil to climb but upwards. He had defeated the queen's remaining enemies, and thus, his own enemies. He had so far preserved his father's wish to protect and preserve the Elizabethan state and the woman that reigned over it. There remained some male and female favourites amongst Elizabeth's circle, of that there is no doubt. But Robert Cecil had made his abilities and position clear – he was now at the pinnacle of his power. The running of the government his father had formed from a vision was now in the hands of Robert Cecil entirely. The queen was at the head of that government and undoubtedly ruled, but Robert was now the *de facto* most powerful man in the kingdom.

By the time of the Essex Rebellion and Devereux's downfall and execution, Robert Cecil was also busying himself with matters outside of conspiracy, rebellions and governance. With the death of his father, he had inherited many houses and lands, but none matched what his brother had inherited. Like his father, Robert was a man of many interests. He was interested in art and became quite the collector. He was such a grand connoisseur in fact, that there are whole studies dedicated to his patronage of the arts. Furthermore, like his father before him, Robert had a great interest in books and a desire for knowledge and learning. By the time he was elevated to his earldom in 1605, he had amassed a great collection of books encompassed in two massive libraries.[18]

However, there is another comparison to his father in terms of his interests, and that is evident in his love for architecture. He wrote to Sir George Carew in 1602, that 'I shall shew myself a good Architector (of which great virtue in me, or rather vice for it hath almost undone me) you shall be *Oculatis testis...*' By this, Cecil was indicating that he would himself would become a great architect and commissioner of great buildings like his father before him, though he had many homes to choose from. Homes that many Londoners would only have dreamt of living in. Robert felt the need to show off his new political prowess, and with the Earl of Essex gone, there was no better time. He now embarked on an architectural pursuit that would eventually result in what became known as Salisbury House, although he was not yet elevated to a peerage at the beginning of its plans and construction, nor would he be given the title during Elizabeth's lifetime.[19] As Robert Cecil's star was rising, Elizabeth was fading. It could even be said that the sun that Elizabeth was, was setting entirely. The queen was old, frail and tired. She had reigned longer than anyone had expected, and though Robert had great respect and reverence for her, he had bigger plans for England which went beyond Elizabeth's mortality. A new great statesman had arrived, and he would guide England into a new age.

Chapter 13

The Queen is Dead, Long
Live the King

Towards the end of 1601, Elizabeth I had survived multiple conspiracies and plots to dethrone and murder her. She had prevailed. It is inconceivable to think that she would have survived without the Cecils, their knowledge and their informants in her service. Her reign had been tumultuous at best, but her choice in William Cecil as her secretary all those years ago, was likely the reason for her long-lasting life and successful reign. By the time the Essex Rebellion was put down, the earl was dead and Robert Cecil ruled the day. The queen was revered by her people as no other English monarch had ever been before. Her final parliament took place in November 1601. By the turn of the century, Tudor England had changed beyond recognition. However, the monopolies scandal had continued, and this called for reform. If Parliament members wished for reform to take place, there was no better time to request it in what was obviously the queen's final years. When Elizabeth agreed to reform particular corruptions and abuses, over 140 members of Parliament went to Whitehall Palace to formally thank the queen for her reforms and services. Elizabeth had always been a great show woman, and her 'Golden Speech' was her final show of affection for her people, thanks for their loyalty and for the service of the men who advised her and ran the government in her name. At this point, there was no sign that the queen was on the way out, but she had become low since the Essex Rebellion and plunged in and out of depression. Her golden speech left more than an impression on her subjects, and even today, her words echo of the end of an era:

> I do assure you there is no prince that loveth his subjects better or whose love can countervail our love. There is no jewel, be it of never so rich a price, which I set before this jewel, I mean your love. For I do more esteem of it than of any treasure or riches, for that we know how to prize, but love and thanks I count invaluable…

And although God hath raised me high, yet this I count the glory of my crown, that I have reigned with your loves...

To be a king and wear a crown is a thing more glorious to them that see it than it is pleasing to them that bear it...

There will never queen sit in my seat with more zeal to my country, care for her subjects, and that sooner with willingness will venture her life for your good and safety than myself, for it is not my desire to live nor reign longer than my life and reign shall be for your good...

...I commit you all to your best fortunes and further counsels. And I pray you, Master Comptroller, Master Secretary, and you of my Council, that before these gentlemen depart into their countries you bring them all to kiss my hand.[1]

Elizabeth's final political years were made up of differing treaties and Cecils' attempts to make peace with Spain. Cecil had led the *Treaty of Vervins* peace party himself within the Privy Council. He, more than anyone, was eager to see peace with Spain and to find some calm in the murky European waters of foreign policy. His influence grew stronger by the day and by 1602, he well may have convinced the queen to finally give up on her vow to never make peace with Spain. The Archduke of Austria, Albert VII, had married Philip III's sister Isabella, and had assured Elizabeth that he wished to sue for peace also. However, many of Elizabeth's advisors were against any proposition for peace after two decades of Spanish threats. The Archduke sent an envoy to discuss peace with Elizabeth in person. Cecil had already drawn up the papers, ever methodical as his father, but the conversation went sour when the envoy spoke as if a peace treaty between Spain and England was all but finalised. Elizabeth changed the subject quickly and Cecil ripped up his proposal faster than he could say 'The Tower'.[2]

Though the Archduke was clearly lying, a peace treaty of some sort may have served Elizabeth well. It may even have given her some form of peace in her final years, but stubbornness ran through her veins and she could not forget the latter years of the 1580s so easily. However, it was not all talk of doom and gloom at Elizabeth's court as so many authors have depicted. Elizabeth was seriously agile for her age by the turn of the century. And while her father had grown fat, smelly and ill by the time he was in his early fifties, and her mother had not lived past her thirties (albeit not through natural means), she was robust and strong. She dressed lavishly, ate ludicrously, danced and sang without any comparison, rode out weekly and took walks on her own without any help. It must be noted that to have reached her late sixties was quite the feat for the period, even for a queen. However, though her mind remained razor sharp academically, the final threat of rebellion from Essex pushed her over the edge. She became seriously melancholic, moody, suspicious and even paranoid in the final two years of her life. Sir John Harington even reported that she kept a sword by her table and at times, thrust it into the air in 'great rage'.[3]

While Elizabeth was ageing, and going through the motions of mental decline, her secretary, Robert Cecil, had other things on his mind besides making peace with Spain. Cecil was in a precarious situation. His father's legacy and his own career hung in the balance as Elizabeth aged. Though she was suffering from some form of mental decline, she made recoveries here and there. She was also healthy physically, or so it seemed. There was no direct sign that she would die soon, but the succession crisis loomed nonetheless. Elizabeth herself refused to discuss the inevitability of her own demise, the succession and who she wished to take her place. The problem was Elizabeth did not want to die, nor for another to take what had been hers for over four decades. Cecil was eager to settle the succession, by whatever means. His means of finding a solution that would suit England and his own skin, however, verged on the treasonous. Robert Cecil was no fool. He was well aware by the time of Devereux's trial and execution, that the earl had himself been in contact with representatives of James VI of Scotland, the Protestant son of Mary Stuart. It appeared that Devereux had been in communication for some time with the Earl of Mar. Whether or not this was another existing conspiracy on the earl's part and that of James Stuart mattered little to Cecil. James himself certainly knew of the succession crisis in England. He was also acutely aware of his mother's and father's claims to the English throne, even during Elizabeth's youth. As a Protestant, and due to his distancing of himself on a personal level with his mother and her Catholic cause, James was not the worst possible candidate for the throne once Elizabeth was gone, and Cecil knew this.[4]

Robert was well aware that any form of communication with James personally was dangerous if Elizabeth were to find out. Especially if the topic had anything to do with the succession. If Robert was to be found guilty of treason, his father's great name and legacy would be destroyed forever, and Cecil power would no doubt have been extinguished. However, if he did not act in favour of James and take the opportunity to preserve his position and career, he was well aware that many in England, including those who had even some small claim to Elizabeth's throne upon her death, were opposed to Cecil influence and power. Indeed, if the succession were to go any other way, Robert Cecil may have found himself in a precarious situation anyway. He quickly set out to enamour himself with the Scottish king, making him a friend rather than promising him the throne outright. The Earl of Essex had portrayed Cecil as his enemy and an enemy of the English State. But as Loades mentions, James knew who wielded true power in England, and if the Scottish king could find support in anyone for his claim to the English succession, he knew his best bet was Robert Cecil.[5]

Robert Devereux was not the only man in secret correspondence with representatives of King James. Lord Henry Howard had also been sending letters to James's agents in a bid to secure his own future when the inevitable occurred. Since the Earl of Essex's fall, James had been sure to keep in with Elizabeth, sending the Earl of Mar to congratulate her. However, Elizabeth could always smell a rat, and she was well aware that many in Scotland, England and even men under her own nose, would have been happy for her to declare James as her heir. But Elizabeth was as cautious as ever. James had often vied for his 'future right' – indicating his right to inherit the crown as the descendant of Henry VIII's daughter. Elizabeth was clever enough to reprimand James for his presumptions and reminded him that the succession depended on her will, and also her death: 'Remember that a bird of the air, if no other instrument, to an honest king shall stand instead of feigned practices.' By this she was indicating her knowledge of the current talks and correspondence of James's hopes for succession.[6] The queen was no fool, but was she ever aware of Cecil's intentions to actually pursue a Stuart succession upon her death? Probably not.

With Devereux out of the way, Elizabeth became more and more dependent on Cecil for advice. Despite her concerns for James's demands, she was aware that the succession crisis had never truly gone away, nor would it. In a bid to push James back into favour with the queen, Cecil suggested that Elizabeth restore a pension for James of £5,000 to be paid in instalments. Whether this was a way to appease the queen, King James, or both is anyone's guess. When Cecil had discovered the secret letters between Mar and the late Devereux, he didn't simply jump into correspondence with James, offering him the crown upon Elizabeth's death. First, he had to weigh the pros and cons, and consider the consequences. His father had not educated him at his side for decades for him to destroy the Cecil name within his first decade of power. It took around two weeks for Cecil to decide on his course of action. In hindsight, we know that he chose to write to James and discuss the possibilities of him succeeding the crown, and we know that it was successful. However, he was unaware of the outcome and consequences of his actions at the time, and one can only image his anxiety, and excitement. When he did write to James, he was careful to use ciphered code in order to hide sensitive details. For example, Elizabeth was referred to as '24', James was '30' and Cecil was '10'. However, most letters were written between Mar and James or a lawyer named Bruce, to put off any suspicion.[7]

The notion that James, as a Protestant would inherit Elizabeth's throne, strengthen the Protestant cause and eliminate a Catholic succession whilst also uniting England and Scotland may have seemed straightforward. However, it was anything but. The problem for many English Protestants was not only the fact that James was Scottish and therefore a foreigner, but that he was the son of the Catholic martyr, Mary Stuart, who had many a time attempted to remove Elizabeth from the throne and brought on the wrath of Spain. There were also many who believed that James would secretly convert to Catholicism afterwards. English sentiments of the time were weary regarding the accession of a foreign king and son of a Catholic. The Jesuit exile named Robert Persons was partly responsible for the growing debate in England concerning a Stuart succession due to his publication of *A conference about the next succession for the crown of England*. Persons suggested the succession of the Monarchy was not in fact a divided decision, but merely an election that suited the people of a particular inclination. He also argued that in terms of a Lancastrian inheritance by blood and discordancy that the Spanish Infanta was actually the true heir and not James VI of Scotland. While most English nobles and subjects would have declined the idea of a Spanish succession, James's possibility of inheritance was also severely damaged.[8]

The idea of a monarchy that was elected rather than ordained by God was not new. In fact, when Elizabeth was ill with smallpox in the early 1560s, William Cecil's Protestant vision for England had not taken hold entirely and there was a serious crisis regarding the succession. William posed the idea that a temporary republican government could be formed in the event of her death in order to ensure that Protestantism would remain the dominant denomination in England. This was in stark contrast to earlier Tudor reigns. Indeed, Mary Tudor had been accepted after she challenged Jane Grey's claim which was stipulated by Edward VI's will. Mary had won, and despite her Catholicism, it was mostly believed that she was the true heir due to her blood, not her religion. However, a decade or so later, the Cecil proposal for a council acting as a political body on behalf of a dead queen was strongly considered. The succession was no longer necessarily about the hereditary right of the individual, but their religion and capabilities as a monarch.[9] By the time Robert Cecil was running the show, it was clear to many that he was the way to the throne for any potential heir. Arbella

Stuart was also a contender for the throne, but was never truly considered by Robert and would have dismissed the notion anyway.

In April 1601, Robert Cecil took the plunge. A meeting was apparently arranged secretly at the Strand in the duchy chambers. Nobody else in the English court or government were aware of this plan. There's no evidence of substance to suggest the conversation that took place. However, if it did, it is likely that Robert wished to protect the queen firstly at all costs, and to ensure the integrity of her reign. Secondly, there was the concern for secrecy. In no way was it to get out that they were in correspondence regarding the succession and that James was to be the next king.[10] Thereafter, the interesting coded correspondence between Cecil and James began. They were not the deceptive letters of Mary's Stuart's conspiracy, but the coded numbers used were enough to keep the contents safe from detection. It is ironic that decades earlier, Robert's father and James's mother were sworn enemies, who struggled over the succession of the crown. In the end, Mary's demise was due to her coded letters, discovered by William Cecil's men. Now, their offspring were secretly plotting a Stuart succession using coded letters. What William may have thought of his son's conspiracy we may never know. However, due to Burghley's closeness to the queen and suspicion of the Stuarts, it could be said that he would not have entirely approved. Robert was not willing, however, to give up his own future prospects and the power and influence his father had carved out. A letter from James to Robert reveals the first hint of the plan put in motion:

> I AM MOST heartily glad that 10 [Cecil] hath now at last made choice of two so fit and confident ministers[11] whom with he hath so honourably plain in the affairs of 30 [James]... When it shall please God that 30, she shall no surelier succeed to the place than he shall succeed in bestowing as great or greater favour upon 10 as his predecessor doth bestow upon him...[12]

What James is saying here, is that he intends to keep Robert in the position of secretary or even raise him higher if he is successful in succeeding to the throne upon Elizabeth's death.

The discussion of the Stuart succession cannot only be unraveled by referring to letters written on behalf of Cecil to James and vice versa, but in the correspondence between Bruce and Henry Howard also. Howard summed up perfectly the necessity of including Robert Cecil in the plan for James to succeed Elizabeth in a letter written to Bruce on 4 December 1601:

> But now, dear Mr. Bruce, that you may judge in what a world
> we live of factions and phantasies, I must let you know that,
> whereat you will wonder much, and I believe with reason...
> how impossible it is to cut the sinews of Cecil's motion in
> our estate; and that, like a raging billow, he doth rather break
> himself than the rock against which he beats, finding the same
> difference to be between King James's greatness growing, and
> his own false glory diminishing...[13]

Though Devereux was gone, Cecil had other opponents to contend with.
Walter Raleigh was one major opposition to any possibility of Elizabeth
paying favour to James significantly or naming him as her successor while
she was still alive. Not only was she totally opposed to any discussion of
her death or succession, but many of her favourites opposed a Scottish or
any foreign succession. Lord Cobham, Cecil's brother-in-law, was another
obstacle. Together, Cobham and Raleigh represented the faction of those
opposing James's succession, with Cecil and Howard representing those
(albeit unknowingly to Elizabeth) in favour of it. Howard then wrote to James
personally after his communication with Bruce, relaying the words and
thoughts of Cecil. He discussed Cecil's hopes to guide and advise James –
whether this be on the succession or meaning afterwards is subjective but
the language is clear. The Cecil faction were eager to pursue their enterprise,
but were extremely cautious and concerned for the opposition that would
come. They were particularly concerned about Henry Percy, the 9th Duke
of Northumberland, who was Devereux's nephew, as he allied with Raleigh,
and was wholly opposed to a Stuart succession:

> Both Cecil and I do humbly beseech your Majesty, that none
> of the elect in the place do, by and words, cast out to the Duke,
> or any of his complices, (that have been recommenders of
> Raleigh's hypocrisy), give notice of the dealing of Cobham or
> Raleigh in the matter of this peace or tax those ill affections to
> him, upon the manifest discovery of courses and endeavours
> so far opposite. For there is as little hope of altering their
> minds absolutely fixed upon the poles of the ambition by plain
> dealing, which persons have no ends besides their own...[14]

Howard's warning not only indicated the fragility of Cecil's correspondence
with James, whether it had been through others or not, and their difficulty
in not knowing what direction to take and how to proceed. Clearly, they felt

that it was beneficial for the queen and that they were working on her behalf. But the truth was, Cecil was unaware of how Elizabeth would react if the correspondence became known, or if his plans were revealed. If the queen knew of his endeavour and motives, there was little she could have done. She relied on Cecil, as much as he relied on her. Cecil and Howard not only shared the same ideals and hopes for England and the preservation of the Protestant faith and Cecil regime, they were also cut from the same cloth. Indeed, in Howard, Cecil saw a man with equal talent in politics. As Alford mentions, their plan and correspondence with James was deemed necessary and indeed was significant in terms of managing a dynasty that had previously been 'authoritarian'. The Tudors had always ruled with an iron fist, and despite the power and influence of the Cecils, like any noble or advisor they were always one mistake away from the Tower, or the axe. The death of Elizabeth, however devastating it may have been for the nation as a whole, would allow for a shift in power that was unprecedented. Elizabeth would never give up her own personal power, but as the last Tudor, she represented a different time. Robert Cecil wanted to push England into a new age.[15]

Robert Cecil would not live to see the execution of Charles I, Cromwell's republic, or the formation of what is now called constitutional monarchy. However, his plans to override Elizabeth's refusal to discuss the succession and hand over power before she had even died were revolutionary. The idea that a group of advisers could plan and discuss the probability of the monarch's demise and the best heir to sit on the throne was as close to electing a monarch as was possible for the time. Despite his secrecy however, it is clear that Cecil was loyal to Elizabeth until her dying day. Howard summed up his position as a royal servant:

> upon the multiplicity of doubts his mind would never have been at rest, nor he would have eaten or slept quietly; for nothing makes him more confident, but experience of secret trust, and security of intelligence.[16]

As Loades has mentioned, despite Cecil's plans for the future succession, he was genuinely dedicated to Elizabeth in the final years of her reign, and intended to work hard for her. He himself stated that he was willing to 'labour like a pack horse'. The queen was now frail and difficult, yet he remained by her side whatever her mood or disposition. He was not unaware that Elizabeth's favour for his father and her patronage was the sole reason for his position and his ability to discuss further plans for England's future at all. He also made it clear to James that he was unwilling to assist him in becoming king until Elizabeth had died, and that any pretence otherwise would not even be considered. By the beginnings of 1602, Elizabeth had just previously given her Golden Speech and conducted what was unknowingly her last parliament. Despite the queen's warm words of thanks to the men who advised her and governed the country, the discussions of the day had seen more than a few tense and hostile words between Raleigh and Cecil. Cracks were beginning to show and as the queen aged and weakened, so too did the England she represented. Where factions had thought to be long extinct during her first thirty years on the throne, these final years brought hostility and a divide in court and government. While Elizabeth lived, the seal could be kept shut tight. But as her life drew to a close, Robert was busy preparing himself for what was to come. The strain on his health was evident, and like his father, he found it harder and harder to get around – not due to gout, but due to his own disability. Catholic conspirators were again on the rise as Elizabeth declined, and there were several on the council. Though they supported James VI's cause, they were hopeful that his reign would be more tolerant than Elizabeth's latter years.[17]

Throughout Elizabeth's reign, she had long attempted to show religious tolerance. As her reign went on, Robert's father William had his work cut out for him. Numerous Catholic rebellions in the name of James's mother Mary threatened the very core of Elizabethan governance. Because Catholics were a minority by the end of Elizabeth's reign, they were even more dangerous to the stability of her power. The Cecils were the backbone of the defence against Catholic conspiracy, due to their genius intelligence network. Since Henry VIII's break with the Catholic Church and his Act of Supremacy, a role which Elizabeth took on in her own reign, the battle of religions in England and foreign interference made any hopes of religious reconciliation between the majority and minority impossible, due to the Catholic refusal to recognise the Monarch's authority over the Church. Elizabeth was just as eager for tolerance at the beginning of her reign, but by the time Mary Stuart had been executed and the Spanish Armada had been defeated, tensions between English Catholics and Protestants only intensified. By denying Elizabeth's religious policy, Catholics were viewed with suspicion by the government. The *Act of Supremacy* and the *Act of Uniformity* which Elizabeth's first Parliament had passed may have seemed genius on paper, but the enforcement of denying Elizabeth's position and authority were brutal, and this was considered high treason. Towards the end of her reign however, recusancy fines were put in place for those who stayed loyal to the Catholic Church. This benefitted Elizabeth as both a punishment and also arguably increased her income. To avoid further unrest and rebellion, the death penalty for disobedience existed. This was Parliament's way of keeping the minority just that – a minority.[18]

It is interesting to note that though Robert Cecil was more staunch than his father, his tenure as secretary for Elizabeth was very different to William's. Firstly, William had witnessed multiple rebellions during his life, during four Tudor reigns. By the time the Armada was off the coast of England, old Lord Burghley had built up an unmovable intolerance and distrust of Catholics – whether they be English or otherwise. It is therefore not surprising that despite his son being more devout, William had a more severe and less tolerable approach towards the disloyalty and disobedience of Catholics. Cecil had indeed witnessed many of the rebellions of Elizabeth's reign, and had even worked alongside his father during Elizabeth's greatest crisis. He may have been equally as suspicious of Catholics as any other Englishman, but he knew that if he was to continue to have a role in governance after Elizabeth's death and upon James's accession, then tolerance was key, because that is what James wanted.[19]

James VI of Scotland may well have been a zealous Protestant, and overwhelmingly suitable as Elizabeth's successor, but his tolerance towards Catholic subjects would likely have made any Protestant Englishman of some standing quiver in their boots. In the letters between James and Cecil, the king seemingly approved of a more tolerant approach towards the minority. But he also approved greatly of Cecil's policy towards Catholics and was keen on the policy of recusancy, and both discussed the notion that Catholics could actually be loyal to the crown without an oath. James was also clearly willing to leave all Catholics in peace if their priests were to be exiled, for it was the power of Catholic priests that he feared the most. Even when it would become clear that James was to inherit the throne, he was clever enough to assure his future subjects that tolerance would be possible if they conformed to his laws of the land.[20]

By the end of 1602, Elizabeth's mental and physical health were in decline. She lived in fear of rebellion and assassination, which was only further triggered by the Earl of Essex's recent revolt and subsequent execution. Even her favourites were capable of threatening her reign and life, and it had taken its toll. Elizabeth had always been a bad sleeper, and we now may refer to her condition as insomnia. Whatever the case, the strain in the latter years of her reign did little to lighten her spirits. She went in and out of melancholic states, and this led many to become 'weary of an old woman's government'. Elizabeth had always stated that she herself was the 'sun'. But the sun that once shone so bright, was now setting. Many who saw James as the rightful heir to the throne viewed him as a new 'rising sun', and began to pay attention towards him when they realised Elizabeth would not last the year. Just as they had when Mary I lay dying in her bed. This was done more subtly, however. It was no secret that the Elizabethan's had become detached from their virgin queen, and this only further plunged Elizabeth into a depression, of which she would never really return. She shut herself up in her private rooms for some peace, and perhaps even to die in private away from the eyes of her court. In terms of her physical health, she had all but lost her appetite, and likely lost a lot of weight. Some even described that in her last days, the queen was in a 'pitiable state'.[21]

Many attempted to coax Elizabeth out of her state but with little success. In January 1603, the frail queen travelled from Whitehall to Richmond Palace. It would be her last journey. From almost the moment she arrived, Elizabeth became seriously ill. She was also plagued by waves of guilt for Mary Stuart's execution. When the news was brought to her that her old friend Katherine Howard had died, this was the final nail in the coffin. Elizabeth had now lost most, if not all, of her lifelong friends. The lack of sustenance, sleep and mental strain all contributed to her rapid deterioration. In her final days, Elizabeth stood or paced, refused food, sleep, or to even sit or lay down. Finally, she was persuaded to take to her bed. From there, she declined further, and her throat became so swollen and sore that she could not speak. After decades of refusing to marry, produce an heir, battling with her cousin, Mary Stuart and refusing to name her son James as her heir, Elizabeth gave in. When the Lord Admiral asked her if James, King of Scots was to be her heir, with all her strength, she lifted her hand from the bed and drew a circle around her head, suggesting that the crown was to be his. Or at least, that's how they interpreted it. Elizabeth I then drifted in and out of sleep before finally dying in the early hours of 24 March. She had reigned for almost forty-five years and had not yet reached her seventieth birthday.[22]

The Tudor dynasty was now extinct, and a not so new dynasty was on the rise. But there was another family still intent on making their mark. The Cecils had never known an England without a Tudor monarch, excusing the small blip of Jane Grey's reign, if it could even be called that. Elizabeth had brought England stability, wealth and a true place on the European political plane – an identity. The ministers and advisors she chose spoke volumes of her own wisdom. Yet, without men like William and Robert Cecil at her side, men who were truly loyal, she may never have persisted, may never have survived, and may never have become the Gloriana that we continue to revere to this day. She was an icon even during her own lifetime, and yet every icon has its maker. The Cecils may have been servants to the crown, but the crown also owed a great deal of gratitude and loyalty to the Cecils. Nobody was more aware of this than the new king, James I of England. True to his word, he would keep Robert Cecil at his side as his secretary and advisor, and true to his word – Cecil would advise him. With a new government came rebirth, reform and regeneration. The Tudors had been successful because of their ability to heed good counsel. If the Stuarts were to be equally as skillful and memorable, then they too would have to do the same.[24]

Despite James being Mary Stuart's son and a Scotsman, he was a direct descendent of Henry VII, albeit through a female line. He was also a Protestant and favoured by Elizabeth, despite never being declared her heir officially. To the public, it was time for a new monarch and indeed, a new king. England had not had a true born king of royal blood in fifty years. Indeed, many had never even known England to have a king. Many Englishmen were eager to have a man on the throne again and as Elizabeth aged, the authority of queens was continuously questioned. Elizabeth's court was excited at the prospect of having a royal family again – a king, a queen, princes and princesses. Once again, childhood chatter and laughter would be heard in Richmond and Hampton Court Palace. James was also deemed suitable as he had already been King of Scotland for decades. He was genuinely liked among his subjects, and he had a view of religious tolerance that had not been witnessed in Elizabeth's reign for years.[25]

But where did Robert Cecil really fit in all this? If we are to assume that Robert was completely tolerant of Catholics and willing to allow James free rein on terms of religious policy however, we would be mistaken. Robert was willing to go so far, but James depended on his support to become king in the first place. If all were to go smoothly without much opposition, Robert had to guide the new king, who was waiting eagerly for his English inheritance. If Cecil could not control the direction of this unfamiliar tolerance, Catholics could end up gaining more influence than Protestants. This was far from what he wanted. He therefore came up with a plan to make the Catholics destroy themselves from within. In February 1602, he and an entourage travelled to Rome. This was because there was a major rift between the Jesuits and secular priests which led to Catholic priests being imprisoned. The growing dominance of the Jesuits in England was by far too much for Cecil to stomach. The petition he brought was a way of reprimanding the Jesuits for their actions. Toleration of Catholics was one thing for Cecil and Elizabeth to consider, but to tolerate two warring sides of the same religion when tensions between Protestants and Catholics already existed was too dangerous to consider. By 1 January, it was made clear that Catholics loyal to Elizabeth should stay in England. Jesuits were forced into exile. By the time James became king, there was no sign of any opposing sides of Catholicism, at least within public view. In a way, Cecil had made an official promotion of toleration avoidable by linking his actions against Catholic conspiracy and tensions to his support of James's accession. Therefore, the new king's hands were tied, and evidently, power still belonged to the Cecils.[26]

James I's reign as England's first Stuart monarch has drawn the attention of many scholars, especially recently. Indeed, it seems that he is owed more recognition as a good king than he has been allowed in the past. He was an experienced king, well adept at negotiation and balancing power between his advisors and council. His idea of a more religiously tolerant regime may well have seemed genuine, but even more so was his wish to unite the two kingdoms of Scotland and England. In hindsight, this makes sense of course, and historians often praise him for his vision. However, his contemporaries did not share this vision and though both kingdoms had one king, they remained separate states.[27] In many ways, James was more than capable of being a successful king for England. Like Cecil, he was well educated in court etiquette, politics, the sciences, political philosophy and spoke many languages. In every sense he seemed the prodigal prince. However, again, his contemporaries had much to say about his abilities as a strong ruler. For much of his reign over Scotland, he was considered a relatively impoverished king compared to other European rulers. When he was proclaimed King of England, a newly wealthy and powerful nation that had defeated the Spanish and proven itself a mighty political power, he probably couldn't believe his luck.[28]

The first few days after Elizabeth's death were the most important in making James's accession a success. The days between Elizabeth's death and his official succession were actually considered lawless and governmentless, despite James's promise to keep Cecil in his position of power. This meant that Robert's move towards pushing James as the successor were technically without legal merit. Yet, the queen had given as much indication as possible that her cousin should succeed her. The proclamation of James's new reign was announced at Whitehall. The king was not surprised. After a number of councillors had taken route towards their new master in Edinburgh, he was already drafting a letter of thanks to Cecil for his endorsement: 'How happy I think myself by the conquest of so wise a councillor'. James then later instructed Cecil on the formation of the government which Cecil himself had already drawn up to his own liking. It was simply James's duty to approve it but outwardly it would have been deemed James's decision. As men flocked to James in Scotland, Cecil readied England for a new reign. He would not meet James in person as king until 18 April. By that time the king and his entourage had made their way across the border and into York, plans for his coronation were already underway. James arrived in his new capital of London on 7 May. Robert's ascendency to a peerage finally began, and he was made Lord Cecil of Essendon.[29]

Robert Cecil rightly deserved his new elevation, of that there can be no doubt. The relatively smooth accession of a Scottish king to the English throne was a great feat. However, a title was by no means necessary in terms of Cecil's standard of living. Indeed, by 1602, just a year into James's reign, he was already one of the richest men in the realm. Like his father, his ability for gaining an income from a multitude of sources matched his political cunning. As he inherited his father's position from the Court of Wards, he gained an income of around £2,900 between 1600 and 1603. Clearly the change in monarch had little impact on his investments. Indeed, his inheritance of lands from his father and that of his own investments and acquisition brought him in an annual income of around £6,000 – a vast sum for the time. Indeed, by the time James was settled on the throne and Cecil's position at his side were indisputable, he was likely the richest subject in the kingdom.[30]

James may well have been happy to praise Cecil prior to his accession, but with him firmly on the throne and his position unquestionable, it would only be a matter of time before the two men were at loggerheads. James was very much like a younger Elizabeth, cautious, but also sure of himself, his legitimacy and right to reign. He knew he depended on the Cecils, but he was not willing to give in to their every whim. He was king, and this was a time before constitutional monarchy. During the final days of Elizabeth's reign, the Earl of Tyrone had finally surrendered and it seemed that the war with Ireland would finally come to a close with the new reign. Cecil was eager for peace on all fronts in fact and the many years of war had seriously depleted the treasury. Despite this, James was soon discussing foreign policy and making decisions that would have an impact on Anglo-Spanish and Anglo-French diplomacy, without council or approval. This was unheard of for the past four decades as Elizabeth had always conceded to the wise decisions of her council, even when she disagreed. Before long, plots were forming in the background, notably the Bye Plot which involved the Cobhams.[31]

With James's coronation plans in the works, conspiracy threatened the new regime before it had even really begun. Cecil was already aware of the growing hostility towards James's accession among a minority of young noble men. The main conspirators were none other than Henry Brooke – Lord Cobham, George Brooke – Lord Cobham's younger brother. There were several other notable conspirators however. There was already an existing investigation of a Jesuit conspiracy leading up to the coronation and Cecil had his best men on the job. The plot was simple enough. Those sympathetic to the Catholic cause were to come together as one body, arrive at Greenwich at night during the summer, kidnap James and imprison him in the Tower. He would act as their hostage and then they would make their demands. Their plan was then to put James's cousin, Arbella Stuart, on the throne. They would then remove the king's s councillors – that also implied Cecil, round them up, prosecute them and then replace them with their own choice of men. However, without any military support and general backing or patronage, the plan soon came to nothing and the members disbanded. Eventually the whole plot was unravelled by a number of interrogations and betrayals. Seven men were brought to trial on 15 November and three men were executed shorty after. Lord Cobham's father was once well acquainted with Lord Burghley, yet their sons would end up on completely opposing sides.[32]

Walter Raleigh and Lord Cobham would both end up imprisoned in the Tower for many years, with the former eventually being executed years later. Raleigh and Cecil had once been friends, and despite their differing attitudes towards politics and succession, they had both remained amicable – until now. Before long, they would unfortunately become enemies of divided court factions. The plot to remove James and his government and replace him with Arbella may not have seemed so ridiculous to the conspirators as it was shocking to James. But it was Cecil's decisiveness that saved the new king from a likely usurpation. James's reaction to the plot at such an early stage in his reign was one of fear, but this worked well for Cecil. Soon enough, James would again be consulting with Cecil regarding domestic and foreign policy. Eventually, a treaty was signed on 19 August 1604, known as the *Treaty of London*. On paper, it concluded the almost twenty-year war between England and Spain. This was likely the final straw for Raleigh and what pushed him to treason, as the idea of peace with the Spaniards was beyond him. The peace was now celebrated and Cecil was again granted a further title of Viscount Cranborne.[33] Cecil's vision was finally being realised. He had settled the succession, put down his opponents, mended the Anglo-Spanish relationship, and was now raised to a peerage as his father had been. His power and influence seemed to have no bounds. However, if he thought that a treaty with Spain and a Stuart on the throne were enough to end Catholic conspiracy in England, he was wrong. Soon enough, a much more treacherous and dangerous plot would be woven, and it would be up to Cecil to unravel it. This would prove to be his greatest obstacle and victory, but would ultimately cement his position and legacy in history, as one of England's greatest statesmen.

Chapter 14

Gunpowder

When James left Scotland on 5 April 1603, he promised his people that he would return to Scotland within three years. He borrowed what he could for his journey – around 10,000 Scottish merks according to Croft's evaluation. When he had arrived in York, after crossing at Berwick, the new king walked to the Minister, apparently to hear the Easter service. This would in fact be James's first attempt at public relations with the English. According to Croft, his journey towards the Capital southwards became like a procession. Even Cecil himself commented that he enjoyed being a part of the 'spectacle of happiness'. The English were said to show their delight in having a new king and eagerly shared their emotion and interest. However, the somewhat bewildering emotional reaction of the English was likely more out of relief for a peaceful transition of monarchy, than anything else. Again, most people had never known another monarch besides Elizabeth, and so any notion of a king on the throne was lost to the common memory. In Elizabeth's time, women ruled the land. Even the new Scottish king's mother had been a queen regnant in her own right. The smooth transition of power may well have been seen as a good omen, but the first plot of James's reign – the Bye Plot, was only a taste of what was to come.[1]

Though James had long been married and had children – male heirs, and his accession was smooth enough, he would have to fight just as hard as Elizabeth to keep his grip on power. He had married Anne of Denmark, the second daughter of Frederick II of Denmark, by proxy in 1589. As the bride was travelling across to England, a storm pushed her ship back to Denmark, and James took it upon himself to 'rescue' her. This was perhaps his only romantic gesture, if it could even be called that. The marriage may have proven fruitful, but was anything but harmonious. Both James and Anne had strong and domineering personalities. Anne was an extravagant queen. Her husband tolerated her frivolous spending habits, despite not being the richest king in Europe. They had six children together, but only three would live to adulthood. Henry Frederick was born in 1594, and upon his father's accession to the English throne, he became the Prince of Wales. England finally had another possible 'King Henry'. The second child that lived to adulthood was Elizabeth, named for the late virgin queen, and their third son would be the ill-fated 'spare', whom they named Charles. Though James was notorious for having male favourites, and there has often been hints by some scholars and authors that he may have been homosexual or more likely bisexual, James never took on a mistress and remained faithful to Anne, at least in that regard, for the entirety of their marriage. In fact, the reason why the couple could not have anything more than a platonic marriage of convenience, was simply because they shared no common interests. The fact that their marriage proved fruitful at all would have simply been down to duty.[2]

Anne had indeed performed her wifely and queenly duties to perfection. But by the time the couple had relocated to England, discussions surrounding Anne's religion were causing some alarm. For some time, there had been reports that Anne had secretly written to the Pope expressing her true faith in the Catholic religion and that she had even converted to Catholicism. Though James wished his reign to be tolerable, for the majority of his English subjects and nobles, a Catholic consort was as intolerable now as it was twenty years previously. The first printed written reference to Anne's clandestine Catholicism dates to 1604, after she and her husband had been proclaimed and anointed as king and queen. It has been stated that Anne's conversion was strategic, and that she professed her true faith to the Pope to secure his endorsement for their claim to the English throne and for the protection of her and her children and their rights to inherit it. Whatever the case may be, the rumours regarding the queen caused further tension between Catholic and Protestant opponents, rather than easing any existing divisions. Cecil vehemently denied that Anne was a Catholic and what made it even more confusing for those who saw her as a potential supporter for the Catholic minority, is that she attended Protestant services and refused to take the sacrament at his coronation ceremony.[3]

Though James's accession could not have come about as smoothly, or perhaps at all, without the influence of Cecil, the new king was eager to push much of the administrative work on his secretary. Indeed, Thomas Cecil had reported to his brother that during his stop at Theobald's on his way towards London in April 1603, James had exclaimed to him that though he [Robert] was but a little man, he [James] would shortly load up his shoulders with business. Little did James know that Cecil was well capable of running the show on his own, with the king's hand simply required to sign his royal approval. Cecil's stature and deformity would be used time and again against him and many in James's and Anne's court made comments or gave him nicknames such as 'the little beagle'. However, Cecil would use this to his own advantage as he had with Elizabeth. He used the nicknames given to him by the king and court as a means of proving the importance of his abilities as a politician and secretary despite the difficulties his deformity presented.[4]

Cecil had his own family to contend with. Though his wife had died prior to James's accession, he remained close with his children and his relationships with both William and Frances mirrored that of his father's with his children by Mildred Cooke. Cecil was a loyal servant and a family man as his father had been. So, when the Cobhams conspired against the new regime in 1603, and therefore against Cecil himself, he had no choice but to protect the crown and his own position as this was also the inheritance of his own children. The fact that his wife Elizabeth had not lived to see her brothers' treason, and particularly her younger brother George's execution, was perhaps somewhat of a comfort to Cecil. His children flourished and his daughter Frances caught the eye of the Princess Elizabeth, and the pair became close friends.

By 1605, the new king had settled in well, and Cecil continued to busy himself with much of the administrative work he had under Elizabeth. His newfound position and title gave him a new edge and sense of authority. His main concerns were the royal treasury and the ever-growing danger of Catholic conspiracy. By early 1605, he was so busy that he could no longer attend the House of Commons. On 4 May 1605, he was further elevated to the earldom of Salisbury. The new lavish home which he had been building in London would thereafter be known as Salisbury House. His elevation seems to have been simply due to James's wishes. Cecil had proven himself as a most diligent advisor, secretary and spymaster. His role as Master of the Court of Wards and Lord Privy Seal also continued. The problem of money was never far from Cecil's mind. Though he was one of the richest peers in the land, the king was practically a pauper. It did not help that both the new king and queen spent lavishly.[5]

By early November 1605, Cecil was kept as busy as ever. Indeed, he had settled well into his role. His influence on the king, despite the odd disagreement, was ever-growing. As Jenny Wormald indicated, Cecil's hand was in every pocket in the kingdom. His influence and opinion were never far. But this often met with some opposition. An example of this was when the Warden of All Souls college wrote to Cecil turning down his suggestions of the newly elected fellows for the month of November, despite the king sharing his suggestions. As Wormald states, it was not unusual for educational institutions to be pressured by the crown and those on the council in the selection of new members. But why is this important in relation to the events that occurred? Just four days earlier, it had been discovered that there existed a Catholic conspiracy to kill the king, the queen, the king's ministers, judges, leaders of government and many more, possibly even the king's children and Cecil himself. The plan was to fill the cellars of Parliament with barrels of gunpowder, and blow it all up when the king was present. Therefore, All Souls' worry regarding the king's and Cecil's suggestions of new members based on academic standards just days after a plot to destroy the new regime is perhaps one of the greatest ironies of the Gunpowder Plot.[6] What is more fascinating was the fact that for Cecil, it was business as usual, despite almost being blown to pieces only days before. This poses even further questions.

Prior to the plot coming to light or even being planned, many of the men that put their hand to it were being watched closely. Firstly, by Elizabeth's government, and secondly by James's. Lord Percy, for example, had been involved in some way in the Essex Rebellion during Elizabeth's final years. Guy Fawkes himself and another conspirator named Thomas Winter had also travelled to Spain in order to gain military assistance and restore Catholicism as England's dominant religion. Indeed, the fact that the men involved in the unfolding plot of 1605 entered into such a venture, knowing that many of them were being closely watched by Cecil's men shows either their desperation at this point for the emancipation of Catholics, or their audacity. Or, it could simply indicate their lack of ability to evade detection. Perhaps all of these factors must be taken into consideration. The fact that many of these men were from aristocratic, privileged, backgrounds, whether Catholic or not, actually lends to the genuineness of their convictions. But how was the plot started? Who was the instigator? And at what point did Cecil learn of it?[7]

The fact that many of the men involved in the plot were of high birth and lived privileged lives in comparison to that of the Catholic minority of the common English people speaks volumes of their disdain for the new regime. They had much to lose, and they would have been aware that there was every chance that they could. It is also indicative of James's true wish for 'tolerance' in the first two years of his reign. Whether his intentions to remain tolerable of Catholics or not, considering Cecil's influence is one matter. However, as always, James would learn that it was more complicated than simply granting tolerance, as tolerance was never enough – Elizabeth herself had learned this the hard way. The Bye Plot had done little to loosen the new king's reserve. The general consensus of those involved in this new plot to kill the king was simple; their hatred for him, as a Scot and Protestant, and his failure to grant Catholics relief from persecution, despite the whole kingdom knowing of his wife's sympathies. As Sidney stated, they felt deceived, and little had changed since the death of the late queen. The straw that broke the camel's back was the recusancy fines of early 1605 which both the king and Cecil favoured. Thirteen men put their names to the plot, and though it is generally agreed that Guy Fawkes is the most notable member of the conspiracy, he was not the founder, for this was Robert Catesby. Catesby was a member of a prominent but Catholic family, who had suffered since their refusal to swear the Oath of Supremacy. There were many men like this involved in the plot: Thomas Winter, John Wright, Robert Keyes, Thomas Bates, John Grant, Robert Winter, Ambrose Rookwood, Guy Fawkes, Thomas Percy, Christopher Wright, Sir Edward Digby and Francis Tresham. These were the main conspirators known but there were many others involved that were absolutely necessary for the planning of this plot.[8]

As many of the conspirators came from noble backgrounds, they were aware that during the opening of Parliament, the king, queen, commons and chief ministers would all be together in one large room. Though a plot of such magnitude was a huge risk, if successful, it may have allowed them to put a Catholic on the throne. Despite their level of education, influence and wealth however, the men involved were no match for Cecil's many agents in every corner of London. As Loades mentioned, the conspiracy itself was discovered unbeknown to those involved, very early on in its planning. The genius of Cecil was as his father's and Walsingham's – to allow his enemies to feel they had the upper hand, to further incriminate themselves beyond any notion of redemption, and take down their enterprise themselves. This was his father's legacy, and this was the legacy of Elizabeth's spymaster. Robert Cecil, in his formidable silence and ability to watch a conspiracy unfold, had finally come into his own. Cecil hoped that his spies across London would catch at least one of the thirteen in the act in some form or another. It is unsurprising in hindsight, that this man was to be Guy Fawkes. On the evening of 4 November, Cecil was alerted that there was some activity in the cellars of the Palace of Westminster where Parliament was to be held the next day. Of course, he was probably aware of the plan that he was to be blown to pieces already. When men were sent to search the cellars after the report that night, Guy Fawkes was discovered amongst thirty-two small barrels of gunpowder. It was his task to lay there during the night and to keep hidden until Parliament had commenced the next day. He was then tasked to light the fuse and blow the king and commons to kingdom come. The fact that the plot was so easily unraveled by Cecil's network and that Fawkes was caught red-handed underlines the incompetence of those involved.[9]

As Wormald states, 'the very fact that a small group of people planned something so cosmic as the destruction of the entire "establishment" makes it seem almost predictable that the scheme was bound to go wrong.' It was due to the men outside of the 'thirteen' that led to the plot's discovery. This is not to say that it was Cecil's only evidence for the plot, not by any means is this true. However, it was the Monteagle letter written to William Parker, Lord Monteagle, in late October which warned of the gunpowder plot. It gave a warning for him not to attend parliament if he wished to live that was the main reason for Fawkes's discovery on 4 November. Monteagle may have been a Catholic, but he was a respected member of the House of Lords. What the conspirators were not aware of, was his loyalty to the new king and to the crown. He himself could not warn the king in person as the king was away from court, hunting. Monteagle was quick to act. He quickly made his way to Cecil who was in the company of men like Suffolk, Northampton, Worchester and Nottingham. James was then later shown the letter upon his arrival and the conspiracy which Cecil and many others had long suspected was imminent was finally confirmed. James himself would later state that he discovered the plot, but as it happens, Cecil's secretary, Levinus Muncke, stated the opposite, and that the plot had long been suspected.[10]

Many of the men that were involved in the plot had once served the crown in some capacity. Guy Fawkes, for example, who was born in 1570 in York. It appears that his family were Protestant, and that he was the only son. His parents were respectable enough and his father was a Registrar of the Consistory Court. However, his mother remarried a Catholic and therefore, it appears that the origins of his faith can be found in his childhood. He later served in the Spanish army and assisted the capture of Calais in 1595. He was also tasked with seeking aid from Spain for the Jesuits upon Elizabeth I's death. He only returned to England in 1604 it seems, on Catesby's request. Like many of the thirteen, Fawkes was absolutely a devout Catholic. The problem however for most involved was the fact that they came from a long line of aristocratic and noble families. Some men involved, such as Sir Digby, had even been previously knighted by James.[11]

Though some members of the thirteen had been under surveillance for some time, the question remains: how did they get the gunpowder under the cellar of parliament? Fawkes had been acting as what Sidney refers to as a porter of some sort outside of the Parliament cellars which had been available to rent. When he noticed that one cellar in particular was being vacated, he informed another conspirator, Percy, who then rented the cellar, stating that he wished to use it as storage for coal. By the time the cellar was filled with barrels of powder, the thirteen had become suspicious as

Parliament had been continuously pushed forward in 1605. It was Francis Tresham who informed Monteagle and others of the looming danger to their lives. Prior to the final meeting of the thirteen before their plan was to take place, Tresham had already long betrayed them.[12]

Mounteagle may well have had familial connections with some of the conspirators and shared their faith as a member of the minority religion, but he was also a well-respected nobleman and had little opposition to the new regime. He may well have been Catholic, but he outwardly conformed to Protestantism, likely to protect his family, political career and wealth. Indeed, some have suggested that could have been one of Cecil's spies. He had met with Catesby for example, several times from the beginnings of the plot to just a month prior to its discovery. In fact, when the letter was delivered to Cecil and his dining guests, it could almost be suggested that the party were expecting it. However, Monteagle was also careful to secretly warn the thirteen, as his Catholic servant named Warde was also present when the letter was read aloud. Warde was a friend of one of the conspirators – Winter. The conspirators were soon warned that they had a Judas in their midst. This worked nicely for Monteagle, as he was able to warn his Catholic brothers, whilst also appearing loyal to the crown. Later, when he died in 1622, he received the last rights of the Catholic Church.[13]

When Fawkes was questioned on 5 November, what exactly the conspirators' plans were after blowing up the king, queen, commons and both Protestant and Catholic peers, he answered that the plan was to simply pray for the souls of those who were Catholic. This shows that though Cecil was already aware of the plot, to what extent is unclear, the Monteagle letter was the downfall of the Gunpowder Plot and that Tresham's betrayal sealed all their fates. Fawkes also stated that though they had not wished for a foreign Catholic ruler, but an English one after the deed was done, they had not exactly been able to plan for the future due to the need of secrecy. Luckily for Cecil, there was no plan for any foreign invasion thereafter.[14]

Fawkes, in the Tower, had confessed. Much of what he said may already have been known to Cecil. Whatever the case, the other twelve men were not arrested straight away for fear that others involved would have time to flee. Cecil wanted all those involved to be taken down for their treachery. On 7 November, two days later, a proclamation of the arrest of only eight men was issued. Most of the men, particularly the eight arrested, were in some small way involved in the Essex Rebellion of Elizabeth's reign not five years prior. Monteagle then gave a further list of co-conspirators and Cecil then went about having them arrested. Even the Spanish Ambassador was suspected of being involved. Cecil had uncovered a plot that would likely have ended the king's and queen's lives, the lives of many innocent members of the House of Commons, probably that of many civilians and even possibly his own life. Yet it was perhaps his greatest moment. It was also proof that any form of tolerance would no longer be possible. After the trials of those involved, with many executions including the most infamous of Fawkes, and the life imprisonment of others, anti-Catholic legislation was brought about, and due to the Gunpowder Plot, the vision of internal peace in England between Protestants and Catholics was impossible. However, there was another question of union in discussion – that of uniting England and Scotland. In this, Cecil had his work cut out for him.[15]

For some time, James had been approaching the idea of one united single kingdom of England and Scotland. He was king of both, and in general, his idea may have seemed more practical than anything else. However, there were many factors to consider. Cecil was tasked with furthering these discussions and coming to some plan of action. For the English, the idea of amalgamating with the Scots was too much to bear. Many Scots were also adamant to keep their own national identity. Of the few Scots that had made their way to England with the king, there were only three on the Privy Council and others had to put up with a high degree of hostility and violence, as Loades has noted. After the first Parliament, Cecil had tasked a committee of men to come to some conclusion on the matter. The committee came back the following year in 1605, with a general approval of the motion, but there were to be changes made in terms of Scottish legislation. The Scots for their part were eager to hold onto their own laws and authority in their land and therefore, it was difficult to make any progress based on the hostility between two very different kingdoms. The idea of Great Britain as we know it now, was simply that – an idea. Though the plan that James and Cecil came up with was put into motion, it would only come to fruition long after they themselves were gone. The idea was eventually dropped by 1607. Though Cecil and James failed to bring about a united Scotland and England, the Cecil administration continued on. Recusancy laws continued, and Catholics remained under governmental suspicion. For his service to the crown, Cecil was invested into the Order of the Garter – a great privilege for a second son born without a title. By 1608, he had become Lord Treasurer, an office once held by his father.[16]

It seemed that the legacy of the great Lord Burghley had finally come full circle and his son had successfully succeeded his father as the most influential and powerful man in the kingdom besides the king himself. He even received Hatfield House – once the home of Elizabeth before she had become queen. This is where much of the Cecil collection of papers remains today, and Hatfield remains as much a part of the Cecil legacy as it does Elizabeth's. Little did a young William Cecil know when he flocked to a new queen's home all those years before, that his own son would one day be awarded it for his service to the crown.

In 1610, Cecil was tasked with another difficult matter, increasing the crown's income and stabilising the king's finances. He was also to come up with a way of ridding the king of his crippling debts. If religious tolerance and the unity of England and Scotland are deemed to have been ambitious, James's and Cecil's Great Contract was over-ambitious. In essence, it was Cecil's idea that the crown would receive a large annuity in return for yielding all rights to wardship and purveyance – meaning it would no longer purchase the necessary royal household items at inflated prices. This was a problem due to the lack of royal funds as it was to do with James's own extravagant spending, something he inherited inadvertently from Elizabeth. This was a time of peace, and yet despite an end to war with Spain or France, internal tensions continued to fester. The removal of wardship and purveyance was radical, but it would have increased the crown's income substantially, removed James's debts, and allowed Cecil to settle the kingdom's financial situation.[17]

However, the House of Commons was opposed to the idea. They were deeply suspicious as a whole of the notion of the king gaining such an independent, large revenue. This wealth itself was deemed a threat to the stability of the current regime and gave the king more power over Parliament – therefore power to dissolve it. Some historians have stated that by the end of November, James had changed his mind and his terms. However, others note that James did not change his terms by November, but only later retracted his endorsement of the idea when the Commons rejected it. Furthermore, not all courtiers and politicians were opposed to it. However, the overwhelming opposition towards the Great Contract in general as a political undertaking was thereafter directed towards Cecil. The fact that the House of Commons outwardly opposed his ideas to raise the crown's revenue gave the already existing anti-Cecil factions a new platform for their spite. It also seems that the House of Commons were more apprehensive about a new form of taxation. Cecil's idea was innovative, but he was a man ahead of his time. The notion of permanent taxation to give the monarch an income had never been done. The country was at peace, and during peace, heavy taxation was not necessary as there was no war to fund.[18]

After the failings of the Great Contract, it was difficult for Cecil to push for any further radical reform of the government, whether that had to do with taxation, the king's revenue or otherwise. It is often believed that Cecil fell out of favour with the king after his failings of 1610. However, the king's affections for the man who gave him his throne never truly diminished. The period from 1610 until Cecil's death has often been referred to as his 'decline' or 'fall'. Yet, there remained much substance to the son of the great Lord Burghley. The king had long been known to have male favourites. Again, whether this was down to his sexuality or otherwise matters little in understanding Cecil's position in his final years. As he had struggled with Elizabeth's favouritism of the Earl of Essex, Cecil now found himself struggling with the king's new favourite, Sir Robert Carr. Not only was Carr the king's favourite, but he became a popular courtier, and his influence allowed for his own following to grow. A following that was generally opposed to Cecil's influence and power. Indeed, many historians have concluded that it was Carr who influenced James's final decision to draw back his support for the Great Contract in late 1610. Indeed, Cecil had seriously misjudged the Common's reaction towards his idea and the king's reaction to the opposition. The king was deeply offended that he had to retract his support and he blamed Cecil. Unfortunately for Cecil, his final years are mostly remembered for his failings. In hindsight, his approach was fairly modern. Yet, England of 1610 was not yet ready for such rapid change.[19]

Cecil's final years may be remembered for his political errors, but we must also consider the physical decline in his health. Whether this was due to the strain of his duties and the failure of the Great Contract cannot be determined. Yet, it seems that multiple factors contributed to his ill health. If Cecil could not get the backing of the government of which his master, the king presided over, then what purpose did he serve? Indeed, Cecil made a true enemy in Carr when he criticised the king's grant of £20,000 to his favourite. This, however, is only one interpretation of Cecil's so called 'decline'. In fact, the truth is much more complicated than what has previously been interpreted. There is evidence to suggest that while the king mistrusted Cecil after his failings of 1610, he ultimately depended on Cecil's influence, power, and administrative genius right up until the latter's final days. Whether Cecil's influence remained as strong as it was prior to 1610 has been long discussed by historians.[20]

With Cecil's Great Contract pushed aside, the king and Parliament continued to discuss the solutions for the crown's crippling financial situation. The House of Commons may have been far too conservative and untrustworthy of Cecil's radical ideas, but a solution was still needed nonetheless. The king needed a supply of cash, and he was sure he would get it. However, the House of Commons were opposed to granting any revenue for the king's personal use, and therefore, James remained as much a pauper as king of England as he was as king of Scotland. Indeed, with Cecil's failings in the final months of 1610, the king was put under enormous pressure from the Commons and he was openly criticised for his financial generosity to Scotland – the country of his birth and birthright as king. In the end, the parliament remained divided and they paused coming to any conclusion for that November. When a meeting was held with the king in person and the council came up with further ideas, the king rejected them. However, tensions continued to brew. Cecil's informants had found that a particular group of men opposed to any Scottish influence on English affairs were petitioning for the king to have his Scottish followers removed. This was reported to the king by his new secretary named Sir Thomas Lake, who was no friend of Cecil's. It appears that Lake brought this information to the king and upon the king confronting Cecil on the matter, the Lord Treasurer denied any knowledge of malice.[21]

With Lake's and Carr's growing influence on the king, and the king's frustrations with Cecil after the failure of the Great Contract, it is no wonder that the Lord Treasurer found himself in a difficult position. However, is it a fair assumption to refer to his final years as his 'decline'? Can we really base Carr's rise to favouritism on Cecil's failure to secure an agreement on the Great Contract or vice versa? Indeed, it appears that Secretary Lake seemed more interested in stirring the pot and insinuating far more resentment between both men than there probably was. In a letter to Cecil, Lake discussed the Commons' reaction to Cecil's proposal and Carr's influence on the king. Indeed, Lake may have been suggesting that Carr was trying to cause some discord between James and the Commons, and not simply with Cecil alone. Whatever Carr's intentions were and whatever we can take from Lake's meddling, it would appear that both were unsuccessful. When, at the end of the year, Parliament was dissolved temporarily, both the king and Cecil likely agreed it was the best decision.[22]

Cecil may well have believed he was on the way out of favour by the end on 1610, but the fact that he remained in his position is evidence enough that the failures of that year had not quite finished him. However, the Lord Treasurer had reason enough to fear the king's wrath. One of the most well-known of James's letters to Cecil, sometime after the failure of the Great Contract and the threat to his Scottish followers, reveals how the king really felt: 'Your greatest error hath been that ye ever expected to draw honey out of gall, being a little blinded by the self love of your own council in holding together this Parliament, whereof all men were despaired, as I have oft told you, but yourself alone.' However, the king also made sure to let Cecil know that though he had misjudged the Commons' reaction to his contract, this did not mean he had lost the favour of his master:

> My little beagle... I wonder what should make you to conceive
> so the alteration or diminishing of my favor towards you...
> for I am sure I never gave you any such occasion, and all that
> know me do know I never use to change my affection from any
> man except the cause be printed in his forehead.[23]

As poignant as this letter is, it is often forgotten that with his deteriorating health, Cecil also depended much on his family, as had his father. His wife was long dead, but he was still a father. He continued to be as busy as ever, and though he was shaken by his failings in 1610, Cecil continued conducting both domestic and foreign affairs. There has been some suggestion that the quality of his administration waned due to his increasingly ill health. Indeed, his ability to advise and conduct his duties on behalf of the king itself, depended on his ability to attend the king. James was not Elizabeth, and the current council was not the one of the ailing Lord Burghley's day. The king and council were not willing to flock to Cecil's home every time his health weakened, simply to conduct the affairs of state. His job in itself was no easy task, and though his health was declining, there remained no better man for the job. Parliament was also postponed in April 1612, due to Cecil's ill health. This in itself could suggest the king and Commons' respect for the Lord Treasurer and also their inability to conduct matters without his presence. There may have been those who opposed Cecil's power, but in all, most supported the man who had given his life to the crown and state. With no notable candidate to take the reins, Cecil had to endure. Whether he wished to retire due to his declining health is another matter entirely. The evidence suggesting his hand in almost all state affairs, particularly in State Papers up until 1612, could indicate that he was unwilling to yield to another. In fact, during his final months, he was more popular than ever. Men continued to write to him for favour, and many were grateful for the patronage he offered them.[24]

Throughout his final seven years of influence and power, Cecil, much like his father, spent lavishly. The fact that his power under James as monarch would only last that long meant that his money was in fact well-spent. Indeed, he became a wealthy businessman under the patronage of James I. He not only served in a position that allowed for numerous grants, offices, and therefore revenues, but he was also shrewd enough to invest in land, which after developed into shops, general business and homes, he was able to generate a generous income. As Loades states, we cannot know for sure every avenue of the Lord Treasurer's income, but if he was worried about the king's finances, he was not worried about his own. His family greatly benefitted from this, and likely lived more lavishly than the royal household. To put it into perspective, most peers made an annuity of around £4,000. Towards the end of his life, Cecil was making up to £24,000. He was therefore able to spend up to £12,000 a year on luxuries alone. Something the king was fighting in Parliament for.[25]

Though Cecil and Carr may not have been on the best terms, Lindquist has suggested a more nuanced interpretation of their rivalry. Cecil's final two years were not his strongest, politically and physically. However, if the king's letters are one reason to consider his favour was never lost, his joint appointment with the Earl of Suffolk as Lord Lieutenant of Dorset in 1611 is another. Indeed, it could be considered that James was able to bestow favour on more than one man, and despite his interest in Carr, the latter would never rise as high as Robert Cecil, even after his death. The lieutenancy of Dorset was yet another honour bestowed upon the Lord Treasurer. Yet, it also presented more work for the ailing Cecil. When James had granted the office to Cecil and Suffolk, he had already had the pleasure of visiting Cecil's home in Cranborne, from which his son, William Cecil, Viscount Cranborne's title derived. Cecil was sure to groom his son for a life of service to the crown just as his own father had for him. Indeed, as Elizabeth had favoured Robert Cecil as his father's protégé, James took a liking to young William Cecil. As Cecil began to slow down, due to his ill health, it was only natural that his son took on some of his duties.[26]

Cecil was also fond of Queen Anne and had a particular interest in Henry, the Prince of Wales, and thus, James's heir. It is often stated that there existed some bad feelings between the Prince of Wales and Cecil. Some have indicated that this derived from his disproval of a marriage between Henry and the Spanish Infanta. Such a marriage would not only have finalised the peace between England and Spain however. Spain remained a Catholic country and an influential European power. It seems however that there is little evidence to suggest any tension between the Prince of Wales and Lord Treasurer. Quite the opposite.

Towards the end of 1611, Cecil was no longer the man he once was. He was never the strongest individual by any means and he had always been more fragile than he let on. With his disability making his daily tasks more and more difficult as his health in general decline, it is no wonder that he struggled in his final year.[27] The king often gave him breaks from his duties.

Cecil tried many remedies and took the waters at Bath. However, when he left for Bath, he remained just as influential and powerful as he had been upon James's accession. Therefore, it is important that his final years should be re-evaluated. His health was most certainly bad, and indeed, he made more than one political blunder. But his power remained. On his way back from taking respite, Robert Cecil was apparently crippled by pain. Eventually, he could take no more, and died in Marlborough on 24 May 1612. Aged just forty-eight, he had not lived a life as long as his father's, but considering his disability and declining health over a number of years, he had lived a relatively long and full life. Though he was not as affectionate with his own children as his father had been, his son William was with him in his final moments, and this says much about the relationship between the two.[28]

Though his father was a great record keeper and diarist, Robert Cecil did not keep a diary and kept his writings to that of his duties. There are numerous letters between Robert and his father, the king and others, but many details of his own life are missing and therefore he remains one of the most elusive Cecils. For such an important figure, it is strange that we do not know for certain what Cecil died of. Some have suggested cancer, while others suggest that he died from scurvy, which brought on open sores amongst other gruesome symptoms. Cecil's enemies were quick to accuse him of contracting syphilis, and it was suggested he had at least one mistress. However, there is little to no evidence to suggest that Cecil had any interest in debauchery or simply taking on a mistress or marrying again. Indeed, these personal thoughts of the Lord Treasurer are lost to us, if they even existed at all. It is more likely that such rumours derived from the slander of those who wished to smear his legacy.[29]

Though Robert Cecil's relationship with his children and family was complicated, he was nonetheless greatly loved and missed by his children. We know little of his half-brother Thomas's reaction to his death, or whether they were close towards the end of his life, but he had many supporters, friends and allies. The king likely felt the loss of his beloved 'beagle' the most, and indeed, Robert Cecil would not be replaced for years. Since the 1590s, he had dedicated his life to the service of the crown and the Protestant state. Yet, he had more foes than friends, and there were many who did not mourn his death, especially James's favourites at court. He did however, ensure that the succession after Elizabeth's death went as smoothly as possible; he protected the integrity of his father's legacy, had accumulated massive wealth, lands and beautiful homes, and ensured that his father's vision of a strong, Protestant England remained. However, he was also a man, with human desires, feelings and vices. He married, had children to secure his dynasty, and ensured that the Cecil name would be engrained in English history and politics for years to come. Overall, Robert Cecil proved to be just as successful as a statesman as his father, and it was due to his diligence, intelligence and determination that he ensured the preservation and continuation of the Cecil dynasty. Upon his death, his son William became the 2nd Earl of Salisbury and the influence, wealth and power of this great family continued. In truth, the *Regnum Cecilianum* had not ended, it had only just begun.[30]

Epilogue

The Legacy of a Great Family

William and Robert Cecil's legacy remains impeccably intact today. Their individual contributions to what is now Great Britain cannot be understated. Both men were fiercely loyal to the crown and the monarchs that they served. However, it is important to note that though they served Elizabeth and James, they also served themselves. Neither men were the typical courtier of the day. Indeed, it can be argued that father and son were not courtiers, whereas William's father and grandfather definitely were. The Cecil family had long served the Tudors by the time Robert's and Thomas's sons, both named William for their grandfather, came into their own, the political structure of England had changed rapidly. In essence, this was due to their grandfather's service, diligence, genius and overall sense of duty to the state and crown. Robert Cecil was perhaps even more radical in his vision for England than his father. However, though his ideology can be seen in some sense in Britain's political basis today, his contemporaries did not share his vision. Lord Burghley, on the other hand, was far more cautious than his son. Both men were cut from the same cloth, but both were very different.

After Robert's death, he was not replaced for some time, and indeed, his many enemies rejoiced upon his death. It must be noted that though his final years were politically damning to a degree, his overall success as a politician and statesman far outweigh his failures. Such was the same with Lord Burghley. But what became of their ancestors? Who were they? How did they serve? What was the level of their influence? And where are they now? William Cecil's eldest grandchildren not only inherited his name as well as their fathers' titles, but also the legacy of Lord Burghley. Politics and duty to the crown was in their blood. But with two very influential and powerful men to live up to, it is no wonder that we forget the other Cecils. The Cecil name, lineage and dynasty as it were, took two different directions, both legitimate, but both originating from two very different and perhaps distant brothers. Both the noble houses of Exeter and Salisbury remain intact today. In fact, both trace their lineage right back to the first Cecils to serve the crown in the late fifteenth century. Thomas Cecil, as mentioned before, was a politician, but he was much better suited to the army and was well able to command a room. He inherited Burghley House as the eldest son, and the Cecil family home is now a representation of the Great Lord Burghley's legacy. In the late eighteenth century, the earldom of Exeter was raised to that of Marquis. Then, at the dawn of the nineteenth century, the earldom of Salisbury was also raised to the same. Between the seventeenth and late eighteenth centuries, many Cecils, such as Sir Edward Cecil, a younger son of the first Earl of Exeter became a solider. However, many others served in local public offices and as their lineage continued to grow and expand, so did their patronage and influence. Many were MPs and served the crown directly in government.[1]

The Earl of Salisbury's lineage also continued and remains just as intact as the Exeter line does today. Indeed, many of Robert Cecil's descendants were granted offices and titles of their own, further expanding their political and social reach in British society. Many would take on higher roles such as the 3rd Earl of Salisbury, who as Loades mentions, mirrored that of his grandfather's and great-grandfather's careers as he served on the Privy Council. They seem to have survived the ten years of English republicanism under Oliver Cromwell after the execution of Charles I. During disputes between Charles II after the restoration, and his brother, the Catholic James II, the 3rd earl resigned from his position on the council. He, in fact, supported the accession of James II as a Catholic contender to the throne. Times were changing, but it was too much for Charles to stomach and it politically restrained the Salisbury line for a time. One can only imagine William and Robert Cecil's reaction after their decades of attempting to avoid a Catholic succession.[2]

It was another Cecil, Robert Gascoyne Cecil, who was the 3rd Marquis of Salisbury, elevated to that title as previously mentioned during the late 1860s, that really breathed some fresh air into the political scope and legacy of the Cecil family. Indeed, many of the Cecils held offices throughout the past few hundred years since the death of the first Earl of Salisbury. However, their actual political influence and ideology was somewhat dismal until 'Gascoyne' was elevated further during Queen Victoria's reign. He was held in high regard by the queen and was a popular politician of the time. Like his forefathers before him, he was a man of true conviction and vision. He was the representative of Victorian political change as William Cecil had been during Elizabeth I's reign. But what made him different? Born in 1830, some years before Victoria became queen, he likely did not remember a time without her as queen. His domestic and foreign policy and approach towards political strategy has been discussed by political historians for decades. He was a member of the Conservative party during his political career and he even served as Prime Minister on three separate occasions over a period of fourteen years, as mentioned by Weston.[3]

Prime Minister Cecil had a lifelong political rivalry with another politician of the opposing Liberal Party, William Ewart Gladstone. Though it cannot be said that this mirrored the factional rivalry for political dominance between Robert Cecil and Robert Devereux, it does nonetheless serve as an example of the continuation of the Cecil vision for political power, influence and dominance. Cecil's political theory, ideology and arguments were strikingly new for the day, and as a leader of the Conservative party and government, he was genuinely successful and admired. Of course, his ideology, such as his ancestor's, the first Earl of Salisbury's, ruffled some feathers and many were not ready for the changes in governance that he suggested. However, this time, his political agenda took hold in a country that was experiencing rapid social and economic change. Not to mention that the Industrial Revolution was well under way. Indeed, as Weston noted 'With high energy and maturing political skills, Salisbury undertook to cement a firm alliance between the authority of an aristocratic, hereditary house and the popular will…and thanks to him there developed a distinctive Conservative ideology that shaped his political party's policy in the decade before 1914.' It would be during Cecil's tenure as Prime Minister and the leader of the Conservative party which dominated British politics, that would see Britain become more than just a powerful European island nation. In every way possible, Gascoyne's vision for Britain as a domineering empire which spread across so many nations that it was said of which the sun never set, outweighed his ancestor Lord Burghley's vision. It perhaps even outweighed that of the first Earl of Salisbury's expansion of British territory and the uniting of two kingdoms under one ruler.[4]

Upon his death, he was succeeded by his son James, the 4th earl but it would be his second son Edgar, much like that after the death of Lord Burghley, who became a rising star. He lived a life of politics as any other Cecil, but was a talented lawyer and served in the House of Commons. He was rewarded for his services during the First World War and his vision for peace. Other Cecils became notable scholars, secretaries, minor politicians and authors. The list of their talents goes on, but it is their political influence that remained their greatest legacy.[5]

Many of the great Cecil houses have lasted just as the two separate noble houses of Exeter and Salisbury have. Theobalds is gone, but Hatfield survives and now houses the thousands of letters and papers written by William and Robert Cecil. The fact that much of their papers survives despite centuries of political and social changes, not to mention numerous wars, is in itself a miracle, and yet, there is still so much to go by. The houses that remain intact and conserved are a testament to the incredible legacy of the Cecil family and their influence. Burghley House served as home to six generations of the Cecil family, descended from Lord Burghley's eldest son from his first marriage, Thomas Cecil. The current and eighth Marquis Michael Cecil now lives in British Columbia with his wife and children. His son Andrew Cecil is now Lord Burghley and is also married. They also currently reside in British Columbia, but return to the UK and Burghley House regularly. The house and the integrity of William Cecil's dynasty, represented by his favourite home is now in the care of the Burghley House Preservation Trust. The Marquis's cousin is the director of the trust and lives in Burghley House with her husband and their children. Not only does this mean that the Cecil ancestral home is open to the public who can marvel in the Cecils' extraordinary eloquence as innovative architects and designers, but it also remains a family home. This is what it was built for, and so it reminds us that though William Cecil was perhaps one of the greatest statesmen of English history, he was also man who valued his family, and family life deeply.[6] The current and 7th Marquis of Salisbury, also known as Baron Gascoyne-Cecil is Robert Michael James Gascoyne Cecil. He also carried on the Cecil family legacy and serves as a politician for the British Conservative party. The family are also landowners and are well connected to the current royal family and the late queen, Elizabeth II.

During the mid-sixteenth and early seventeenth centuries, the Cecils dominated English politics in ways that had never been accomplished before. There had been many great men to rise under the patronage of the Tudors from the very beginning of the dynasty's reign. However, many men such as Thomas Wolsey and Thomas Cromwell lacked the genius shown by William and Robert Cecil. Their ability to rise to favour, steer their monarchs through periods of great social, economic and political changes, not to mention numerous threats both domestic and foreign was the reason for their success as politicians and advisors. In preserving the legacy and integrity of the Tudor and Stuart dynasties, they inadvertently established and preserved their own. The Cecil family legacy as shrewd politicians derived from the very first great statesman, William Cecil, and because of him, we owe much to our love and fascination with Elizabeth I. Without the Cecils at her side, Elizabeth may never have lived and reigned as long and successfully as she did. We now refer her as Gloriana, and remember the Elizabethan period as the 'Golden Age'. However, it was in truth, as much the *Regnum Cecilianum* as it was Elizabethan and Britain owes a great deal of gratitude to the Cecils in terms of its success as an island nation as it does any monarch or other politician of the past. The Cecils were and remain one of the most fascinating, enigmatic and extraordinary families in British history.

Author's Final Note

The Cecil family, and in particular William Cecil, Lord Burghley, have fascinated me for a number of years. Though I am predominantly a historian of women's history, I was nonetheless compelled to delve into the lives of Tudor England's greatest statesmen. The intention of this book was not to record or discuss the entirety of William's and Robert's political careers, for this is not what I wished to present. What I hope the reader takes from this work, is that the Cecils were not simply cold, calculated and genius statesmen, but real men with courage, dreams, families and above all, flaws. There were living, breathing men who both loved and suffered loss. The lives of the Cecil women have also been almost entirely brushed over. Yet, their stories add as much substance to the tale of a fascinating family. There have been multiple works based on the Cecils and their political careers and lives, notably that by David Loades, Conyers Read, Alan Gordon Smith and Stephen Alford, all of whom I greatly admire. However, I wished to present a more nuanced and human interpretation of the men who steered England through the dawn of the Early-Modern period. I hope the readers of this work enjoy it as much as I enjoyed writing it.

David Lee

Endnotes

Chapter 1 – The Origins of a Great Family

1. John Nichols, *The progression and public processions of Queen Elizabeth*, (London, 1832), p. 242. It was also spelt Syssyllte in relation to a place or origin, as can be seen in The Cecil Papers, Pedigree of the Cecil family, from 'Syssyllte', Vol. 143/4, Before Aug. 1598, https://www-proquest-com.jproxy.nuim.ie/cecilpapers/docview/1858030728/citation/B5A833618EA34A2EPQ/16?accountid=12309 (12 Apr. 2021).
2. A Tudor Times Insight, *Sir William Cecil: Elizabeth I's Chief Minister* (eBook), (2015), p. 8.
3. *The Cecil Papers, Feb. 1548/9 in Calendar of the Cecil Papers in Hatfield House: 1306-1571, vol. 1,* (London, 1883), pp. 58-80, British History Online, http://www.british-history.ac.uk/cal-cecil-papers/vol1/pp58-80 (20 Apr. 2021). Also see Martin, A. S. Hume, *The great Lord Burghley: a study in Elizabethan statecraft* (eBook), (London, 1898), p. 4, Internet Archive Online, https://archive.org/details/greatlordburghl00humegoog/page/n30/mode/1up (12 Apr. 2021).
4. Edward Nares, *Memoirs of the life and administration of the Right Honourable William Cecil, Lord Burghley: containing an historical view of the times in which he lived, and of the many eminent and illustrious persons with whom he was connected; with extracts from his private and official correspondence, and other papers, now first published from the originals,* Vol. 1, (London, 1828), p. 13, Internet Archive Online, https://archive.org/details/memoirsoflifeadm01nare/page/13/mode/1up (12 Apr. 2021).
5. B.W. Beckingsale, *Burghley: Tudor statesman, 1520-1598*, (London, 1967), p. 4.
6. *The Cecil papers, Pedigree of the Cecil family, from owyn, temp. regis Harold, to William Cecil, Vol. 143/2,* (before Aug. 1598) Online at ProQuest, https://login.jproxy.nuim.ie/login?url=https://www-proquest-com.jproxy.nuim.ie/government-official-publications/cecil-family-2-pedigree-owyn-temp-regis-harold/docview/1858029879/se-2?accountid=12309 (12 Apr. 2021).

7. Beckingsale, *Burghley: Tudor statesman*, p. 4.
8. David Loades, *The Cecils: privilege and power behind the throne*, (London, 2019), pp 13-15.
9. Beckingsale, *Burghley: Tudor statesman*, pp. 9-10.
10. Nares, *Memoirs of...Lord Burghley*, vol. 1, p. 5.
11. Nares, *Memoirs of...Lord Burghley*, vol. 1, pp. 14-15.
12. Beckingsale, *Burghley: Tudor statesman*, p. 7.
13. Alan Gordon Smith, *William Cecil: the power behind Elizabeth*, (Holoulu, 1934), p. 5.
14. *Ibid.*
15. Lisa Hilton, *Elizabeth, renaissance prince: a biography*, (London, 2015), p. 76.
16. Smith, *William Cecil*, pp. 5-6.
17. *Ibid.*
18. Nares, *Memoirs of...Lord Burghley*, vol. 1, pp. 15-16.
19. Nares, *Memoirs of...Lord Burghley*, vol. 1, p. 41.
20. Beckingsale, *Burghley: Tudor statesman*, p. 11.
21. Smith, *William Cecil*, p. 6.
22. Beckingsale, *Burghley: Tudor statesman*, pp 15-16.
23. Smith, *William Cecil*, p. 8.
24. Beckingsale, *Burghley: Tudor statesman*, p. 12.
25. Smith, *William Cecil*, pp. 8-9.
26. Beckingsale, *Burghley: Tudor statesman*, pp. 18-19.
27. *Ibid.*
28. Francis Peck, *Desiderata curiosa: a collection of divers scarce and curious pieces relating chiefly to matters of English history...* Vol. 1, (London, 1779), p. 80, Internet Archive online, https://archive.org/details/desideratacurios00peck/page/82/mode/1up (14 Apr. 2021).
29. Beckingsale, *Burghley: Tudor statesman*, p. 21.
30. Nares, *Memoirs of...Lord Burghley*, vol.1, p. 60.
31. Hume, *The great Lord Burghley*, p. 10.
32. Nares, *Memoirs of...Lord Burghley*, vol. 1, pp. 71-72.
33. Beckingsale, *Burghley: Tudor statesman*, p. 23.
34. Loades, *The Cecils*, p. 26.
35. Nares, *Memoirs of...Lord Burghley*, vol. 1, p. 73.
36. Beckingsale, *Burghley: Tudor statesman*, pp. 25-26.
37. Hume, *The great Lord Burghley*, p. 16.
38. Beckingsale, *Burghley: Tudor statesman*, p. 27.
39. Linda Porter, *Katherine the queen: the remarkable life of Katherine Parr*, (London, 2011), pp. 302-303.

40. The Religious Tract Society, *Writings of Edward the sixth, William Hugh, Queen Catherine Parr, Anne Askew, Lady Jane Grey, Hamilton, and Balnaves*, (London, 1831), pp. 29-31.
41. Robert Lemon (ed.), *Calendar of state papers, domestic series, Edward VI., Mary, Elizabeth, 1547-1580*, (London, 1856), p. 8, Internet Archive online, https://archive.org/details/cu31924091775258/page/n7/mode/2up (15 Apr. 2021).
42. Beckingsale, *Burghley: Tudor statesman*, p. 28.
43. Lemon, *Calendar of state papers, Edward VI*, p. 8.
44. Loades, *The Cecils*, pp. 30-31.

Chapter 2 – The Path to Power

1. Loades, *'The Cecils*, p. 31.
2. Anna Whitelock, *Mary Tudor: England's first queen*, (London, 2010), pp. 132-133.
3. Chris Skidmore, *Edward VI, the lost king of England*, (London, 2008), pp. 87-88.
4. Smith, *William Cecil*, p. 20.
5. Charles Wriothesley, *A chronicle of England during the reigns of the Tudors from A.D. 1485 to 1559*, Vol. 2, ed. William Douglas Hamilton, (London, 1877), p. 10, online at Google Books, https://play.google.com/books/reader?id=u7rvU_OylIAC&pg=GBS.PP5 (21 Apr. 2021).
6. Skidmore, *Edward VI*, pp. 102-105.
7. Smith, *William Cecil*, p. 23.
8. Loades, *The Cecils*, pp. 33-34.
9. Hume, *The great Lord Burghley*, p. 118.
10. Loades, *The Cecils*, p. 36.
11. Wriothesley, *Chronicle of England*, p. 30-31.
12. Wriothesley, *Chronicle of England*, p. 36.
13. Loades, *The Cecils*, p. 36.
14. Smith, *William Cecil*, pp. 23-24.
15. Leanda De Lisle, *Tudor: the family story*, (London, 2013), pp. 251-253.
16. Hume, *The great Lord Burghley*, p. 24.
17. Smith, *William Cecil*, p. 25.
18. W. H. Charlton, *Burghley: the life of William Cecil, lord Burghley, lord high treasurer of England etc.*, (Stamford, 1847), Google Books Online, https://books.google.ie/books?id=8uQ5AAAAcAAJ&printsec=frontcover&dq=

LORD+BURGHLEY&hl=en&sa=X&ved=2ahUKEwjp1P7zw
ZvwAhUro3EKHQ3XCHIQ6AEwAHoECAAQAg#v
=onepage&q=LORD%20BURGHLEY&f=false (26 Apr. 2021).

19. Smith, *William Cecil*, p. 25.
20. Smith, *William Cecil*, p. 26.
21. Charlton, *Burghley*, p. 14.
22. Smith, *William Cecil*, p. 26.
23. Loades, *The Cecils*, p. 40. Also see Lemon, *Calendar of state papers, Edward VI*, p. 30.
24. *Ibid.*
25. Loades, *The Cecils*, p. 39.
26. Charlton, *Burghley*, p. 15.
27. David Loades, *Mary Tudor*, (London, 2012), p. 56.
28. *Ibid.*
29. Smith, *William Cecil*, pp 28-29.
30. *Ibid.*
31. Loades, *Mary Tudor*, p. 57.
32. Lemon, *Calendar of state papers, Edward VI*, p. 33.
33. Skidmore, *Edward VI*, p. 243.
34. Lemon, *Calendar of state papers, Edward VI*, p. 46.
35. Loades, *Mary Tudor*, p. 57.
36. Loades, *Mary Tudor*, p. 59.
37. Nicola Tallis, *Crown of blood: the deadly inheritance of lady Jane Grey*, (London, 2016), p. 146.
38. Royall Tyler (ed.), *Calendar of state papers, Spain, Vol. 11, 15 Jun. 1553*, (London, 1916), pp. 48-56, British History Online, http://www.british-history.ac.uk/cal-state-papers/spain/vol11/pp48-56 (3 May. 2021).
39. Tallis, *Crown of blood*, p. 146.
40. Loades, *The Cecils*, pp. 26-27.
41. Lemon, *Calendar of state papers, Edward VI*, p. 51.
42. *Ibid.*
43. *Calendar of the Cecil Papers in Hatfield House, 12 May. 1553*, pp. 106-134 (30 Apr. 2021).
44. Loades, *Mary Tudor*, p. 59.
45. Smith, *William Cecil*, p. 30.
46. Skidmore, *Edward VI*, p. 258.
47. Wriothesley, *Chronicle of England*, p. 85.
48. Lemon, *Calendar of state papers, Edward VI*, p. 54.
49. Tallis, *Crown of blood*, p. 151-152.
50. *Ibid.*

51. *Ibid.*
52. Loades, *Mary Tudor*, pp. 60-63.
53. *Ibid.* Also see Wriothesley, *Chronicle of England*, pp. 87-89.
54. Loades, *The Cecils*, p. 47.

Chapter 3 – Heretics and Martyrs

1. Wriothesley, *Chronicle of England*, p. 88.
2. Whitelock, *Mary Tudor*, p. 173.
3. Peck, *Desiderata curiosa*, p. 8.
4. Loades, *The Cecils*, p. 48.
5. Judith M. Richards, *Elizabeth I*, (Oxon, 2012), p. 27.
6. *Ibid.*
7. Loades, *The Cecils*, p. 49.
8. Whitelock, *Mary Tudor*, p. 196.
9. Loades, *The Cecils*, p. 49.
10. Rawdon Brown (ed.), *Calendar of state papers, Venice, Aug. 1554, 16-20, vol. 5*, (London, 1873), pp. 531-567, British History online, https://www.british-history.ac.uk/cal-state-papers/venice/vol5/pp531-567 (6 May. 2021).
11. *The Cecil Papers, Lord Burghley - Family and Historical Memorandum, vol. 140/13 1554*, Online at ProQuest, https://login.jproxy.nuim.ie/login?url=https://www-proquest-com.jproxy.nuim.ie/government-official-publications/cecil-family-2-pedigree-owyn-temp-regis-harold/docview/1858029879/se-2?accountid=12309 (6 May. 2021).
12. Smith, *William Cecil*, p. 35.
13. *Ibid.*
14. *Ibid.*
15. Wriothesley, *Chronicle of England*, p. 96.
16. Loades, *Mary Tudor,* p. 66.
17. Charlton, *Burghley*, pp. 22-23.
18. Loades, *The Cecils*, p. 51.
19. Loades, *The Cecils*, p. 52.
20. Smith, *William Cecil*, p. 36.
21. Smith, *William Cecil*, p. 37.
22. *Ibid.*
23. Whitelock, *Mary Tudor*, p. 296.
24. Whitelock, *Mary Tudor*, pp. 253-256.
25. *Ibid.*

26. Nares, *Memoirs of Lord Burghley,* vol. 1, pp. 625-626.
27. Nares, *Memoirs of Lord Burghley*, vol. 1, pp. 636-639.
28. Loades, *The Cecils,* pp. 52-54.
29. Loades, *The Cecils*, pp. 54-56.
30. *The Cecil Papers, Lord Burghley - Family and Historical Memorandum,* (7 Jun. 2021).
31. Loades, *The Cecils*, p. 56.
32. Wriothesley, *Chronicle of England*, pp. 141-142.
33. Hume, *The great Lord Burghley*, p. 67.
34. Loades, *The Cecils*, pp. 57-58.
35. '*Words spoken by her majesty to Mr. Cecil*', from Hatfield House, 20 Nov. 1558, (The National Archives, TNA SP12/1, no. 7).
36. Hume, *The great Lord Burghley*, pp. 69-70.

Chapter 4 – A New Regime

1. Loades, *The Cecils*, p. 59.
2. Stephen Alford, *The watchers, a secret history of the reign of Elizabeth I*, (London, 2013), p. 34.
3. Alford, *The watchers*, p. 35.
4. Edward Nares, *Memoirs of the life and administration of the Right Honourable William Cecil, Lord Burghley: containing an historical view of the times in which he lived, and of the many eminent and illustrious persons with whom he was connected; with extracts from his private and official correspondence, and other papers, now first published from the originals*, Vol. 2, (London, 1828-31), p. 33, Internet Archive online, https://archive.org/details/memoirsoflifeadm02nareuoft/page/n9/mode/2up (4 Jul. 2021).
5. Nares, *Memoirs of...Lord Burghley*, vol. 2, p. 21.
6. Nares, *Memoirs of...Lord Burghley*, vol. 2, p. 22.
7. Smith, *William Cecil*, p. 47.
8. John Guy, *Elizabeth: the forgotten years*, p. 11.
9. Smith, *William Cecil*, p. 47.
10. Richards, *Elizabeth I*, p. 50.
11. Stephen Alford, *The early Elizabethan polity: William Cecil and the British succession crisis, 1558-1569*, (Cambridge, 1998), pp. 9-10.
12. Smith, *William Cecil*, pp. 47-48.
13. *Ibid.*
14. *Ibid.*

15. Loades, *The Cecils*, p. 62.
16. Alford, *The early Elizabethan polity*, pp. 54-55.
17. Edward, Lord north to Sir William Cecil, 30 Jan. 1559, (*Calendar of the Cecil Papers...*, *Vol. 1*) https://www.british-history.ac.uk/cal-cecil-papers/vol1/pp150-165 (24 July 2021).
18. Lord William Paget to Sir Thomas Parry and Sir William Cecil, 3 Feb. 1559, (*Calendar of the Cecil Papers...*, Vol. 2) https://www.british-history.ac.uk/cal-cecil-papers/vol1/pp150-165 (24 July 2021).
19. Loades, *The Cecils*, p. 64.
20. Alford, *The early Elizabethan polity*, pp. 54-55.
21. Alford, *The early Elizabethan polity*, p. 64.
22. Alford, *The watchers*, P. 44.
23. Alford, *The early Elizabethan polity*, p. 59.
24. Alford, *The watchers*, P. 45.
25. Loades, *The Cecils*, p. 74.
26. Hume, *The great Lord Burghley*, p. 96.
27. Conyers Read, *Mr secretary Cecil and queen Elizabeth*, (London, 1955), p. 161.
28. Alford, *The early Elizabethan polity*, p. 70.
29. Guy, *Elizabeth*, p. 13.
30. *Ibid.*
31. A Tudor Times Insight, *Sir William Cecil,* p. 30.
32. Philippa Jones, *Elizabeth: virgin queen*, (Lincolnshire, 2017), pp. 187-188.
33. Antonia Fraser, *Mary Queen of Scots*, (London, 2009), p. 204.
34. Fraser, *Mary Queen of Scots*, p. 206-209
35. Guy, *Elizabeth*, pp. 13-14.

Chapter 5 – The Hunt for a King

1. William Cecil to Sir Nicholas Throckmorton, 14 July 1561, British Library (BL), Add. MSS 35830, fol. 159v.
2. Loades, *The Cecils*, pp. 64-65.
3. Queen Elizabeth to the Estates of Scotland, Dec. 1560, (*Calendar of the Cecil Papers...*, Vol. 1) https://www.british-history.ac.uk/cal-cecil-papers/vol1/pp243-256#highlight-first (28 Aug. 2021).
4. Wallace T, MacCaffrey (ed.) and William Camden, *The history of the most renowned and victorious princess Elizabeth, late queen of England: selected chapters*, (London, 1970), p. 29.

5. Josephine Ross, *The men who would be king: the courtships of Elizabeth I*, (New York, 2012), p. 83.
6. Loades, *The Cecils*, p. 65.
7. Letter from Bishop de Quadra to the Duchess of Parma, 11 Sept. 1560, *Calendar of state papers, Spain (Simancas)*, Volume 1, 1558-1567, ed. Martin A. S. Hume (London, 1892), pp. 174-176. British History Online, https://www.british-history.ac.uk/cal-state-papers/simancas/vol1/i-lxiii#highlight-first (4 Sept. 2021).
8. Loades, *The Cecils*, p. 67.
9. R. Dudley, John Applyard and James Gairdner, 'The death of Amy Robsart' in *The English Historical Review*, vol. 1, no. 2 (1886), pp. 235-259 at pp. 235-236.
10. *Ibid.*
11. *Ibid.*
12. Ross, *The men who would be king*, pp. 68-70.
13. Hilton, *Elizabeth*, pp. 138-140.
14. Ross, *The men who would be king*, pp. 75-77.
15. Hilton, *Elizabeth*, pp. 140-141.
16. 'Introduction', in *Calendar of State Papers, Spain (Simancas)*, Volume 1, 1558-1567, ed. Martin A. S. Hume (London, 1892), pp. i-lxiii. British History Online http://www.british-history.ac.uk/cal-state-papers/simancas/vol1/i-lxiii (accessed 4 September 2021).
17. Hilton, *Elizabeth*, p. 151.
18. Susan Doran, 'Religion and politics at the court of Elizabeth I: The Habsburg marriage negotiations of 1559-1567' in *The English Historical Review*, vol. 104, no. 413 (1989), pp. 908-926 at p. 914.
19. *Ibid.*
20. Doran, 'Religion and politics', p. 916.
21. A Tudor Times Insight, *Sir William Cecil*, p. 34.
22. Alford, *The early Elizabethan polity*, pp. 142-146.
23. Alford, *The early Elizabethan polity*, pp. 147-149.
24. Alford, *The early Elizabethan polity*, pp. 155-157.
25. Anne McLaren, 'The quest for a king: gender, marriage, and succession in Elizabethan England' in *Journal of British Studies*, vol. 41, no. 3 (2002), pp. 259-290 at pp. 268-269.
26. *Ibid.*
27. Ross, *The men who would be king*, p. 78.
28. Leah S. Marcus, Janel Mueller, Mary Beth Rose, *Elizabeth I: collected works*, (Chicago, 2002), p. 105.
29. Alford, *The early Elizabethan polity*, p. 158.

30. Alford, *The early Elizabethan polity*, pp. 159-163.
31. A. M. F Robinson, 'Queen Elizabeth and the Valois princes' in *The English Historical Review*, vol. 2, no. 5 (1887), pp. 40-77 at pp. 44-45.
32. Robinson, 'Queen Elizabeth and the Valois Princes', pp. 49-51.
33. A Tudor Times Insight, *Sir William Cecil*, p. 35.
34. *Ibid.*
35. Donald Stump and Susan M. Felch, *Elizabeth and her age*, (New York, 2009), pp. 274-276.
36. Loades, *The Cecils*, pp. 172-174.

Chapter 6 – The Spirit's Circle

1. Loades, *The Cecils*, p. 142.
2. Alford, *The early Elizabethan polity*, p. 4.
3. Loades, *The Cecils*, p. 23.
4. Loades, *The Cecils*, p. 131.
5. Mary Dewar, *Sir Thomas Smith: A Tudor intellectual in office*, (London, 1964), p. 5.
6. Dewar, *Sir Thomas Smith*, p. 12.
7. Dewar, *Sir Thomas Smith*, pp. 82-85.
8. Chisholm, Hugh (ed.) 'Throckmorton, Sir Nicholas', in *The Encyclopædia Britannica* (Cambridge University Press, 1911), vol. 26, p. 891.
9. *Ibid.*
10. John Cooper, *The queen's agent: Francis Walsingham at the court of Elizabeth I*, (London, 2011), pp. 5-6.
11. Robert, Hutchinson, *Elizabeth's spy master: Francis Walsingham and the secret war that saved England,* (London, 2007), p. 28.
12. Cooper, *The queen's agent*, p. 39.
13. Conyers Read, 'Walsingham and Burghley in Queen Elizabeth's Privy Council' in *The English Historical Review*, Vol. 28, No. 109 (1913), pp. 34-58 at p. 34.
14. *Ibid.*
15. Read, 'Walsingham and Burghley', pp. 34-36.
16. Louis Adrian Montrose, 'Celebration and insinuation: Sir Philip Sidney and the motives of Elizabethan courtship' in *Renaissance Drama*, vol. 8 (1977), pp. 3-35 at p. 4.
17. Loades, *The Cecils*, p. 217.
18. Loades, *The Cecils*, p. 141.
19. Montrose, 'Celebration and insinuation' pp. 10-12.

20. Alford, *The early Elizabethan polity*, pp. 12-13.
21. Sir Ralph Sadler, *The state papers and letters of Sir Ralph Sadler*, Vol. 1, (Edinburgh, 1809), p ii, Haiti Trust Online, https://babel.hathitrust.org/cgi/pt?id=uc2.ark:/13960/t4dn4dv58&view=1up&seq=16&skin=2021(accessed 30 Oct. 2021).
22. Sadler, *State papers*, p. ii–vi.
23. Sandra Vasoli, *Anne Boleyn's letter from the tower*, (2015), pp. 35-38.
24. Extracts from P.W. Hasler (ed.), *The history of Parliament: The house of commons 1558-1603*, (London, 1981), The History of Parliament online, https://www.historyofparliamentonline.org/volume/1558-1603/member/sadler-sir-ralph-1507-87#footnote2_mhp83ee, (31 Oct. 2021).
25. *Ibid.*
26. Hilton, *Elizabeth*, p. 43.
27. Catherine L. Howey, 'Dressing a virgin queen: court women, dress, and fashioning the image of England's queen Elizabeth I' in *Early Modern Women*, vol. 4 (2009), pp. 201-208 at p. 204.
28. F. Elrington Ball, *The Judges in Ireland 1221-1921*, vol. 1, (London, 1927), p. 213-214, Internet Archive Online, https://archive.org/details/judgesinireland10000unse/page/214/mode/2up, (31 Oct. 2021).
29. *Ibid.*

Chapter 7 – Patronage and Influence

1. Loades, *The Cecils*, pp. 138-140.
2. Loades, *The Cecils*, p. 141.
3. Conyers Read, *Lord Burghley and Queen Elizabeth*, (London, 1965), p. 33.
4. Read, *Lord Burghley*, pp. 33-34.
5. Loades, *The Cecils*, pp. 141-142.
6. Nares, *Memoirs of Lord Burghley*, vol. 2, pp. 543-544.
7. *Ibid.*
8. Nares, *Memoirs of Lord Burghley*, vol. 2, p. 545.
9. Loades, *The Cecils*, p. 143.
10. Read, *Lord Burghley*, p. 35.
11. *Ibid.*
12. Donald R. Kelley, 'Martyrs, myths, and the massacre: the background of St. Bartholomew' in *The American Historical Review*, vol. 77, no. 5 (1972), pp. 1323-1342 at p. 1324.
13. Nares, *Memoirs of Lord Burghley*, vol. 2, pp. 549-550.
14. Read, *Lord Burghley*, pp. 66-68.

15. Read, *Lord Burghley*, p. 77.
16. *Ibid.*
17. Read, *Lord Burghley*, p. 87.
18. Read, *Lord Burghley*, pp. 101-102.
19. Thomas Smith, *De repvblica anglorvm: The maner of gouernement or policie of the realme of England* (London, 1584), pp. 111-112.
20. Norman Jones, 'William Cecil, Lord Burghley, and Managing with the Men-of-Business' in *Parliamentary History*, vol. 34, issue 1 (2015), pp. 45-61 at pp. 47-49.
21. Jones, 'William Cecil', p. 51.
22. Loades, *The Cecils*, pp. 144-149.
23. Loades, *The Cecils*, pp. 149-150.
24. Nicola Tallis, *Elizabeth's rival: the tumultuous tale of Lettice Knollys, Countess of Leicester*, (London, 2017), pp. 164-165.
25. Tallis, *Elizabeth's rival*, pp. 161-167.
26. Loades, *The Cecils*, pp. 155-156.
27. Loades, *The Cecils*, p. 157.
28. Stump and Felch, *Elizabeth and her age*, pp. 274-276.
29. Loades, *The Cecils*, p. 169.

Chapter 8 – A Family Man

1. A Tudor Times Insight, *Sir William Cecil*, pp. 57-58.
2. 'William Cecil: family life', Tudor Times online, https://tudortimes.co.uk/people/william-cecil-family-life/a-growing-family, (3 Dec. 2021).
3. A Tudor Times Insight, *Sir William Cecil*, pp. 58-59.
4. A Tudor Times Insight, *Sir William Cecil*, p. 59. Also see Smith, *William Cecil*, p. 81.
5. Smith, *William Cecil*, p. 81.
6. Loades, *The Cecils*, p. 71.
7. Loades, *The Cecils*, pp. 205-206.
8. Smith, *William Cecil,* p. 177.
9. 'William Cecil: family life', Tudor Times online, https://tudortimes.co.uk/people/william-cecil-family-life/a-growing-family, (4 Dec. 2021).
10. Smith, *William Cecil*, p. 177.
11. *Ibid.*
12. Alan, H. Nelson, *Monstrous adversary: the life of Edward de Vere, 17th Earl of Oxford*, (Liverpool, 2003), p. 46.
13. Smith, *William Cecil*, pp. 177-178.

14. Read, *Lord Burghley*, pp. 124-128.
15. *Ibid.*
16. *Ibid.*
17. *Ibid.*
18. *Ibid.*
19. Read, *Lord Burghley*, p. 132.
20. Smith, *William Cecil*, p. 178.
21. Read, *Lord Burghley*, pp. 132-135.
22. A Tudor Times Insight, *Sir William Cecil*, p. 64.
23. Read, *Lord Burghley*, p. 129.
24. Nelson, *Monstrous adversary*, p. 218.
25. Loades, *The Cecils*, p. 222.
26. Loades, *The Cecils*, pp. 223-225.
27. *Ibid.*
28. Read, *Lord Burghley*, p. 276.
29. Loades, *The Cecils*, pp. 203-204.
30. Loades, *The Cecils*, pp. 205-207.
31. A Tudor Times Insight, *Sir William Cecil,* p. 64.
32. Read, *Lord Burghley*, pp. 407-408.
33. *Ibid.*
34. Read, *Lord Burghley*, pp. 446-447.
35. Read, *Lord Burghley*, p. 125.
36. Conyers Read, 'Lord Burghley's household accounts' in *The Economic History Review*, vol. 9, no. 2 (1956), pp. 343-348 at p. 343.

Chapter 9 – Treachery and Victory

1. The National Archives Online, https://www.nationalarchives.gov.uk/spies/ciphers/mary/ma3.htm, (31 Dec. 2021).
2. Read, *Lord Burghley*, pp. 287-288.
3. *Ibid.*
4. Alford, *The watchers*, pp. 179-180.
5. Alford, *The watchers*, pp. 180-184.
6. Alford, *The watchers*, pp. 188-192.
7. G.R., Elton, *England under the Tudors*, (London, 1974), p. 368.
8. Fraser, *Mary queen of Scots*, pp. 591-593.
9. Read, *Lord Burghley*, pp. 340-343.
10. Read *Lord Burghley*, pp. 343-344. Also see Steve Arman, Simon Bird, and Malcolm Wilkinson, *Reformation and Rebellion 1485-1750*, (Oxford, 2002), p. 28.

11. R. Kent Tiernan, 'Walsingham's Entrapment of Mary Stuart' in *American Intelligence Journal*, vol. 34, no. 1 (2017), pp. 146-156.

12. Read, *Lord Burghley*, pp. 344-345. Also see Anthony Babington to Mary Stuart, the Babington postscript and cipher, 1586, SP 12/193/54 and SP 53/18/55, The National Archives online, https://www.nationalarchives. gov.uk/spies/ciphers/mary/ma2_x.htm (4 Jan. 2022).

13. Read, *Lord Burghley*, pp. 344-345. Also see Derek Wilson, *Sir Francis Walsingham: a courtier in an age of terror*, (London, 2007), p. 120.

14. Read *Lord Burghley*, p. 345.

15. Wilson, *Sir Francis Walsingham*, pp. 119-121.

16. Wilson, *Sir Francis Walsingham*, pp. 121-124.

17. Loades, *The Cecils,* pp. 172-175.

18. Loades, *The Cecils,* pp. 181-182.

19. James Grant, *Life of Mary, queen of Scots*, (London, 1828), pp. 190-194.

20. Alford, *The watchers*, pp. 243-245.

21. Read, *Lord Burghley*, pp. 371-372.

22. Alford, *The watchers*, pp. 243-245.

23. Meaghan J. Brown, "The hearts of all sorts of people were enflamed': manipulating readers of Spanish armada news' in *Book History*, vol. 17 (2014), pp. 94–116 at pp. 94-96.

24. Camden, *Elizabeth*, pp. 308-313.

25. Smith, *William Cecil,* pp. 232-237.

26. Garrett Mattingly, *The "invincible" armada and Elizabethan England*, (New York, 1963), pp. 12-15. Also see Smith, *William Cecil,* pp. 232-237.

27. Susan Frye, 'The myth of Elizabeth at Tilbury', in *The Sixteenth Century Journal*, vol. 23, no 1 (1992), pp. 95-114 at pp. 95-97.

28. Richards, *Elizabeth I*, pp. 140-144.

29. Loades, *The Cecils,* pp. 188-189.

30. Richards, *Elizabeth I*, pp. 140-144.

31. Richards, *Elizabeth I*, pp. 144-145.

32. Read, *Lord Burghley*, pp. 435-436.

33. Loades, *The Cecils,* pp. 189-190.

Chapter 10 – The Final Decade

1. Wilson, *Sir Francis Walsingham*, p. 134.

2. Read, *Lord Burghley*, p. 464.

3. Loades, *The Cecils,* p. 226.

4. Read, *Lord Burghley*, p. 467.

5. Loades, *The Cecils,* pp. 226-227.

6. Sarah-Beth Watkins, *Elizabeth I's last favourite: Robert Devereux, 2nd Earl of Essex*, (Hampshire, 2021) pp. 46-51.

7. William Acres (ed.), *The letters of Lord Burghley, William Cecil, to his son Sir Robert Cecil, 1593-1598*, (London, 2017), p. 2.

8. Acres, *The letters of Lord Burghley*, p. 40.

9. Loades, *The Cecils,* pp. 232-235.

10. Watkins, *Elizabeth I's last favourite*, pp. 82-83.

11. Loades, *The Cecils,* p. 236.

12. Walter Bourchier Devereux (ed.), *Lives and letters of the Devereux, Earls of Essex in the reigns of Elizabeth, James I., and Charles I: 1540-1646, Volume 1*, (London, 1853), pp. 389-390. Also see Watkins, *Elizabeth I's last favourite*, pp. 83-84.

13. Devereux, *Lives and letters of the Devereux*, p. 291. Also see Read, *Lord Burghley*, p. 524.

14. Read, *Lord Burghley*, p. 525.

15. Loades, *The Cecils,* pp. 236-240.

16. Acres, *The letters of Lord Burghley*, pp. 242-243.

17. *Ibid.*

18. Christopher Maginn, *William Cecil, Ireland, and the Tudor state*, (Oxford, 2012), p. 2.

19. Watkins, *Elizabeth I's last favourite*, pp. 96-98.

20. Read, *Lord Burghley*, p. 527.

21. Loades, *The Cecils*, p. 196.

22. Smith, *William Cecil,* p. 260.

23. Read, *Lord Burghley*, p. 545.

24. Acres, *The letters of Lord Burghley*, pp. 292-293.

25. Loades, *The Cecils*, p. 197.

26. Helen Castor, *Elizabeth I: 1558-1603*, (London, 2018), p. 90.

27. Nigel Llewellyn, 'Honour in life, death and in the memory: funeral monuments in early modern England', in *Transactions of the Royal Historical Society*, vol. 6 (1996), pp. 179-200 at p. 187.

Chapter 11 – The Cecil Succession

1. Loades, *The Cecils*, p. 198.

2. Smith, *William Cecil,* p. 241.

3. Loades, *The Cecils*, p. 205.

4. Richard Milward, 'Cecil, Thomas, first earl of Exeter (1542–1623), courtier and soldier' in *Oxford Dictionary of National Biography*

online, (2004) https://www.oxforddnb.com/view/10.1093/ref:odnb/9780198614128.001.0001/odnb-9780198614128-e-4981 (31 Jan. 2022).

5. *Ibid.*

6. Loades, *The Cecils*, pp. 206-207.

7. Alford, *The watchers,* pp. 310-311.

8. Robert Lemon (ed.), *Calendar of state papers domestic, Elizabeth, 1581-90, Volume 181* (London, 1865), pp. 256-265, British History online, https://www.british-history.ac.uk/cal-state-papers/domestic/edw-eliz/1581-90/pp256-265 (5 Feb. 2022). Also see Pauline Croft, 'The reputation of Robert Cecil: libels political opinion and popular awareness in the early seventeenth century' in *Transactions of the Royal Historical Society*, vol. 1 (1991), pp. 43-69 at p. 46.

9. Read, *Lord Burghley*, pp. 408-409.

10. Will of William Cecil, Lord Burghley (copy) 1 March 1597/8. Proved 13 November 1598, The national archives, Kew, (PROB 1/3). Also see Loades, *The Cecils*, p. 241.

11. Croft, 'The reputation of Robert Cecil', p. 48.

12. Guy, *Elizabeth*, pp. 351-355.

13. Elton, *England under the Tudors*, p. 470. Also see Loades, *The Cecils*, p. 243.

14. Loades, *The Cecils*, pp. 242-245.

15. Loades, *The Cecils*, pp. 192-193.

16. Guy, *Elizabeth*, pp. 243-244.

17. Natalie Mears, 'Courts, courtiers, and culture in Tudor England' in *The Historical Journal*, vol. 46, no. 3 (2003), pp. 703-722 at p. 708.

18. *Ibid.*

19. Robert Shepard, 'Court factions in early modern England' in *The Journal of Modern History*, vol. 64, no. 4, (1992), pp. 721-745 at p. 737.

Chapter 12 – Crisis and Rebellion

1. Watkins, *Elizabeth I's last favourite*, pp. 105-110.

2. Guy, *Elizabeth*, pp. 309-313.

3. Hilton, *Elizabeth*, pp. 307-309.

4. L.W., Henry, 'Contemporary Sources for Essex's Lieutenancy in Ireland, 1599' in *Irish Historical Studies*, vol. 11, no. 41 (1958), pp. 8-17 at p. 10 (footnotes).

5. Hilton, *Elizabeth*, pp. 307-309.

6. Loades, *The Cecils*, pp. 242-245.

7. Bradley J. Irish, 'The dreading, dreadful Earl of Essex' in *Emotion in the Tudor court: literature, history, and early modern feeling*, (Illinois, 2018) p. 145.

8. Watkins, *Elizabeth I's last favourite*, pp. 116-118.

9. Castor, *Elizabeth I*, pp. 92-93.

10. *Ibid*. Also see De Lisle, *Tudor*, p. 385.

11. *Ibid*.

12. Loades, *The Cecils*, pp. 250-251.

13. Guy, *Elizabeth*, pp. 338-343.

14. Guy, *Elizabeth*, p. 344.

15. Stump and Felch, *Elizabeth and her age*, pp. 500-503.

16. *Ibid*.

17. Hilton, *Elizabeth*, p. 315.

18. Manolo Guerci, 'Salisbury house in London, 1599-1694: The Strand Palace of Sir Robert Cecil' in *Architectural History*, vol. 52 (2009), pp. 31-78 at pp. 32-34.

19. *Ibid*.

Chapter 13 – The Queen is Dead, Long Live the King

1. Stump and Felch, *Elizabeth and her age*, pp. 503-505.

2. Guy, *Elizabeth*, pp. 347-348.

3. Tracy Borman, *The private lives of the Tudors: uncovering the secrets of Britain's greatest dynasty*, (London, 2016), p. 368.

4. Loades, *The Cecils*, pp. 250-251.

5. *Ibid*.

6. Guy, *Elizabeth*, pp. 366-367.

7. Guy, *Elizabeth*, p 368.

8. Rei Kanemura, 'Kingship by descent or kingship by election? The contested tide of James VI and I' in *Journal of British Studies*, vol. 52, no. 2 (2013), pp. 317–342 at p. 321.

9. Kanemura, 'Kingship by descent or kingship by election?', p. 329.

10. Loades, *The Cecils,* pp. 253-254.

11. Likely indicating Mar and Bruce.

12. Loades, *The Cecils,* pp. 253-254.

13. Edmund Goldsmid (ed.), *The secret correspondence of Sir Robert Cecil with James VI. King of Scotland, Volume 1,* (Edinburgh, 1887) p. 31.

14. Goldsmid, *The secret correspondence of Sir Robert Cecil,* p. 44.

15. Alford, *The watchers,* p. 324.

16. *Ibid.*
17. Loades, *The Cecils,* pp. 254-255.
18. John J. LaRocca, '"Who Can't Pray with Me, Can't Love Me": Toleration and the Early Jacobean Recusancy Policy' in *Journal of British Studies*, vol. 23, no. 2 (1984), pp. 22-36 at pp. 24-25.
19. *Ibid.*
20. *Ibid.*
21. Borman, *The private lives*, pp. 368-369.
22. Borman, *The private lives*, pp. 370-371.
23. Borman, *The private lives*, pp. 371-372.
24. Elton, *England under the Tudors*, pp. 474-475.
25. Borman, *The private lives*, p. 373.
26. Loades, *The Cecils,* pp. 258-259.
27. Robert Zaller, 'Review of: King James by Pauline Croft', in *Albion: A Quarterly Journal Concerned with British Studies*, vol. 36, no. 2 (2004), pp. 300-303 at p. 301.
28. Godfrey Davies, 'The Character of James VI and I', in *Huntington Library Quarterly*, vol. 5, no. 1 (1941), pp. 33-63 at p. 37.
29. Loades, *The Cecils,* pp. 259-260.
30. Loades, *The Cecils,* pp. 261-263.
31. *Ibid.*
32. Mark Nicholls, 'Treason's reward: the punishment of conspirators in the Bye Plot of 1603', in *The Historical Journal*, vol. 38, no. 4 (1995), pp. 821-842 at pp. 821-830.
33. Loades, *The Cecils,* p. 266.

Chapter 14 – Gunpowder

1. Pauline Croft, 'Foreword: 'The translation of a monarchy': the accession of James VI and I, 1601-1603' in *King James*, (Hampshire, 2002), British History online, https://archives.history.ac.uk/history-in-focus/Elizabeth/index.html (13 Mar. 2022).
2. Davies, 'The Character of James VI and I', pp. 41-42.
3. Albert J. Loomie, 'King James I's Catholic consort' in *Huntington Library Quarterly*, vol. 34, no. 4 (1971), pp. 303-316 at pp. 304-306.
4. Catherine Loomis, '"Little man, little man": early modern representations of Robert Cecil' in *Explorations in Renaissance Culture*, (2011), The Free Library online, https://www.thefreelibrary.com/%22Little+man%2C+little+man%22%3A+early+modern+representations+of+Robert...-a0273078550 (13 Mar. 2022).

5. Loades, *The Cecils,* pp. 269-270.
6. Jenny Wormald, 'Gunpowder, treason, and Scots' in *Journal of British Studies*, vol. 24, no. 2 (1985), pp. 141-168 at p. 141-142.
7. Philip Sidney, *A history of the gunpowder plot: the conspiracy and its agents*, (London, 1904), pp. 15-20, Internet Archive online, https://archive.org/details/historyofgunpowd00sidnuoft/page/41/mode/1up?view=theater, (19 Mar. 2022.
8. *Ibid.*
9. Loades, *The Cecils,* pp. 266-267.
10. Wormald, 'Gunpowder, treason, and Scots', pp. 142-144.
11. Sidney, *A history of the gunpowder*, pp. 39-54.
12. Sidney, *A history of the gunpowder*, pp. 59-64.
13. Sidney, *A history of the gunpowder*, pp. 70-72.
14. Wormald, 'Gunpowder, treason, and Scots', pp. 165-166.
15. Loades, *The Cecils,* pp. 267-270.
16. Loades, *The Cecils,* pp. 270-271.
17. Eric Lindquist, 'The failure of the great contract' in *The Journal of Modern History*, vol. 57, no. 4 (1985), pp. 617-651 at pp. 617-621.
18. *Ibid.*
19. Eric Lindquist, 'The last years of the first earl of Salisbury', in *Albion: A Quarterly Journal Concerned with British Studies*, vol. 18, no. 1 (1986), pp. 23-41 at pp. 23-26.
20. *Ibid.*
21. Lindquist, 'The last years of the first earl of Salisbury', pp. 26-30.
22. *Ibid.*
23. Lindquist, 'The last years of the first earl of Salisbury', pp. 31-32.
24. Lindquist, 'The last years of the first earl of Salisbury', pp. 32-34.
25. Loades, *The Cecils,* p. 273.
26. Lindquist, 'The last years of the first earl of Salisbury', p. 36.
27. Loades, *The Cecils,* p. 279.
28. Loades, *The Cecils,* pp. 280-281.
29. Loomis, '"Little man, little man"'.
30. Loades, *The Cecils,* pp. 280-282.

Epilogue – The Legacy of a Great Family

1. Loades, *The Cecils,* pp. 282-284.
2. *Ibid.*

3. Corinne Comstock Weston, 'Lord Salisbury: conservative political leader and preeminent politician in Victorian England' in *Proceedings of the American Philosophical Society*, vol. 142, no.1 (1908), pp. 74-80.
4. *Ibid.*
5. Loades, *The Cecils,* pp. 282-284.
6. 'The family now' online at Burghley, https://www.burghley.co.uk/about-us/the-family/the-family-now (24 Mar. 2022).

Bibliography

Calendar of State Papers (online and printed)

Brown, Rawdon, (ed.), *Calendar of state papers, Venice, Aug. 1554, 16-20, vol. 5*, (London, 1873), pp. 531-567, British History online, https://www.british-history.ac.uk/cal-state-papers/venice/vol5/pp531-567.

Calendar of the Cecil papers in Hatfield House: 1306-1571, vol. 1, (London, 1883), British History online, https://www.british-history.ac.uk/cal-cecil-papers/vol1.

Calendar of the Cecil papers in Hatfield House: 1572-1582, vol. 2, (London, 1888), British History online, https://www.british-history.ac.uk/cal-cecil-papers/vol2?page=1.

Calendar of the Cecil papers in Hatfield House: 1583-1589, vol. 3, (London, 1889), British History online, https://www.british-history.ac.uk/cal-cecil-papers/vol3.

Calendar of the Cecil papers in Hatfield House: 1590-1594, vol. 4, (London, 1892), British History online, https://www.british-history.ac.uk/cal-cecil-papers/vol4.

Calendar of the Cecil papers in Hatfield House: 1594-1595, vol. 5, (London, 1894), British History online, https://www.british-history.ac.uk/cal-cecil-papers/vol5.

Calendar of the Cecil papers in Hatfield House: 1596, vol. 6, (London, 1894), British History online, https://www.british-history.ac.uk/cal-cecil-papers/vol6.

Calendar of the Cecil papers in Hatfield House, Pedigree of the Cecil family, from owyn, temp. regis Harold, to William Cecil, Vol. 143/2, (before Aug. 1598), ProQuest online, https://login.jproxy.nuim.ie/login?url=https://www-proquest-com.jproxy.nuim.ie/government-official-publications/cecil-family-2-pedigree-owyn-temp-regis-harold/docview/1858029879/se-2?accountid=12309.

Calendar of the Cecil papers in Hatfield House, Lord Burghley - Family and Historical Memorandum, vol. 140/13 1554, ProQuest online, https://login.jproxy.nuim.ie/login?url=https://www-proquest-com.jproxy.nuim.

ie/government-official-publications/cecil-family-2-pedigree-owyn-temp-regis-harold/docview/1858029879/se-2?accountid=12309.

Hume, Martin A., *Calendar of state papers, Spain (Simancas),* Volume 1, 1558-1567, (London, 1892), https://www.british-history.ac.uk/cal-state-papers/simancas/vol1.

Lemon, Robert, (ed.), *Calendar of state papers, domestic series, Edward VI., Mary, Elizabeth, 1547-1580,* (London, 1856), p. 8, Internet Archive online, https://archive.org/details/cu31924091775258/page/n7/mode/2up.

Lemon, Robert, (ed.), *Calendar of state papers domestic, Elizabeth, 1581-90, Volume 181* (London, 1865), pp. 256-265, British History online, https://www.british-history.ac.uk/cal-state-papers/domestic/edw-eliz/1581-90/pp256-265.

Tyler, Royall, (ed.), *Calendar of state papers, Spain, Vol. 11, 15 Jun. 1553,* (London, 1916), pp. 48-56, British History Online, http://www.british-history.ac.uk/cal-state-papers/spain/vol11/pp48-56.

The National Archives

Anthony Babington to Mary Stuart, the Babington postscript and cipher, 1586, SP 12/193/54 and SP 53/18/55), The National Archives online, https://www.nationalarchives.gov.uk/spies/ciphers/mary/ma2_x.htm.

Will of William Cecil, Lord Burghley (copy) 1 March 1597/8. Proved 13 November 1598, The national archives, Kew, (PROB 1/3).

'Words spoken by her majesty to Mr. Cecil', from Hatfield House, 20 Nov. 1558, (The National Archives, TNA SP12/1, no. 7).

'Secrets and spies', The National Archives Online, https://www.nationalarchives.gov.uk/spies/ciphers/mary/ma3.htm.

The British Library

William Cecil to Sir Nicholas Throckmorton, 14 July 1561, British Library (BL), Add. MSS 35830, fol. 159v.

Other primary sources (online and printed)

Acres, William (ed.), *The letters of Lord Burghley, William Cecil, to his son Sir Robert Cecil, 1593-1598,* (London, 2017).

Bourchier Devereux, Walter (ed.), *Lives and letters of the Devereux, Earls of Essex in the reigns of Elizabeth, James I., and Charles I: 1540-1646, Volume 1*, (London, 1853).

Goldsmid Edmund, (ed.), *The secret correspondence of Sir Robert Cecil with James VI. King of Scotland, Volume 1,* (Edinburgh, 1887).

MacCaffrey, Wallace T., (ed.) and William Camden, *The history of the most renowned and victorious princess Elizabeth, late queen of England: selected chapters*, (London, 1970).

Marcus, Leah S., Mueller, Janel, Rose, Mary Beth, *Elizabeth I: collected works*, (Chicago, 2002).

Sadler, Sir Ralph, *The state papers and letters of Sir Ralph Sadler*, Vol. 1, (Edinburgh, 1809), p ii, Haiti Trust Online, https://babel.hathitrust.org/cgi/pt?id=uc2.ark:/13960/t4dn4dv58&view=1up&seq=16&skin=2021.

Stump, Donald, and Felch, Susan M., *Elizabeth and her age*, (New York, 2009).

Smith, Thomas, *De repvblica anglorvm: The maner of gouernement or policie of the realme of* England (London, 1584).

Secondary sources

Books (online and printed)

Alford, Stephen, *The early Elizabethan polity: William Cecil and the British succession crisis, 1558-1569*, (Cambridge, 1998).

Alford, Stephen, *The watchers, a secret history of the reign of Elizabeth I*, (London, 2013).

Arman, Steve, Bird, Simon, and Wilkinson, Malcolm, *Reformation and Rebellion 1485-1750*, (Oxford, 2002).

A Tudor Times Insight, *Sir William Cecil: Elizabeth I's Chief* Minister (eBook), (2015).

Ball, F. Elrington, *The Judges in Ireland 1221-1921*, vol. 1, (London, 1927), p. 213-214, Internet Archive Online, https://archive.org/details/judgesinireland10000unse/page/214/mode/2up.

Beckingsale, B.W., *Burghley: Tudor statesman, 1520-1598*, (London, 1967).

Borman, Tracy, *The private lives of the Tudors: uncovering the secrets of Britain's greatest dynasty*, (London, 2016).

Castor, Helen, *Elizabeth I: 1558-1603*, (London, 2018).

Charlton, W. H., *Burghley: the life of William Cecil, lord Burghley, lord high treasurer of England etc.*, (Stamford,

1847), Google Books online, https://books.google.ie/ books?id=8uQ5AAAAcAAJ&printsec=frontcover&dq=LORD+ BURGHLEY&hl=en&sa=X&ved=2ahUKEwjp1P7zwZvwAhUro3 EKHQ3XCHIQ6AEwAHoECAAQAg#v=onepage&q=LORD%20 BURGHLEY&f=false.

Chisholm, Hugh, (ed.) 'Throckmorton, Sir Nicholas', in *The Encyclopædia Britannica*, (Cambridge University Press, 1911), vol. 26.

Cooper, John, *The queen's agent: Francis Walsingham at the court of Elizabeth I*, (London, 2011).

Croft, Pauline, *King James*, (Hampshire, 2002).

De Lisle, Leanda, *Tudor: the family story*, (London, 2013).

Dewar, Mary, *Sir Thomas Smith: a Tudor intellectual in office*, (London, 1964).

Elton, G.R., *England under the Tudors*, (London, 1974).

Fraser, Antonia, *Mary Queen of Scots*, (London, 2009).

Grant, James, *Life of Mary, queen of Scots*, (London, 1828).

Guy, John, *Elizabeth: the forgotten years*, (London, 2016).

Hilton, Lisa, *Elizabeth, renaissance prince: a biography*, (London, 2015).

Hutchinson, Robert, *Elizabeth's spy master: Francis Walsingham and the secret war that saved England*, (London, 2007).

Hume, Martin, A. S., *The great Lord Burghley: a study in Elizabethan statecraft* (eBook), (London, 1898), Internet Archive online, https:// archive.org/details/greatlordburghl00humegoog/page/n30/mode/1up.

Jones, Philippa, *Elizabeth: virgin queen*, (Lincolnshire, 2017).

Maginn, Christopher, *William Cecil, Ireland, and the Tudor state*, (Oxford, 2012).

Mattingly, Garrett, *The "invincible" armada and Elizabethan England*, (New York, 1963).

Milward, Richard, 'Cecil, Thomas, first earl of Exeter (1542–1623), courtier and soldier' in *Oxford Dictionary of National Biography* online, (2004) https://www.oxforddnb.com/view/10.1093/ ref:odnb/9780198614128.001.0001/odnb-9780198614128-e-498.

Nares, Edward, *Memoirs of the life and administration of the Right Honourable William Cecil, Lord Burghley: containing an historical view of the times in which he lived, and of the many eminent and illustrious persons with whom he was connected; with extracts from his private and official correspondence, and other papers, now first published from the originals*, Vol. 1, (London, 1828), Internet Archive online, https://archive. org/details/memoirsoflifeadm01nare/page/13/mode/1up.

Nares, Edward, *Memoirs of the life and administration of the Right Honourable William Cecil, Lord Burghley: containing an historical view of the times in which he lived, and of the many eminent and illustrious persons with whom he was connected; with extracts from his private and official correspondence, and other papers, now first published from the originals*, Vol. 2, (London, 1828-31), Internet Archive online, https://archive.org/details/memoirsoflifeadm02nareuoft/page/n9/mode/2up.

Nelson, Alan, H., *Monstrous adversary: the life of Edward de Vere, 17th Earl of Oxford*, (Liverpool, 2003).

Nichols, John, *The progression and public processions of Queen Elizabeth*, (London, 1832).

Loades, David, *'The Cecils: privilege and power behind the throne'*, (London, 2019).

Peck, Francis, *Desiderata curiosa: a collection of divers scarce and curious pieces relating chiefly to matters of English history…* Vol. 1, (London, 1779), Internet Archive online, https://archive.org/details/desideratacurios00peck/page/82/mode/1up.

Porter, Linda, *Katherine the queen: the remarkable life of Katherine Parr*, (London, 2011).

Read, Conyers, *Mr secretary Cecil and queen Elizabeth*, (London, 1955).

Richards, Judith M., *Elizabeth I*, (Oxon, 2012).

Ross, Josephine, *The men who would be king: the courtships of Elizabeth I*, (New York, 2012).

Sidney, Philip, *A history of the gunpowder plot: the conspiracy and its agents*, (London, 1904), Internet Archive online, https://archive.org/details/historyofgunpowd00sidnuoft/page/41/mode/1up?view=theater.

Smith, Alan Gordon, *William Cecil: the power behind Elizabeth*, (Holoulu,1934).

Skidmore, Chris, *Edward VI, the lost king of England*, (London, 2008).

Tallis, Nicola, *Crown of blood: the deadly inheritance of lady Jane Grey*, (London, 2016).

Tallis, Nicola, *Elizabeth's rival: the tumultuous tale of Lettice Knollys, Countess of Leicester*, (London, 2017).

The Religious Tract Society, *Writings of Edward the sixth, William Hugh, Queen Catherine Parr, Anne Askew, Lady Jane Grey, Hamilton, and Balnaves*, (London, 1831).

Vasoli, Sandra, *Anne Boleyn's letter from the tower*, (2015).

Watkins, Sarah-Beth, *Elizabeth I's last favourite: Robert Devereux, 2nd Earl of Essex*, (Hampshire, 2021).

Wilson, Derek, *Sir Francis Walsingham: a courtier in an age of terror*, (London, 2007).

Whitelock, Anna, *Mary Tudor: England's first queen*, (London, 2010).

Wriothesley, Charles, *A chronicle of England during the reigns of the Tudors from A.D 1485 to 1559*, Vol. 2, ed. William Douglas Hamilton, (London, 1877).

Journal articles

Applyard, John, Dudley, R., and Gairdner, James, 'The death of Amy Robsart' in *The English Historical Review*, vol. 1, no. 2 (1886), pp. 235-259.

Brown, Meaghan J., "The hearts of all sorts of people were enflamed': manipulating readers of Spanish armada news' in *Book History*, vol. 17 (2014), pp. 94–116.

Comstock Weston, Corinne, 'Lord Salisbury: conservative political leader and preeminent politician in Victorian England' in *Proceedings of the American Philosophical Society*, vol. 142, no.1 (1908), pp. 74-80.

Croft, Pauline, 'The reputation of Robert Cecil: libels political opinion and popular awareness in the early seventeenth century' in *Transactions of the Royal Historical Society*, vol. 1 (1991), pp. 43-69.

Davies, Godfrey, 'The Character of James VI and I', in *Huntington Library Quarterly*, vol. 5, no. 1 (1941), pp. 33-63.

Doran, Susan, 'Religion and politics at the court of Elizabeth I: The Habsburg marriage negotiations of 1559-1567' in *The English Historical Review*, vol. 104, no. 413 (1989), pp. 908-926.

Frye, Susan, 'The myth of Elizabeth at Tilbury', in *The Sixteenth Century Journal*, vol. 23, no 1 (1992), pp. 95-114.

Guerci, Manolo, 'Salisbury house in London, 1599-1694: The Strand Palace of Sir Robert Cecil' in *Architectural History*, vol. 52 (2009), pp. 31-78.

Henry, L.W., 'Contemporary Sources for Essex's Lieutenancy in Ireland, 1599' in *Irish Historical Studies*, vol. 11, no. 41 (1958), pp. 8-17.

Howey, Catherine L., 'Dressing a virgin queen: court women, dress, and fashioning the image of England's queen Elizabeth I' in *Early Modern Women*, vol. 4 (2009), pp. 201-208.

Irish, Bradley J., 'The dreading, dreadful Earl of Essex' in *Emotion in the Tudor court: literature, history, and early modern feeling*, (Illinois, 2018).

Jones, Norman, 'William Cecil, Lord Burghley, and Managing with the Men-of-Business' in *Parliamentary History*, vol. 34, issue 1 (2015), pp. 45-61.

Kanemura, Rei, 'Kingship by descent or kingship by election? The contested tide of James VI and I' in *Journal of British Studies*, vol. 52, no. 2 (2013), pp. 317–342.

Kelley, Donald R., 'Martyrs, myths, and the massacre: the background of St. Bartholomew' in *The American Historical Review*, vol. 77, no. 5 (1972), pp. 1323-1342.

Lindquist, Eric, 'The failure of the great contract' in *The Journal of Modern History*, vo. 57, no. 4 (1985), pp. 617-651.

Lindquist, Eric, 'The last years of the first earl of Salisbury', in *Albion: A Quarterly Journal Concerned with British Studies*, vol. 18, no. 1 (1986), pp. 23-41.

LaRocca, John J., '"Who Can't Pray with Me, Can't Love Me": Toleration and the Early Jacobean Recusancy Policy' in *Journal of British Studies*, vol. 23, no. 2 (1984), pp. 22-36.

Llewellyn, Nigel, 'Honour in life, death and in the memory: funeral monuments in early modern England', in *Transactions of the Royal Historical Society*, vol. 6 (1996), pp. 179-200.

Loomie, Albert J., 'King James I's Catholic consort' in *Huntington Library Quarterly*, vol. 34, no. 4 (1971), pp. 303-316.

Loomis, Catherine, '"Little man, little man": early modern representations of Robert Cecil' in *Explorations in Renaissance Culture*, (2011), The Free Library online, https://www.thefreelibrary.com/%22Little+man%2C+little+man%22%3A+early+modern+representations+of+Robert...-a0273078550.

Mears, Natalie, 'Courts, courtiers, and culture in Tudor England' in *The Historical Journal*, vol. 46, no. 3 (2003), pp. 703-722.

McLaren, Anne, 'The quest for a king: gender, marriage, and succession in Elizabethan England' in *Journal of British Studies*, vol. 41, no. 3 (2002), pp. 259-290.

Montrose, Louis Adrian, 'Celebration and insinuation: Sir Philip Sidney and the motives of Elizabethan courtship' in *Renaissance Drama*, vol. 8 (1977), pp. 3-35.

Nicholls, Mark, 'Treason's reward: the punishment of conspirators in the Bye Plot of 1603', in *The Historical Journal*, vol. 38, no. 4 (1995), pp. 821-842.

Read, Conyers, 'Lord Burghley's household accounts' in *The Economic History Review*, vol. 9, no. 2 (1956), pp. 343-348.

Read, Conyers, 'Walsingham and Burghley in Queen Elizabeth's Privy Council' in *The English Historical Review*, Vol. 28, No. 109 (1913), pp. 34-58.

Robinson, A. M. F., 'Queen Elizabeth and the Valois princes' in *The English Historical Review*, vol. 2, no. 5 (1887), pp. 40-77.

Shepard, Robert, 'Court factions in early modern England' in *The Journal of Modern History*, vol. 64, no. 4, (1992), pp. 721-745.

Tiernan, R. Kent, 'Walsingham's Entrapment of Mary Stuart' in *American Intelligence Journal*, vol. 34, no. 1 (2017), pp. 146-156.

Wormald, Jenny, 'Gunpowder, treason, and Scots' in *Journal of British Studies*, vol. 24, no. 2 (1985), pp. 141-168.

Zaller, Robert, 'Review of: King James by Pauline Croft', in *Albion: A Quarterly Journal Concerned with British Studies*, vol. 36, no. 2 (2004), pp. 300-303.

Other online sources

Extracts from P.W. Hasler (ed.), *The history of Parliament: The house of commons 1558-1603*, (London, 1981), The History of Parliament online, https://www.historyofparliamentonline.org/volume/1558-1603/member/ sadler-sir-ralph-1507-87#footnote2_mhp83ee.

'The family now' online at Burghley, https://www.burghley.co.uk/about-us/ the-family/the-family-now.

'William Cecil: family life', Tudor Times online, https://tudortimes.co.uk/ people/william-cecil-family-life/a-growing-family.

Index